# Turning
### the
# Tables

# Turning the Tables

## FROM HOUSEWIFE TO INMATE AND BACK AGAIN

## TERESA GIUDICE

*with* K.C. BAKER

G

*Gallery Books*

NEW YORK   LONDON   TORONTO   SYDNEY   NEW DELHI

Gallery Books
An Imprint of Simon & Schuster, Inc.
1230 Avenue of the Americas
New York, NY 10020

First Gallery Books trade paperback edition June 2016

GALLERY BOOKS and colophon are
registered trademarks of Simon & Schuster, Inc.

For information about special discounts for bulk purchases,
please contact Simon & Schuster Special Sales at
1-866-506-1949 or business@simonandschuster.com

The Simon & Schuster Speakers Bureau can bring authors to your live event.
For more information or to book an event, contact the Simon & Schuster Speakers
Bureau at 1-866-248-3049 or visit our website at www.simonspeakers.com.

Interior design by Jaime Putorti

Manufactured in the United States of America

10 9 8 7 6 5 4 3 2 1

Library of Congress Cataloging-in-Publication Data
Names: Giudice, Teresa. | Baker, K.C.
Title: Turning the tables : from housewife to inmate and back again / Teresa Giudice with
K.C. Baker.
Description: New York : Gallery Books, 2016.
Identifiers: LCCN 2015047685 (print) | LCCN 2015048704 (ebook) |
Subjects: LCSH: Giudice, Teresa, | Television personalities—United States—Biography. |
Real housewives of New Jersey (Television program) | Women prisoners—Connecticut—
Danbury—Biography. | BISAC: BIOGRAPHY & AUTOBIOGRAPHY /
Entertainment & Performing Arts. | BIOGRAPHY & AUTOBIOGRAPHY / Rich &
Famous. | BIOGRAPHY & AUTOBIOGRAPHY / General.
Classification: LCC PN1992.4.G565 A3 2016 (print) | LCC PN1992.4.G565 (ebook) |
DDC 791.4502/8092—dc23

ISBN 978-1-5011-3511-8
ISBN 978-1-5011-3510-1 (hardcover)
ISBN 978-1-5011-3512-5 (ebook)

*For Gia, Gabriella, Milania, and Audriana*

*I thank God every day for blessing me with each one of you.*
*You are my everything.*

*I am so proud of you, especially for your strength and grace*
*during the time I was away. Seeing how strong you all were—*
*and the love you showed me—helped me get through all of this.*

Vi voglio tanto bene con tutto il mio cuore.

*I LOVE, LOVE, LOVE, LOVE you all to infinity and beyond.*

*Love, Mommy*

Life isn't about waiting for the storm to pass,
but learning to dance in the rain . . .

—VIVIAN GREENE

# CONTENTS

# AUTHOR'S NOTE

Names and identifying characteristics of all inmates and others I met at Danbury have been changed, and in some instances, those described are composites.

# LETTER TO THE READER

*T*o the world, my life seems like an open book. People think they know everything there is to know about me from what they have seen on TV and read in the tabloids.

But they don't. Not even close.

I want people to get to know the *real* me. I want the world to see who I really am—not what the media or *The Real Housewives of New Jersey* has made me out to be. Don't get me wrong. I'm blessed to be a *Real Housewife*. It opened up so many new worlds for me and brought the most amazing, life-changing opportunities my way. Bravo, Sirens Media, and Andy Cohen have been so good to me, and for that, I will always be grateful. Andy has been so supportive of me through everything. He kept in touch with me in prison, to make sure I was OK. I love him for that.

But at the same time, I feel like I have been misunderstood. A lot of people have said they think I'm mean. Look, I'm not proud of everything I've said and done in the public eye. But I'm not a bitch. I'm good-hearted, laid-back, and a caring mom, but like every other person out there, I'm not perfect. My parents raised me to be a good person, which is something I've strived to be my whole life. I have always been a hardworking student, a faithful employee, a good wife and mother—and never broke the law in my life. I never meant to, anyway. As you read my story, you will come to know that my children, my husband, and my family are all that matter to me, not money or fame. As I have seen firsthand, fame can be a tremendous blessing and a horrendous curse.

I guess because I'm a strong person and *very* confident, some people think that I'm the nastiest person out there or whatever else they choose to project onto me. I think some people don't get the way I express myself. Sometimes the first thing I think of is what comes out of my mouth—and it's taken the wrong way, which evidently causes problems. Whenever that happens, I think, *Uh-oh—I didn't mean to say that that way* . . . That's something I need to work on.

My family and friends who know me totally get me. But with new people I meet, I find that once they get to know me, they come to see that I'm very genuine, down-to-earth, fun, and loyal. If I love you, then I love you with all my heart. When one of my bunkies in prison really started to get to know me, she took me aside one day and said, "Wow. You're such a sweet person. You're so different than the way they portray you on TV and nothing like what I've read. I can see that you only care about Joe, your daughters, and your parents." (I do. I worry about my parents' health all the time and I pray every day for my family . . .)

What you see with me is what you get . . . but the media doesn't always show the real me. They don't always give the full side of the story. I can't completely blame them, but I can open my heart to all of you, in my own words. I love life. I am blessed to be happy and healthy, and surrounded by amazing family and friends. I would never hurt my loved ones—or anyone—in any way. I don't have that in me. But I've found out the hard way that there are other people out there who *do* want to hurt you. Who wish for bad things to happen to you. My problem is that I am too trusting and see the good in everyone, which has gotten me into a lot of trouble over the years.

At the same time, though, being in the business I'm in, you need to have thick skin. I definitely do and it's something that helped me a lot in prison. I'm sweet but not a pushover, and I stand my ground when I have to. I've also learned to keep my guard up more. It's too bad, but it's what I have to do now.

Before all this happened, I thought I had the perfect life. What I have now realized is that *no one* has a perfect life. Everyone carries a cross in this lifetime. A lot of my time on this earth has been a fairy tale. But as you may know, I have gone through some very tough times, too. Tough times I've had to weather with the entire world watching, judging everything I've done without knowing all the facts . . .

In 2014, I was sentenced to fifteen months at the Federal Correctional Institution in Danbury, Connecticut, for federal bankruptcy fraud and conspiracy to commit wire and mail fraud. Going to prison was very difficult for my family and me. I missed my girls, my husband, my parents, my family, and my friends. My parents were heartbroken, but they have been there for me, just like Joe, my daughters, and the rest of my family and my friends. And, of course, my amazing fans. I couldn't have gotten through prison without the Trehuggers. You have no idea.

Since I went to prison, I've learned a lot about life—and so much about myself. I've met the most incredibly good-hearted people. People with an inner strength I cannot believe. I made some really great friends in prison, who helped me survive since the day I got there.

My faith was one of the things that helped me the most in prison. Praying and getting closer to God helped me get through one of the most difficult times of my life. I took care of my body and mind by walking and running around the track as much as I could, taking exercise classes, doing yoga, eating clean (as clean as you can eat in prison!), going to church, reading inspirational books—and reflecting on how I could use this experience to change my life. I planned to come out of prison a stronger, better person. I wanted the world to see a new Teresa. A different Teresa. Well, actually, the Teresa I always was.

I had so much fun strolling down memory lane for this book, but it also brought back some painful moments. In life, we all go through bad things, but I've found that revisiting tough times forces us to appreciate the good even more. I do. That's for sure.

Thank you for reading my story. I want you to know that I LOVE, LOVE, LOVE, LOVE you all! I couldn't have made it through this ordeal without each and every one of you . . . God bless you and *tanti baci*!

Tanti Baci Love Love Love Love

XOXOXO        You All!

# PROLOGUE

$\mathcal{I}$ had been dreading this moment for more than a year. But here I was, finally, on my way to prison.

After saying goodbye to the loves of my life—my husband, Joe, and my four daughters, Gia, Gabriella, Milania, and Audriana—my lawyer, James J. Leonard, Jr., drove me to the Federal Correctional Institution in Danbury, Connecticut, from my house in New Jersey, so I could surrender myself to the Federal Bureau of Prisons. The prison would be my home for the next year of my life. No amount of preparation could have gotten me ready for this moment.

I was supposed to turn myself in at noon on January 5, 2015. But James, who I call Jim, had talked to prison officials about letting me turn myself in earlier—in the middle of the night—so my daughters wouldn't have to deal with the swarm of reporters, photographers, news vans, and TV cameras we knew would be lying in wait outside my house the morning I was scheduled to surrender. I didn't want them to ambush my family with their popping flashbulbs and intrusive questions. It made me mad that I had to give up my last few, precious hours with my family because of the media and the paparazzi, but I knew I had to do what was best for my girls.

During our almost two-hour drive to the prison, a white van chased us for a bit on I-287N in New York. Before I could duck out of sight, a pap who was riding in the back of the van snapped some pictures of me, Jim, and a friend of his named Mike, a former FBI agent he had brought along for security. I still have no idea who that was, since I don't believe those pictures ever saw the light of day. Good.

When we finally got to the prison, we circled the perimeter trying to find the back entrance (so I could go in unnoticed) and passed a small group of reporters and photographers. They were rubbing their hands together, trying to keep warm. They had been waiting for me, probably for hours at that point. They wanted a quote from me—or even better for their bank accounts, a picture—at one of the worst moments of my life. But they didn't get either, thank God. Jim and the prison made sure of that. Cameras flashed when we turned into the prison entrance, but I ducked down in the backseat so they couldn't get a shot of me. Knowing how much some of the media had hurt me and my family over the years, I didn't feel so bad the paparazzi were standing outside, freezing in the frigid January wind.

We drove onto the prison grounds and made our way up a steep, winding hill. Once we reached the top, I gasped when I saw a huge building surrounded by a towering fence that was topped with a seemingly endless twirl of razor-sharp barbed wire. A chill went through my whole body. I had never been to a prison before, let alone surrendered to one to begin my own sentence. I had only seen foreboding prison walls and fences like this in the movies and on TV (though, ironically, I still have not seen *Orange Is the New Black* . . .

even though the real-life Piper Kerman served her sentence at Danbury, too).

We got out of Jim's Denali and made our way to the intimidating building ahead of us. I pulled my black coat a little tighter as we walked through the gate that led to the prison. It was three in the morning, so it was pitch-black outside. I couldn't even see the moon. I shuddered again, and shoved my hands deeper into my pockets. I still couldn't believe that I was really here.

We entered the building and were met by two officers inside a sterile, white entryway, lined with pictures of President Obama, government officials, and the warden. They greeted us and talked to Jim while I stood quietly next to him, wishing I were anywhere but there at that moment. When it was time for me to go with the officers, I handed Jim my coat and my cell phone before saying goodbye to him and Mike. As I headed toward the area where I would be processed, I turned around one last time and said to Jim, "Tell Joe and the girls I'll be fine and that I love them very much. Tell them not to worry. I'll be okay . . ."

*O*nce Jim and Mike were gone, a female guard guided me past a male officer sitting behind a formica desk and through a metal detector attached to it. It reminded me of the kind of setup I had seen at the airport and in the federal courthouse in Newark, New Jersey, where Joe and I were sentenced three months earlier. She led me down a long, dirty hallway, into what looked like a dingy shower stall, with no curtain, and handed me my "greens"—my prison uniform.

I'm glad I like green. At least my uniform wasn't neon orange . . .

"Change into this," she said, before giving me a white bra, white granny panties, and a pair of white tube socks. While these were new, the pants and shirt had been worn by many, many inmates before me. I took them from her, reluctantly. I couldn't believe that now, here I was, about to live in a prison with more than two hundred other women, potentially getting a job cleaning toilets or washing windows—while wearing clothes that other inmates before me had worn. I tried not to think about the faint stains I saw on the pants the guard had given me, and I couldn't help wondering how the hell I was going to be able to put them on.

This was not happening.

"Before you change," the guard said, "you have to go through a strip search."

*The strip search.*

I had been told that prisoners had to do a "squat and cough" during processing, to make sure they weren't holding any contraband in any of their body cavities. I had heard that prisoners had tried to hide drugs, knives, phones, headphones, lighters, paperwork, and even guns inside their you-know-whats. Knives? Phones? Guns? You gotta be kidding me. *Oh, Madonna mia . . .* Honest to God, the last thing on earth I would ever think about doing is hiding something in my *chuckalina*. All of this was new to me. This was a long way from Jersey—and a really long way from the life I led on *Real Housewives . . .*

I was still wearing the clothes I had on when I left my house— my black velour, rhinestone-emblazoned Fabellini jacket (made for the launch of my line of cocktails), my black Skinny Italian tank top (named after my cookbooks, of course), black leggings, and running shoes. I hadn't thought twice when I was getting dressed for prison a few hours earlier—I just wanted to wear something comfortable for the long ride from my house to my new "home away from home."

In the mere minutes that I had been in prison, I was already looking at things differently: I laughed when I realized what I was wearing. In my real life, I wore this outfit all the time because it was so easy. I threw it on when I was running the girls to school, grocery shopping, cooking dinner, helping with homework, or doing whatever the day had in store for me. And now, I was wearing this outfit—remnants of my family, my home, my successes—in *prison*. I felt like I stuck out like a sore thumb, but at the same time, in that moment, I was still me—rhinestones and all.

The guard watched while I stripped down to nothing and stood there completely naked.

"Turn around, face the wall, squat down, and cough," she said.

*I wanted to die.*

"Open your mouth and stick your tongue out when you cough," she ordered.

I felt sick to my stomach. I was embarrassed and humiliated. I had never felt more vulnerable in my life.

I turned around and did what she said. I thanked God that this was happening in the middle of the night, when no other inmates were there—just this one guard. I did not want an audience watching this—or someone leaking a picture of this mortifying moment to the tabloids. My God . . . that's all I needed.

When that was done, she watched while I put on the uniform she had given me—a V-neck shirt and pants. When I handed her my own clothes, I felt like I was giving her a piece of my soul— things I loved that were almost like a security blanket to me at that point. Now I had nothing else with me that reminded me of home or happier times except a rosary and religious medals Jim had given me before I left for prison, which were among the few things I was allowed to bring with me. The guard also gave me a pair of clunky, black, steel-toed boots to wear. (I had never worn boots like that in my life . . . I'm a high heel girl . . .) Who knew what had happened to the women who wore these things before me? Now here I was, the next inmate adding to their history.

After I got dressed, it was time for my prison photo shoot. For a moment, this reminded me of the many photographs I had posed for in magazines and promos for the show. But here I was, getting my mug shot. Me? Getting a mug shot? Oh my God. I felt numb at this point, so I just stared at the camera. I don't think I even thought of smiling. Everything was really just a blur by then.

Next, I was fingerprinted—something else I had never done in my life. A counselor who was very nice to me placed her hand over mine as she pressed my fingertips onto an old-fashioned ink pad and then onto a white card. I was still feeling out of it, like this was a bad dream, so I was going through the motions at this point, just doing what she told me to do. I was trying not to think about anything that was happening to me.

I was given an ID card that had my picture, name, and registration number on it. I was told that we inmates had to carry it with us everywhere, especially during head count, when the guards would make sure none of us had escaped. After taking a look at the razors on that barbed wire fence and seeing a couple of intimidating-looking guards standing on a hill watching over the property, I wondered who would even try.

I glanced at my picture on the card. This was not my best photo, since it was taken at almost four in the morning. But it wasn't the worst, either. I wondered if someone would try to smuggle that picture of me out of the prison, to give to the tabloids. I had heard that the prison couldn't do that, but after seeing what the media was capable of in the past six years? Nothing would surprise me. (Someone did end up releasing it to the media later on, but I didn't care because I thought it was a good picture.)

After we were done with processing, which they call R&D (for Receiving and Discharge), the female guard led me down another hallway to a dark, dank cell with bars. I sat down on a steel bench. I shivered because it was so cold in there. After the echoes of her steps faded away, I realized just how quiet and how dark a room (if you can call a barred cell a room) could be. It was terrifying in there. I shivered again, more out of fear than from being cold. Thank God she didn't lock me in there, though. She left the cell door open.

I hadn't been handcuffed yet, either, thank goodness. I thought the guards would clamp them on my wrists as soon as I set foot inside the prison, but they didn't. I was actually never handcuffed the whole time I was there, which still surprises me. No "clink, clink" as someone on the show once said. Believe me, I'm not complaining. There was something weirdly freeing about being in prison without being physically constrained. I thanked God many times for that.

I was so tired at this point and wanted to lean up against the wall to rest, but it looked so filthy that I just couldn't bring myself to do it. So I just sat on the edge of the bench, trying hard to keep from crying and to stop my legs from shaking.

I looked around the holding cell at the concrete walls and floor, feeling very alone. That first bout of true silence was paralyzing. I'll never forget it. That's when it truly hit me: *I am really here. I am in prison.*

I began to get emotional, thinking about Joe and the girls back home and what life would be like for them without me there. Gia knew I was going to prison, but at that point, the younger girls did not. I had told Gabriella and Milania I had to go away to work on writing a book about prison, and that to do that, I had to live there. (I told Audriana I was writing a book but didn't say I had to live in a prison to write it because she wouldn't even know what that was.) When I started feeling like I was going to cry, I thought: *OK. I'm here now. I have to do this. What choice do I have?*

My stomach started churning when I began to think about what was going to happen to me—or what could happen to me—in the next twenty-four hours and beyond. Would I get beaten up? Bullied? Would people shout nasty things at me? Could I go to sleep knowing no one was going to hurt me? I had seen so many movies and TV shows about what a horror show life in prison could be. My mind started racing as I ran through all the possibilities, with images I had seen on TV and stories I had read in the news popping into my head, over and over. Then I stopped myself.

*I am going to do this. I am going to be strong—stronger than I've ever been in my life. I have to be strong for Joe and the girls. I'm going to learn from this experience, make the best of it and come out a better person. At the end of the day, I'm still the headstrong person I've always been. I've got to keep it together.*

*I have to . . .*

The guard returned to the cell. "Let's go," she said.

"Um, where are we going?" I asked.

"To the camp, up the hill."

Up the hill? What? I thought I was going to have serve my sentence in that scary building with its barred windows and cells and that barbed wire surrounding it, which reminded me of the kind of maximum security prison in the movie *The Green Mile.*

Another guard, who had a huge scar on her neck, led me out of the cell and down a hallway, where she opened a giant, heavy metal door with an old-fashioned skeleton key, the kind I imagined my great-grandmother used in Italy to lock a chest or armoire. It seemed odd to me that they used keys like this, but then again, everything there seemed strange to me at that point.

She led me outside into a small area inside that huge fence. I couldn't take my eyes off that sharp barbed wire. It looked like it would cut you so deep that you would bleed forever and die if you got caught on it. But it felt so good to breathe in fresh air. When I'd walked into that first building, I thought I was going to be locked inside the bowels of that concrete fortress for months, behind bars in a cement cell with a metal toilet and a sink. But I would now be locked up inside a camp, whatever that was. I took as many deep breaths as I could, as though they were my last, thinking about how claustrophobic I would feel for months on end in there.

A few minutes later, an inmate they called the "town driver" pulled up in a small car, like a Toyota Corolla or something. I don't remember. I slid into the backseat and we drove up a big hill to the women's minimum-security satellite camp at FCI Danbury, where I would be spending the next year of my life. It was still so dark and cold and eerily quiet. It wouldn't stay that way for long. Just as I was about to go to sleep, the women in the prison were about to wake up.

The town driver pulled up to a long two-story building that looked like an old elementary school. It reminded me of a rambling cheerleading camp in Pennsylvania that I had brought Gia to the summer before. I was shocked that the building had no fence and no barbed wire around it at all. I was even more surprised when a guard opened the door right up. She didn't even need a key. It was unlocked. That thirty-foot fence surrounding the building I had just left, which I found out later on was a men's prison, had looked so intimidating to me. I thought the prison would batten down every hatch to make sure no one could get in or get out.

*OK . . .*

The counselor met me inside and led me through a set of double doors and down some stairs, to a long hallway where my room was located. I would be in Room 9. (Piper Kerman, I later learned, was in Room 6 when she first got there.) The counselor handed me some sheets so I could make my bed, which was on a top bunk. A few of the other inmates in there—my new roommates—woke up when we got there, and helped me make my bed, which surprised me. It was so nice of them, especially so early in the morning. I almost gagged, though, when I saw stains on my mattress. Was that urine? Dried blood? Or something else?

*I can do this.*

I was so exhausted, though, that I didn't even care *what* I was lying on at that point, but I was grateful for that sheet. I put my head down on the flat, mushy pillow and pulled a scratchy, beige blanket over me. I shut my eyes and literally crashed. I had been running on adrenaline this whole time. I had been up since the morning before, when Joe and I took the girls to church on our last Sunday together. I was totally drained.

*I have to be strong . . .*

Right before I passed out, I stared up at the exposed, moldy pipes, covered in about an inch of dust, in the ceiling right above my head. Spiderwebs knotted the space in between them, and I thought I saw something move . . .

*How did I end up here?*

# 1

## GROWING UP GORGA

When I was little, I wanted to be a movie star or an entertainer. That's all I could think about. I wanted to be just like Cher.

Every week, my parents and I gathered in the living room of our five-room apartment to watch *The Sonny and Cher Comedy Hour*. I could barely wait until it was on each week. My father, Giacinto Gorga, sat on our green couch with my mother, Antonia, while I lay on the floor, right in front of the only TV set we had in the house at the time. It had a twelve-inch screen and dials to turn up the volume. We didn't have remotes back then and we only had thirteen channels or something.

My brother, Giuseppe, who is two years younger than I am—I call him Joey and he calls me Tre—would only watch some of the programs with us, like *Three's Company* and *Sanford and Son*. He wasn't really into the ones where glamorous women in sequined gowns were singing and dancing onstage. He and I were best friends growing up. We rode bikes together, played board games and cards, and loved making forts in the living room with our blankets and pillows. He always had my back, and would kick me under the dinner table to warn me if I was pushing my dad to the limit while asking his permission for something. My parents and brother were my world growing up, and believe me, I could not have asked God for a better family.

Watching Cher onstage took me to a whole other world. She was so glamorous in her long, slinky gowns, with her glittery diamond earrings. I loved her gorgeous makeup, perma-tan, and those loooong eyelashes. (Which I started wearing All. The. Time. on the show . . .) I thought her huge fame, her undeniable glamour, and her devoted fans (I was, of course, one of them, though I never met her or anyone famous when I was little) were so amazing. As I lay there on the floor of my family's humble little apartment, fantasizing about what it would like to be Cher, I had no idea that one day I would be famous, too. But like Cher and every celebrity out there, I would come to see that fame comes with some of the best things in the world—and some things that threaten to break you.

I wanted to sing and dance like Cher. I thought I was pretty good at it. As a kid, I would put on little shows for my parents all the time in our living room, singing and dancing and pretending I was onstage. As I got older, I wished that my mom had sent me to dancing school or gymnastics class, but she didn't because she literally couldn't take me. She didn't start driving until I was in third grade, when she surprised all of us by getting her license! All on her own! We were all so proud of her. But up until then, when I was seven years old or so, she, Joey and I would walk everywhere, unless our dad drove us. They didn't trust anyone else to drive us anywhere because they were so protective.

The bigger issue was that as an Italian immigrant, my mom simply didn't know how to go about finding classes for me and signing me up, even when she did have her license. My mom has since said that she would have taken me to dance or gymnastics if she'd known I wanted to go. But I knew how hard it was for her to get around, even with a car, so I never asked her about it. I didn't want to burden her with that.

Back then, my parents really didn't see the point of after-school activities, either. They were like, "You have to be home for dinner at five-thirty. No out and about." So I would just take part in whatever activities were offered at school. I was a baton twirler in third grade, played softball in elementary school and in junior high, and played the saxophone in the seventh-grade and eighth-grade band. I gave up on my dream of becoming famous when I became a teenager because I thought it was just hopeless, to be honest. My parents had no Hollywood connections and no idea how to even begin to get me into showbiz. But still, I always wanted to become successful and make something of myself one day. I just didn't know what that would be.

While I love the life my parents gave me and Joey, they definitely didn't have it easy when they came to America. They had a good life in Italy. There, they were surrounded by family and friends everywhere they turned, because Sala Consilina, the town where they grew up, is so tiny. Everyone looked out for everyone else. They were happy there, for sure, but wanted more than what their little hamlet offered. They left the only place they knew because they thought their children would have a better life in America, where anything was possible. Sala Consilina was beautiful but limited in opportunity, and I could not be more grateful for the life and the love they have given me. I had an amazing childhood, thanks to my parents . . . but in order for me to have that incredible childhood, my parents sacrificed a lot.

My dad, Giacinto, came here first, in the late sixties. He moved in with his sister in Paterson, New Jersey, a small city with lots of tall buildings, row houses, and concrete. It was a far cry from Sala Consilina, a small, medieval-looking town nestled in the rolling green and brown hills of the province of Salerno, about two hours from Naples. When I was little, I could always point to where it was on a map because it's right at the beginning of the boot in the southwest of Italy.

My mom, Antonia, grew up as an only child and learned about heartbreak at an early age. She had a sister named Carmela, who passed away when she was fifteen days old. Her mother's (my grandmother's) name was Rosa, but everyone called her Teresa, which is pronounced Tare-ray-za. That's really how you say my name in Italian, although everyone here calls me Ter-ee-sah. I am named after my maternal grandmother. In Italian families, the tradition is to name your children after your husband's parents. But since my mom lost her mother, my dad broke with tradition. He said to my mom, "If we get married and have a daughter, I want to name her after your mother." It was so loving of my dad to say that. My dad's mom totally understood, which is another reason why my parents loved her so much.

Speaking of pronunciations of names, people always ask me why I say my last name different ways. Sometimes I pronounce it Joo-dee-chay or Joo-dih-chay, which is the Italian way to say my husband's last name, which ironically means "judge" in Italian. Other times I will say my last name is Joo-dice, which is the American way to say it. Most people have a hard time pronouncing it the Italian way, so I am sticking with the American way from now on. My husband is fine with that. We had used the Italian pronunciation to make Joe's dad happy, God rest his soul.

While I can easily pronounce words in Italian, people would always laugh when I mixed up or mispronounced words on the show—like when I called a nor'easter a Norwegian, said the word ingrediences (!), stanima instead of stamina, and semolina instead of salmonella. I've read stories that say I am known for my "mixed metaphors and malapropisms." Mala—what? Oh my God. I have no friggin' idea how the heck to even begin to pronounce that one! What can I say? (That's why I had someone help me write this book!) People can laugh all they want. I grew up in a house where my parents spoke Italian all the time, so I spoke two languages, which is why I mix things up sometimes. (I still speak Italian with my parents today . . .) I am blowing all of the haters a big kiss right now. I don't want to hate. I just want to love, love, love, love! But look—it is what it is. And now I definitely know the difference between a nor'easter and a Norwegian . . . well, sort of.

When my mom was a baby, my grandfather, whose name was Pietro, told my grandmother that he was going to leave Sala Consilina for Venezuela to work—and never returned. No one knew if he never returned by choice, or if he was forced to stay. They didn't even know if he was alive or dead. My mother doesn't remember meeting him because he left when she was so young. To this day, my family doesn't know what happened to him. As the years went on, my grandmother tried to find him. She tried to write to him, but wasn't even sure he got the letters. He never answered. That broke their hearts.

After her father (my grandfather) left, my mom and her mother (my grandmother) went to live with my grandmother's parents (my great-grandparents), Rosa and Vincenzo. But my grandmother led a very lonely life. She never left the house, for fear that people would shun her and talk about her because she had no husband. That's how it was back then. She came from a respectable family but felt ashamed that her husband had left, even though she didn't do anything wrong. So she never went out with friends, to the many feasts they held in town (it's the Italian way!), or even to church. She would just stay home and work the land with my great-grandfather and help my great-grandmother cook, sew, make sausages, jar vegetables, and take care of my mom, of course.

Things only got worse for my mom and grandmother as my mom got older. When my mom was nine, my grandmother got very sick. She started to lose a lot of weight and always seemed to have a cold and a cough, so her family took her to see a doctor in Naples. By then it was too late. They told her she was very sick, possibly with lung cancer. They sent her home and she died months later. My mom was an orphan at only ten years old. She was devastated. She and her mother did everything together and were incredibly close. She still had her grandparents, who loved her so much, but said she felt so alone in the world without her mother by her side. Every girl needs her mother, and my mom felt so lost without hers. I can't even imagine what she went through. That's what made it so hard for me to be away from my own girls when I went to prison. They needed their mother, too, even if I was only gone for eleven and a half months.

But that wasn't the end of my mother's pain. While she was still reeling from my grandmother's death, my great-grandfather died a month later because he was so heartbroken over losing his daughter. My mother loved my great-grandfather so much because he was the only father figure she ever had. All of this death and sorrow was a lot for a little girl to take. It was a very dark time for my mother. Again, I cannot even fathom what she went through.

But she went on to have a happy life, thank God. My great-grandmother continued to raise her. She had so much strength and was so good to my mother. Since it was just the two of them, my mom had to learn how to do everything around the house, from cooking and making sausages, to tending the garden and making clothes, just like my grandmother did. That's how she learned to be such an amazing cook and to take care of Joey, my dad, and me so well. What I admire so much about my mom is that while her childhood was filled with such trauma and sadness, she was never bitter or angry over everything that had happened to her. Despite everything she went through, she is one of the kindest people I have ever met. She has a heart of gold (and not one bad bone in her body). She is sweet and loving—and laughs a lot. Even today. I love her so much and am so blessed to have her as my mom.

My dad grew up with his parents, Rosa (yes, another Rosa!) and Giuseppe (whom my brother is named after), two older brothers, Michael and Mario, and two older sisters, Antoinetta and Maria. My dad was the youngest in his family, like Audriana. There was also a brother named Nicola, which means Nicholas in English, who died at six.

They lived in a three-story house made of stone, in the oldest part of Sala Consilina near the main piazza. Underneath the house, which you got to by climbing up a huge flight of stone stairs, were stalls and troughs for the goats, sheep, and pigs they used to keep. They had a huge yard, filled with beautiful fig and cypress trees and an impressive garden, because almost everyone grew their own vegetables. Joe and I visited the house in the show's second season. That was my favorite episode of all time. I was so happy to go back to Sala Consilina to see the relatives that Joe and I have there, since his family is from the same town. It's so beautiful and peaceful there. Most of the people there may not have five-carat diamonds, Chanel bags, McMansions, Ferraris, or yachts, but they are happy. Very happy. Because family is really all you need in this life.

My dad met my mom when he was twenty and she was just thirteen, when she was on her way to a feast to celebrate the Blessed Virgin. My mother didn't give him a second thought, but my father couldn't get her out of his mind. He found out where she lived and began visiting her at her grandmother's house every week, as long as someone else was there, of course. (Italians were very strict back then and still were when I was growing up!) My dad wanted to propose right away, but his father told him he was too young and needed to have a good job and earn some money before he could get married and start a family. But her family wanted them to either get married or break up, because they didn't like the idea of a boy coming around if he wasn't planning to stay forever. So they broke up, but he never forgot about her. (This is my favorite part! It's so romantic!) Five years later, when he was working in America, he wrote to her, telling her that he still wanted to be with her and asked if she wanted to be with him. She replied, "If you are serious, then come back to Italy so we can discuss it." He came right back to Italy and married her eighty-seven days later, on December 27, 1969.

I love looking at their wedding album, which reminds me of scenes from *The Godfather*. After my parents exchanged vows in the church, they walked to the reception hall, with dozens of their friends and family following them in the streets—just like in the movie. They have been married for forty-six years now and are still so in love. They still flirt and make each other laugh every day. They both have a great sense of humor—which is where I get it from!

After my parents got married, they decided to come to America in 1971, with just two suitcases. My mom was pregnant with me when they moved to Paterson (but she didn't know it). Before my mom got here, she said she thought America was paradise. She had seen pictures and fell in love. She said she wanted to explore the world, since she had never set foot outside Sala Consilina in her life. But my dad kept saying to her, "I don't know if you'll really like it . . ."

He was right. Living in a new country was very hard for both of them. Neither spoke English. My mom told me she would cry herself to sleep at night, wondering why they had left Italy. She would say, "I don't have nobody here . . . I don't understand what people are saying. This is terrible . . ." She didn't even know how the money worked, but she said nice people at stores would help her count out her change—and that no one ever stole from her. Yes, it was hard, but they had wanted to come to America—the land of opportunity.

My dad needed a job and began working as a dishwasher at an Italian restaurant, but he learned how to repair shoes at the same time. My father worked day and night and saved everything he could so that he could buy a shoe repair business in Butler, New Jersey. Joey and I would go to work with him on Saturdays when we were little. Most of the time, we just stayed in the back room watching cartoons or playing. Sometimes, though, we would help him sweep or clean or find shoes that customers came to pick up. I loved helping him and always felt so grown up working there.

Sometimes, though, he was too much of a perfectionist. Ten or eleven years ago, a thirty-something-year-old woman brought in a pair of hot Christian Louboutins to repair at the store he bought in Ramsey, New Jersey, after his first store burned down. Now, we all know that Louboutins are known for their signature red soles. They're a total status symbol. But my dad thought the soles looked badly scuffed, so he spray painted the bottoms of these very expensive shoes super-black and then applied a special polish to make them shine. He thought they looked great—just like new. When the woman came to get them, she was like, "These aren't my shoes! My shoes had red soles!" I had to set him straight and tell him, "You cannot spray paint the bottoms of Louboutins!" He didn't want her to be upset, so he spray painted the bottoms red again. She was happy when she saw the red soles again, but at first? Not so much. *Madonna mia!*

After all the years my dad worked at the repair shop, which he really loved, he had to sell his store in Ramsey eight years ago because of his health. He had to have two open-heart valve replacements. On top of that, he just couldn't bear to breathe in the fumes from the chemicals he used in the store. He would get pneumonia all the time. We were sad that he had to sell it, because we have so many happy memories there. The store is still there and I get a little teary-eyed whenever I see it. But, as we all know, with life comes change . . .

When I was growing up in my family, there was a lot of love. We lived a very simple but very happy life. I was raised in a strict Italian Catholic household that had strong values. Loyalty is everything to me. Family is everything to me. You never go against your family in my eyes. That's what I was taught.

My dad was home with us every night after work. We went to

church every Sunday and sat in the same pew at Mass every week. On the weekends, we would sometimes go to my parents' friends' houses or they would come to ours. My dad would play cards with the men. My mom would sit and talk with the women, drinking coffee and having desserts while my brother and I hung out with all the kids.

Even though our apartment was modest, it was so warm and welcoming. I have such good memories from living there. When you walked in the door, the kitchen was right there. That's where we spent most of our time. To the right of the kitchen were three bedrooms right next to each other—my parents' bedroom and then mine and Joey's. Then there was a bathroom and the living room. That was it.

Even though we had no grass in our yard, just asphalt, we lived across the street from the Paterson Falls, which are spectacular. I loved being able to hear the rush of water when we had our windows open. We would always see people going there to take pictures because it's such a famous landmark in our area. They held a big carnival there every year. Joey and I loved going to that carnival. I remember how I couldn't wait to look out the window each year to watch this man walk across the falls on a metal wire. I loved seeing him walk the tightrope because you don't really see things like that a lot anymore. Especially out your window. I was always so worried that he was going to fall! (He never did, thank God . . .)

One thing I loved about living in that apartment house was a massive mulberry tree across the street. Its branches hung down low, so we would go and pick mulberries off the tree when they were ripe and eat them. When Joe and I were little and he would come over to the house with his mom, we would run across the street and pick as many as we could and sit on one of the big rocks under the tree and eat them. Our hands and faces were dark purple from the berries, but we didn't care. I loved the bond that Joe and I shared, even back then. We always felt so comfortable with each other. As kids we joked about how we wanted to marry each other one day, but back then I had no idea that I *was* sitting under that beautiful tree with my future husband!

My dad and I have always been close. He was—and still is—one of the most powerful forces in my life. Growing up, he was like a god to me. He was incredibly strong—emotionally and mentally, but also physically. What always struck me were his strong hands. They were enormous. He wore something like a size 16 ring.

When I was little though, boy, was I terrified of my dad. My father was king. The boss. We always said, "What he says, goes!" He never hit me. He didn't have to. If he was mad, he just shot you this *look*. Whenever he did that, I would be shaking in my shoes. I actually peed my pants when I was in first grade when he was yelling about something I did and gave me that chilling look. Grown men were wary of it! I got so scared that I couldn't help but wet my pants—or run.

As I got older, though, I started to push the limits with him. I wasn't fresh. I just wanted to have my say, like all teenagers do. Sometimes when he told me to do something, I would say, "But . . ." He did not like that. I think he thought I was being disrespectful, but I was just trying to get my point of view across—or get something I really wanted. I remember asking my dad if I could have a sleepover at my friend's house. He said no. "But her parents will be there," I said. "Why can't I?" The answer was *always* no. He couldn't believe that I would dare to continue to ask him about it. Finally, he said,

"You sleep home. I don't want to talk about it again." That was that. No sleepovers.

I remember my mom or my brother shooting me looks to keep quiet when I said, "But . . ." (I laugh now when I think of *all* the crazy things my little spitfire, Milania, comes up with! Like when she said to Joe, "Gimme pizza, you old troll!" I cannot *imagine* what kind of look I would have gotten if I had said that to my dad!)

When my dad got really mad at me, he would slam his hands on the table, just like my brother did at his son's christening on the first episode of Season 3, after he called me "garbage," which started a huge brawl. (I will *never* forget that horrible day . . . *Oh, Madonna mia* . . .)

Unlike me, my brother would never talk back to my father. He would always stay quiet. My mom was a saint. She would never talk back, either. Once in a while she would give him an eye roll, but that was it. As I got older, I always remember my mom saying to me, "If you were married to your father, you would have been divorced already . . ."

My mom and dad were always good at balancing each other out. My mom knew to keep quiet when my dad was fired up and how to speak to him when he calmed down. This really worked for them because they have been happily married for so long. I never heard my mother raise her voice to my dad, who treated my mom like a queen. He would always say to her, "This is how a man treats a woman . . ." I think one reason my brother treats his wife, Melissa, so well is because he learned that from my dad.

Even though my dad could be strict and scary when he shot me *the look*, the funny thing is that today I see that my dad is really just a big teddy bear. My mom is now the boss, although I'm not sure he would admit that. My dad cooks and cleans a lot more now because it's hard for my mom with her rheumatoid arthritis. I think one of the reasons Joe and I have such a strong marriage is because I learned so much from my parents' relationship. He also learned from his parents, Frank and Filomena Giudice, who were happily married for decades, like mine. Joe and I rarely raise our voices to each other and work out our differences in a loving way. I can only hope that Joe and I are able to pass down what we learned from our parents to our daughters. I want them to have the kind of happy marriages we have all had in my family.

I'm grateful that my parents were so strict with me. I never did drugs growing up. I was too terrified of my dad. He would tell me, "If you do drugs and the drugs don't kill you, I will." I always thought of him before doing anything I knew I shouldn't do. Plus, I never wanted to do anything to disappoint my parents in any way. They were so supportive of us, and had given up so much for our happiness, that I never wanted to do anything that would make them think that I wasn't grateful. I was always afraid of what would happen if I ended up in the hospital from taking any drugs. My parents would have had to come and get me, and they would have been devastated. And they would definitely have killed me. Or at least made my life beyond miserable.

My mom is the best mom in the world. So caring and loving. She was always so attentive to my brother and me. We were her life. Her whole world. Growing up, my mom was always home with us. That is how my dad wanted it. We never had a babysitter. My mom would always invite my friends and my brother's friends to our house, so she could keep an eye on all of us and so that she knew where Joey and I were at all times. When I was little, my friends would come over and we would play Barbies for hours.

My dad didn't want my mom to work, although she would come to the shoe repair place every now and then and help him out. She would do any repairs that needed the sewing machine, so she would sew straps on handbags and sandals—that kind of thing.

Dinnertime at my house was sacred. It was family time. It's the same in my house now. My mom had dinner on the table at 5:30 p.m. on the dot every night. We all loved that she made us delicious, healthy home-cooked meals. After we finished dinner, we would have to stay seated at the table for dessert, which was always fruit. We couldn't get up from the table until everyone was done eating. My dad was very big on that. I still carry on that same tradition in my house, too.

My mom was always in the kitchen cooking and baking, like other Italian mamas everywhere. The house always smelled so good. Everything she and my dad made, since he liked to cook, too, was just so delicious. It was all about food in my house. We didn't grow up in a mansion, but our house was the best of the best when it came to food.

Every Sunday, I remember my mom making meatballs and braciole (pronounced *brajole*), thin slices of meat rolled with garlic and parsley and held together with a toothpick. So delicious . . . She would also make her own sauce and stir in homemade sausage, which made it taste even better. I still do that today with my sauce.

I would watch my mom all the time, asking questions about how she prepared things. I would help her cook, too. I think I started helping her when I was five. I would fry eggs in olive oil (like Milania would do with me, later on) and make espresso every night for my dad after dinner. As I got older, especially after I got married, I learned so much from her, which is why I am so good in the kitchen today—and was able to write three *New York Times* best-selling cookbooks!

Everything my mom made was mouthwateringly delicious and done to perfection. During the week she would make us eggplant parmigiana, escarole and beans (which I love to make for my girls now), linguine in white clam sauce or red sauce with crabs, stuffed eggplant, and chicken parmigiana. I love my mom's lasagna, stuffed mushrooms, and homemade pasta. We couldn't get enough of her food. And the smell of her freshly baked bread in the house? Heavenly . . .

My father would always make dinner on Wednesday, his day off. He would roast pork chops or chicken in the oven with onions, potatoes, and vegetables. *Delizioso!*

I loved helping my mom make desserts, too, like *nocché*, which is Italian for bow tie cookies. We would make them for parties and holidays. They taste so good and look so beautiful on the table, but are *a lot* of work.

My mom went all out on Christmas Eve, which was huge for us. We always hung out with our neighbors, who were Sicilians. My mom would invite something like thirty-five people over every year. The kids all played and ran around while the adults laughed, drank homemade wine, and ate all the amazing food my mom spent hours making. (Italian families love to have everyone over all the time, especially for holidays!)

One longtime Italian, Roman Catholic tradition our family followed was the Feast of the Seven Fishes on Christmas Eve to celebrate Jesus's birth. Just like during Lent, when Catholics aren't allowed to eat meat, we are supposed to fast until Jesus is born and can only eat fish while observing the *Cena della Vigilia*—the Christmas Eve vigil dinner. So it was all about the fish that night.

We would have linguine in red sauce with seafood (one of my favorite pasta dishes), seafood salad with octopus, shrimp, and scungilli, another favorite of mine. We would eat a lot of *baccala*—salted cod, which is a southern Italian tradition. We would *mangia* on *baccala* salad, *baccala* in a red sauce, or fried *baccala*, clams casino, mussels in a hot, spicy red sauce baked in the oven, as well as fried shrimp and fried calamari. For dessert, I would help my mom make *struffoli*—fried balls of dough with honey and rainbow sprinkles, which look so beautiful when you serve them. I always loved eating all the fish on Christmas Eve, which is another tradition I uphold at my house now.

At Easter, my mom would make pizza *chiena* or *piena*, a traditional Napolitano recipe. *Piena* means "full"—so it's a thick pie with a crust on top stuffed with ricotta, prosciutto, eggs, and cheese. Absolutely amazing.

One of my favorite childhood memories was going down the Jersey shore with my parents and my brother. Sometimes we would go with Joe's family. We would go for the day every Wednesday and Sunday, since those were my dad's days off. My mom would pack the most delicious sandwiches: prosciutto, fresh mozzarella and eggplant or chicken cutlet. Instead of sprinkling salt and pepper on the sandwiches, she would put homemade jarred eggplant in olive oil or roasted red peppers on the sandwiches. So good! My mom would always pack a big container of iced tea to drink and fresh fruit, like juicy peaches or refreshing watermelon slices. For whatever reason, everything always tasted so good on the beach—and still does.

We would buy badges for the day at beaches like Sandy Hook or Long Branch, and I would spend the day swimming in the ocean, body surfing (hoping I wouldn't lose the top to my bathing suit when I was tossed around in the huge waves!), picking seashells off the beach, playing with sand crabs we dug up, and building sand castles with my dad and my brother. My dad loved to dig a deep hole in the sand, put me or my brother in it, and cover us up to our necks, which would make us laugh! (My mother was always like, "Be careful with them, Giagee!")

My favorite bathing suit back then was a crocheted bikini in rainbow colors. I wish I had a photo of me in that suit, but I don't. My mom didn't take a lot of photos of me and Joey, but I wish she had. I want to be able to see what I looked like every year of my life and share those pictures with my children. That's why I'm now a fanatic when it comes to pictures. I am always taking photos of my daughters doing anything and everything, so they can remember where they come from. What I have learned in this life is that honoring our beginnings—whether they are humble or extravagant—is so important, and I want my girls to be able to look at those photos with my future grandkids!

Growing up with strict Italian, Catholic parents, all I heard my parents say was that they wanted to raise me to be a good girl. They wanted me to be a good wife and mother one day. That's what I wanted to be too. But sometimes it was hard, because the standards they had for my brother, even though he was younger than me, were very different from the standards they held me to because he was a boy, which is typical in Italian families. If my father was king of the house, my brother was the prince. Every night after dinner, I was the one who was expected to help clean up and do the dishes. He would just eat and then take off. I always cleaned my brother's room for him. I would put away my laundry and then his laundry. Every Saturday I would help my mom clean the house. I would dust, mop the floors, clean the bathroom, and vacuum the whole house. He didn't have to do any of this. I never questioned it or got angry about it. This was just the way it was. My brother did have his own responsibilities, too. He would help my dad out in the yard and would always take out the garbage.

While I was a daddy's girl, and still am, my brother was definitely the apple of my mother's eye. My mother was crazy about my brother. She loved him so much. She couldn't pronounce Joey right so she would call him *Jovey mio*—"my Jovey." We both got our love for our own families—and our strength—from our parents, especially my dad. He taught me to stand up for myself and face my challenges head-on, just like he did. I had no idea just how big those challenges would be for me later on in life.

When I was going into fourth grade, we moved from our apartment to a one-family house in a nice neighborhood. I lived in that house with my parents until I was twenty-seven, when I got married. I have a picture of me standing in front of that house on my wedding day. We all spent lots of time in our new yard. My dad would cut the grass, while my mom would be outside every night watering the flowers she loved to plant. My parents had a garden in the backyard, where they grew tomatoes, peppers, cucumbers, and eggplant, just like their families did in Italy. They also installed a full kitchen in the basement, which is totally an Italian thing. They did that because they wanted to keep the kitchen upstairs spotless. The kitchen downstairs was the workhorse kitchen, where all the heavy lifting would take place when it came to cooking—especially for the holidays. Next to the kitchen downstairs, there was a big room with a living room and an area for the table where we ate dinner every night together.

If you thought my parents were strict when I was little, that was nothing compared to when I was a teenager. We would be sitting at the dinner table and my father would pick up a knife and say to me, "You need to walk a straight line on the knife. If you walk crooked on it, you will cut yourself. But if you walk straight, you will be good." He was basically telling me that I always needed to avoid sex and drugs, do right in life, and try not to make any stupid mistakes. He told me that all the time—right up until the day I got married.

For as much of a good girl as I prided myself in being, I did make some mistakes. In seventh grade, I cut school one day with my best friend, Maria. We went to her house because her mom worked and no one was home to catch us. I had my period and felt lousy, and just didn't feel like dragging through the school day. In my house, I had to be dying to stay home from school.

We hung out at Maria's house all day, talking, putting on makeup, and watching TV. I kept a close eye on the clock. I had to get back to school before the last bell rang because my mother picked me up every day. I have to admit, I loved feeling so free!

When I got back to school, I tried to fly under the radar, but one of my teachers saw me and figured out that I had skipped school. The next day I was called into the principal's office. I was shaking like a leaf as I walked down the hall. I had never, ever been in trouble like this before in my whole life. I almost died when the principal told me I was suspended from school for two days, because I knew what my parents would say. That's what scared me the most.

I remember almost wanting to throw up when I told my mom what had happened, because my stomach was in knots. Just as I predicted, she didn't take it well. At all. After I managed to get the words out, she yelled at me and told me I had to go to school unless I was *really* sick. She said I needed to be a good example for my brother. I felt so bad for letting her down. I cried and went to my room and stayed there until dinner. Despite how upset she was with me, she didn't tell my father about it. I was beyond relieved. I was a teenager pushing the limits, but I felt so guilty about disappointing my mom that I never missed school again.

I am proud of the fact that I was a good girl growing up. I know I have made some missteps along the way. I've also had to deal with the many curveballs life has thrown me. Despite all of that, I have always put my family, my love for them, and my values first. I can only hope that my daughters will walk in the same footsteps that I have when it comes to these kinds of things. My strict upbringing also kept me out of a lot of trouble growing up, which is why I am so strict with my own daughters. I am raising them to be good girls, too.

As a teenager, I always wondered what it would be like to date Joe. After all, our families were so close, and even back then, I knew him like the back of my hand. Somehow, though, we knew we had to date others before finding the great love in each other.

In high school, I found myself hanging out with this guy who was the center of a lot of attention. There was another girl who liked him at the same time, and was not happy he liked me so much. She would give me nasty looks—the side eye and the up and down—and would constantly flirt with him. One day, we passed each other in the stairwell between classes and she bumped into me on purpose, making me drop my books. When I stood up, I told her to cut the shit. She started screaming and pushed me, so I pushed her back. I was protecting myself. I had never been in a scuffle like this before, but this girl started it and I reacted to what she did. What did she think I was going to do? Just stand there?

All these people came to watch because they heard we were fighting. When the school officials came, my heart sank. I knew I was going to get in trouble, and I did. Both of us got suspended. I was most terrified of my parents' reaction. While they weren't happy that I got suspended, my father told me he knew that I wouldn't have gotten into it with that girl unless I was defending myself, so he wasn't mad.

I was upset at the suspension but was proud of myself for standing my ground with her. I remember thinking back to this incident when I flipped that table on the first season of *Real Housewives*, when Danielle Staub pushed me to the limit. I am a pretty laid-back person until you push my buttons and keep going. That's when I usually lose it.

Things quieted down for a while after that with that girl in high school, but when another girl set her sights on that same guy, we had to go through the whole thing *all over again*. Just like the first girl, this new one was also jealous of our relationship. So one day, she and her friends waited for me and tried to jump me.

School had just ended for the day, and as I headed outside to the bus, I turned a corner and saw that girl and her friends waiting for me. No one else was around, so I was all alone. Just them and me. After they surrounded me, the girl started hurling a lot of ugly words at me, calling me a *puta* and telling me to stay away from him. I basically said that if he wanted to be with her, he would. Even though we were just yelling at each other at this point, I knew what was going to happen next: they were going to pull my hair, scratch me, push me—and punch me. They were trying to scare me because there were so many of them and only one of me. I wasn't afraid of them. I thought what they were doing was ridiculous. I held my own and stood strong. I didn't back down. I was one tough Italian cookie and they knew it.

Then, out of nowhere, a friend of mine happened to be passing by and saw that I was in trouble. She pulled out a knife and they scattered like mice. I was shocked. I didn't even know she carried a knife on her. Thank goodness she did.

Since I went to school with some tough kids, I learned to be tough and stand up for myself. You had to be strong there. If you showed anyone you were weak, you were done. The good thing about going to school there, though, was that I had friends from all walks of life—black, white, Latina—which taught me to be open-minded and nonjudgmental when it comes to other races and cultures. It's one of the things that helped me in prison, where I also met all kinds of people—and, just like in high school, had friends from all kinds of backgrounds.

In my heart, I think God sent my badass, knife-carrying friend my way that day for a reason. Otherwise, I would have had to defend myself against all of them. I know I could have handled myself and held my own, but still, there were a lot of girls there. Thank God nothing at all happened to me and that my friend was there to back me up. I didn't want another suspension, or for my parents to get upset again.

One thing I learned from that horrible day was that yes, those girls wanted to scare me, but that will never work with me. Doing something like that will just make me come back even stronger. I didn't tell my mom that I was almost attacked because I knew she would be worried about me. But I've never been afraid to stand up to anyone. I don't like fighting, but if I need to stand up for myself, I will. I may have a soft and kind heart, but that doesn't mean I don't have a backbone. Standing strong is just one trait many Italians share, and I'm proud to be able to do that for my family and myself.

People out in the world have said they think I am "pampered and spoiled." That's not true at all. I have always been a hard worker. My parents instilled a strong work ethic in Joey and me from a young age. They always told us to work as hard as we could for our money—and to save, save, save, like they did. I have no problem working hard. I actually like to work. All my employers would always say that I hustled. Later on, at book signings for the four cookbooks I wrote, I would never take a break. I wouldn't stop until everyone waiting in line got an autograph and a picture. I was at one event at a Barnes & Noble until two in the morning, because there were so many people there waiting to meet me! I didn't mind. I wanted to make sure everyone left happy.

I started working at a young age. When I was ten or so, I got my own paper route after begging my father to let me do it. He finally gave in, thinking I would do it for a few weeks and get it out of my system. But I loved it. Unlike other kids, who delivered the newspapers on their bikes, my father would drive me from house to house because he wanted to make sure I was safe. I prided myself as the papergirl who put the newspaper in the mailbox because that was the right thing to do. I would think to myself, "If I throw the newspaper on the lawn or in the driveway and it rains, how will my customers read it?" I got tipped well for my extra efforts. People would tell me they never had someone put the paper in the mailbox before. I just wanted to do the best job possible, something I have tried to do my whole life.

When I was fourteen, my dad helped me get a job at Shoe Town, a shoe store in Ramsey, New Jersey. Since I only worked on Saturdays, I would drive in to work with my dad. He would drop me off at Shoe Town at 8 a.m. and pick me up at 5:15 p.m., when he was done with work. When I got my driver's license, I worked more, especially during vacations and when I was off from school. Eventually, I started working at the Shoe Town in the Preakness Shopping Center in Wayne, New Jersey. That Shoe Town closed awhile ago and is now a Trader Joe's. I smile whenever I drive past there because I loved working there and making my own money. But most of all, I was happy that my parents were so proud of me for being so responsible.

In high school, I started thinking about a future career, so I took the business program there and learned how to type on a typewriter— because we didn't have computers back then—and write shorthand. That kind of thing. I really loved it. After I graduated in 1990, I went to Berkeley College for fashion merchandising and management. I learned so much and graduated two years later with an associate's degree. In the fall we went on a fashion trip with the school to Paris and London . . . a dream trip! I fell in love with both of those cities—especially Paris. I had a hard time understanding what they were saying to me, even though I speak Italian. I would love to take my girls there one day.

All in all, I had a happy childhood. My parents taught me to love and respect them and my family, to love God, to always try to do the right thing, and to be a good wife and mother—all things I am passing down to my own daughters today.

# 2

---

## BECOMING MRS. JUICY JOE

*I*n the very first episode of *The Real Housewives of New Jersey*, I said, "My husband, Joe, is gorgeous. He's built. He's got the big shoulders and the big arms. He's got it going on. He's just absolutely delicious and *juicy*."

Oh . . . some people had *a lot* to say about that. I don't care. I felt that way about him then, and I still feel that way now. Not only is he the love of my life, he's also my best friend. He has always been there for me and has always treated me so well. Joe comes across as a tough guy sometimes, but he is very sweet. We always have a great time together. He's almost always in a good mood and so am I. Joe and I are both very easygoing, and we love to laugh all the time. He has always treated me like a woman should be treated. He's always taken me to nice restaurants since day one and bought me beautiful, thoughtful gifts. He is always so kind and gentle toward me. If you couldn't already guess, I love, love, love, love his body. He is so muscular and built. That's why I started calling him juicy because I love hugging his strong body. I missed him so much when I was in prison—and then some. *Oh, Madonna mia!*

*J*oe has been in my life forever. Our parents are both *paisanos* from the same town in Italy, and they became a lot closer when they moved to America.

Just like he did in Italy, my late father-in-law made it to the top in America, too. He was a very hard worker and very smart. He started his own company doing roofing, siding, and stucco work like he did in Sala Consilina, and did very well with that. He taught Joe and his brother, Pete, the business, too. Joe always said his father was a tough guy to work for, the toughest of the tough. He wanted things done the right way or not at all, and since he was the best at what he did, he taught Joe, Pete, other family members and the people who worked for him how to do everything the right way, so that they would do well, too.

Joe and I grew up together in America. His father was even at the hospital when I was born. My future in-laws brought Joe to the hospital to meet me a day later, when he was just about to turn two. Judging from the pictures I saw of him, he was *so* cute, even then!

Since our parents were friends, we were always together, at home and in school. We both went to St. Mary's, a Catholic school in Paterson. When I was in third grade, I started to think Joe was cute. I liked him a lot. I remember going to the bathroom just so I could walk by his classroom and wave to him. He had dirty blond hair and those green eyes. (That's where my daughters get their light hair.) I'm not sure if I knew what the word "juicy" meant in third grade, but wow, did I have a big crush on him, and he had one on me.

When my parents would bring us to Joe's house so they could spend time with his parents, Joe and I would play house in the basement and would always be the parents, which is so funny. My brother Joey, Pete, and Joe's sister, Maria, would be the kids. Even when we were really little, when the other kids would go upstairs, we would go off in a dark area of the basement and give each other kisses—little pecks. It was so cute.

As Joe and I got older, we liked and dated other people, but we were always in each other's life. From the time he was thirteen or fourteen, Joe always had a girlfriend. In fact, he had many of them over the years. He was a hot guy—buff, strong, and handsome. He had a ton of friends, worked and made his own money, and had a nice car—a 1987 Thunderbird Turbo Coupe. Since he was so independent and got into trouble from time to time (he would joyride in his parents' car at thirteen or fourteen!), a lot of girls viewed him as the ultimate bad boy, so of course, everyone wanted to date him. At one point, I remember my mother warning me about him—that he might not be right for me because he was known as such a bad boy. That made me love him even more . . .

When I was seventeen and he was nineteen, we would meet and go down the shore for the day and spend the day on the beach together. There we could kiss all we wanted. I loved seeing him with his shirt off and he told me he loved seeing me in a hot bikini. That same year, he took me out for Valentine's Day to Shanghai Reds, a fancy restaurant in Weehawken, which is now Chart House. It's right across the Hudson River from Manhattan, so it has some of the best waterfront views in Jersey. He brought me a dozen red roses—and gave me a beautiful tricolor rose ring. I was so touched that he did that. Giving me that ring was a big deal to me because then I knew I was really special to him.

One thing I really admired about Joe was that he was always willing to help my parents out. He is very handy and can fix anything. I remember he got worried because my dad worked in his tiny repair shop for years with no air-conditioning. So one day Joe showed up and installed an air conditioner over the front door of the store so my dad could have some cool air in there. My father was so grateful to him for doing that. Generosity has always been one of Joe's best qualities, and every time he made a gesture like this, no matter how big or small, it turned my world upside down.

I think it was better that we both dated other people before we got serious. I think it happened like it was supposed to happen, because I started running into Joe and seeing him at clubs when he was single, for the most part, and I was, too. He was seeing some girls at the time, but they were nothing serious. I was still talking to my ex, a guy I dated on and off for six years after I graduated from high school, but I realized that he wasn't right for me. (When we broke up once, he sent me twenty-five *dozen* roses, and I didn't want them. I remember my father yelling at the delivery guy to take them all away!) In the back of my mind, I always thought about Joe. That definitely meant something. I guess it was the same for him, too. We both realized that it just felt right to be with each other.

Joe always treated me well, from the beginning. He always took me to nice places, opened doors for me, grabbed my hand and took the lead, and always gave me roses and jewelry. He is a man's man, which I love. (Swoon . . .) The more we were together, the closer we got. We were definitely in love at this point and went practically everywhere together. But here was the problem: how to tell our families. The fact that we were dating was a big deal because our families were so close. As Gorgas, we had spent so much time with the Giudices over the years (little did I know, that would be my last name one day!). Joe and I snuck around while we figured out how to tell them how serious we were about each other, because we didn't know how they were going to take this big newsflash.

Finally, things got so serious between us that Joe decided it was time to let people know we were an item. Joe took me to a big family party—as his date. I think some of his family members were shocked. Everyone was really nice to me, but I could tell they were buzzing about us.

Even though we were nervous about what their reaction would be, my parents said, "If you're happy, then we're happy." Joe's dad loved hearing that we were together. I think Joe's mom was a little surprised, but she seemed fine with it, too.

My brother, Joey, was like, "What? You kidding me?" He was surprised but happy for us, too. He hung around with Joe's brother, Pete, all the time, so they were close. Joey looked up to Joe almost like he was a big brother.

After the families got over their initial shock, everything just fell into place. We both realized that we weren't meant to be together—really together—before this. It happened when it was the right time. Before that, we were too young, and at different places in our lives. It wouldn't have worked out, I'm sure. Joe also knew that if he dated me, he would have to treat me really, really well because our families were so close. His dad was over the moon when he found out we were seriously dating. But still, he gave Joe "the talk." He said, "Make sure you do the right thing with her." He didn't want him to hurt me in any way. He told Joe what he knew already: that I wasn't just a girl to fool around with.

During Memorial Day weekend in 1997, Joe and I went away for his birthday. I wanted to make his birthday extra special, so I arranged to have the place where we were staying totally decorated by the time we got there. The ceiling was covered with balloons. I also had them leave a chilled bottle of champagne there for him. He was so surprised when he walked through the door! He hugged me and kissed me and then . . . well, let's leave it at this: I was the best birthday gift he's ever had.

Little did I know that Joe's plan was to make the weekend even more special. That Saturday night, we went to a restaurant on the water and had a romantic candlelight dinner, drinking and eating filet mignon and lobster until we were stuffed. After dinner, we walked down to the beach and sat on the sand. Joe bought a bottle of champagne from the restaurant bar and brought two glasses with him. I just remember having the most amazing time because we were both madly in love. We were sitting there watching the sunset, listening to the waves crash on the shore, talking and kissing, just the two of us. Everything was so calm, peaceful, and romantic.

We had been drinking for a while, so we were both tipsy. When I saw Joe reach into his sock, I wasn't sure what he was doing. In a flash, he pulled out a gorgeous diamond ring. I started shaking. He got on one knee and said, "Will you marry me, Teresa?" Of course I said yes. We hugged each other so tight before we lay down in the sand and started kissing again. By now it was dark and there was a huge moon in the sky. Everything was perfect. Right out of a storybook. I couldn't stop looking at the gorgeous ring he slid onto my finger. Two and a half carats—a round diamond with two pear-shaped diamonds on the sides . . . I was going to get married!

Then I panicked. Despite how much I had had to drink and that this was one of the most memorable and important moments of my life—one I had dreamt of since I was a little girl—I snapped to and was like, "Oh my God! What about my parents?"

Joe put his arms around me and calmed me down. He said that he had already spoken to my father and gotten his blessing. That's when my dad had "the talk" with Joe. Speaking to him in Italian, he reminded him once again that I was a good girl and that I would be a good wife and mother. Then he took those big hands of his and put them on Joe's shoulders and gave him those crazy eyes, telling him to always honor and respect me, take care of me and love me with all of his heart, just like he did. Joe assured him that he would do all of those things. They looked at each other and hugged. It was such a warm moment between them. My father had always loved Joe, who looked up to him and respected him so much.

Now that I felt better about everything, we went back to the room and called both sets of parents. They were so excited and happy for us. Our moms, of course, were crying.

When we got back from our trip, we had a gigantic engagement party with all of our families—uncles, aunts, cousins and friends— at Villa Amalfi in Cliffside Park. I loved being engaged to Joe and being by his side. I was so proud to be his fiancée. I couldn't wait to be his wife. Mrs. Joe Giudice. But first, we had a wedding to plan . . .

I was so excited—and nervous—on my wedding day, October 23, 1999. I got ready at my parents' house, trying hard not to cry. I thought my dad was going to lose it when I stepped into the living room wearing my dress, which he had helped me pick out. My mom, who also tried not to cry, kept telling me how happy she and my dad were that I was so in love.

After taking lots of pictures, we got into an elegant Excalibur and headed to the Cathedral Basilica of the Sacred Heart in Newark, one of the most ornate churches I have ever seen. My dad helped me out of the limo and gave me a look that said, "My little girl . . ." I tried hard not to cry.

Joe's brother, Pete, who was his best man, was standing at the altar with the other groomsmen. My longtime friend Rosanna, my maid of honor, and my eight bridesmaids fixed my train and made sure my bouquet looked good. I was shaking a little bit when the flower girl and the bridesmaids started walking down the aisle, one by one. Then it was my turn! I hooked my arm into my dad's, and when we heard the wedding march, we started down the long aisle. When I saw Joe standing at the altar waiting for me, he took my breath away. He looked incredibly handsome—and happy, even though I knew he was as nervous as I was.

As my father walked me down the aisle, he was whispering to me in Italian that he was so proud of me and that I was going to be an amazing wife and mother and that I looked more beautiful than he had ever seen me. He also told me he loved me so much. When we got to the altar and it came time to give me a kiss and a hug and give me away, those big, strong hands of his were shaking. He was smiling at me, but had tears in his eyes, too.

Now, you have to understand—this is the man who never cried. My wedding day was the first time he had ever done so in front of me. When I became a mom, I always told my girls that crying is good—a coping mechanism. It's a way to let your feelings out—and then you feel better. But when I was growing up, tears were a big no-no.

So here I was, moments away from getting married, seeing my father, my rock, crying for the first time in my life. All this pent-up emotion started welling up inside of me, so I started tearing up, too.

But I didn't want to break down in front of everyone in church or mess up my makeup, so I put on a stone face—something I have done many times, especially on the show. But I will never forget how absolutely tender that moment was.

I tried not to get teary-eyed again when Joe and I exchanged vows and the priest pronounced us husband and wife. We shared a romantic kiss up on the altar and walked so proudly and triumphantly down the aisle together. I was now Mrs. Joe Giudice . . . I was someone's *wife*. Joe's wife. The man I had loved my whole life. I felt like the whole thing was a beautiful dream.

We left for our honeymoon in Hawaii early the next morning. Everything felt surreal. I was like, "Are we really married? Are we away together and my parents actually *know* about it?" I felt like I finally could be away with my honey without sneaking around. I was as free as a bird, and so protected and secure with Joe. We were just two kids in love. It was amazing to be away with him and waking up to him in paradise. I really did feel like I was floating in love . . . We had fun taking showers together, swimming, fooling around in the coves (!), and being so carefree with each other.

I wanted the best for my honeymoon, so we stayed at the Ritz-Carlton in Kapalua in Maui and at the Grand Hyatt in Kauai. I was told these were the hotels to go to. They were. Our room at the Ritz was stunning. It overlooked the ocean and lush greenery everywhere. I didn't want to leave.

The Ritz was so elegant. The pool overlooking the ocean was one of the biggest I had ever seen. One of the best parts of the trip was when we went to Mount Haleakalā to see the huge volcano there at two in the morning so we could be there for the sunrise. It was cold up there but well worth the wait. The sunrise was one of the most spectacular I had ever seen. We rode bikes down the mountain, but I got scared because we were going so fast, so I ended up taking a bus the rest of the way down, which made Joe laugh. After we spent a week in Maui, we headed to the Grand Hyatt in Kauai for a week. They had a fun bar scene there with music, which we loved. We had a blast at that bar . . . (The Hyatt there still sends us a Christmas card every year, which is incredible since we were there sixteen years ago.)

We went swimming under waterfalls and lagoons at the hotel (and fooled around there, too . . .). We rented this yellow convertible Dodge Prowler, such a cool car, and had fun driving through Kauai, visiting the breathtaking waterfalls and forests. We indulged in many romantic candlelight dinners and went to a couple luaus, where the hula girls danced for us. We tried dancing like them, which was hysterical. You should have seen Joe shaking his hips!

Despite all the fun we were having and how euphoric I felt being away with Joe, I got a little homesick when we first got there. I mean, I lived at home until I was twenty-seven, so I missed my parents so much. I started to cry at one point, but tried not to, because I didn't want Joe to get upset. But he understood. When we sat on the bed in our room and I broke down, Joe put his arm around me and said, "Let's call them." I felt better about everything after I heard their voices. They were so happy we were having such a good time.

It was great to finally be married. I loved being a newlywed and being with Joe all the time. When we got back home, it was fun living together and getting to know each other even better. I would make him scrumptious dinners. We would give each other massages when we were in bed at night. He continued to take me to amazing restaurants and buy me beautiful gifts. He got me whatever I wanted. He never said no . . .

I went straight from living at my parents' house to living at Joe's house, which was a new thing for me. Life without that curfew was so much fun! We would stay out late going to dinner and clubs or drive down to Atlantic City for the weekend or go on lots of vacations together. It was such a relief not having to worry about getting home on time because I was married.

Even though I grew up with two people who made the most incredible food on the planet, I had never actually cooked much myself before I got married because my mom did most of the cooking, especially when I was working. But I would always help her cook on the weekends and on the days I had off. She taught me so much. Joe's mom is an incredible cook, and I wanted to show her that her son would be eating well with me, too. I loved making meals for Joe, but once in a while when I wasn't sure about something I was whipping up, I would call my mom and ask her what to do, and she would talk me through it. I loved doing that with my mom. I would make Joe the most delicious roasted chicken, potatoes, and vegetables in the oven, just like my dad would make for us on Wednesday nights, or veal with peppers, eggplant, and mushrooms, which is one of my favorite dishes. After a while, I started making up my own recipes, and that's when my love of cooking really took off.

When we first got married, I moved into Joe's second-floor apartment in the three-family house he owned in Paterson. When I moved in, there was no mistaking that a guy lived there. This was, after all, his former bachelor pad. He had black leather couches in the living room, gray lacquer furniture in his bedroom, speakers everywhere with surround sound, and a Jacuzzi tub. His apartment also had a small office, a galley kitchen, and a deck where I spent a lot of time.

He had another small bedroom that I used as my closet because he didn't have room in his bedroom for all of my clothes. He couldn't believe how much stuff I had!

I didn't mind that the house looked like a man cave. I didn't want to redecorate—and in turn, spend money on the apartment—because I knew we were going to move and that I would soon be decorating a whole house. I did change the drapes and some other small things, just to give it a bit of a feminine touch.

At this point, Joe was running his businesses and I was working, too. Right after college and before I married Joe, I worked at Nordstrom in Jersey's Short Hills Mall, before I became an assistant buyer at Avenue in Rochelle Park. After that, I landed a great job at Macy's Herald Square, the company's flagship store in New York City, as an assistant buyer in the corporate offices, where we did the buying for all of their stores. I worked hard, and before I knew it, I got promoted to associate buyer. After a great run at Macy's, I went to work for Nine West and later on at Calvin Klein, in their corporate offices, selling handbags to stores like Macy's and Bloomingdale's. (I think people forget—or just don't know—that before I started doing *Real Housewives*, I enjoyed a successful career in the fashion business.)

From the minute Joe and I got married, we wanted to have kids. I was twenty-seven when I got married and Joe was twenty-nine, so we said, "Whenever it happens, it happens." Since we were so in love, we really wanted to have a baby together.

That May, just seven months after we got married, I missed my period. I thought, *There's no way I could be pregnant already*. I drove to CVS and bought a pregnancy test, just in case. I remember how nervous I felt on the drive there and back. As soon as I got home, I took the test while Joe was at work. It came up positive! I thought maybe I did the test wrong, so I went to the store and bought another one, which also came up positive. I still didn't believe I was pregnant. So I went back, yet again, to buy another test.

The test was positive—again. I thought, *Oh my God. I'm really pregnant* . . . I was nervous because I had never spent a lot of time around kids before. I didn't have any little cousins or anything like that, and I never babysat for anyone because I was either working at my dad's repair shop or at Shoe Town.

But I was so excited, too. I couldn't wait to tell Joe. I knew he was going to be so happy! I waited to tell him because I wanted to give him the good news at his thirtieth birthday party. I had been planning a surprise party for him, but now it would be a double surprise. But that plan went out the window fast. I was just too excited. I had to tell him—on the day of the party he didn't know about.

I like to make these important moments unforgettable, so I bought two pairs of booties—one pink and one light blue—and gift wrapped them. I filled our bedroom with pink and pale blue balloons. Since it was his birthday, I handed him the two gifts. I was sitting next to him on the couch in the living room. He opened the first package and looked at the pink booties, but didn't say anything. Then he opened the other package and saw the blue booties. He looked at me like, "What?"

"Now do you know what your gift is?" I said, beaming.

He leaned in toward me and took my hands in his, asking me if we were really going to have a baby. When I said yes, he leaned me back on the couch and started kissing me.

"But there's more!" I told him. I led him into the bedroom, where he saw all the balloons. I told him I wanted to go to the deck and let them all go, so we could send them to heaven and ask God for a healthy baby. Joe and I stood together on our deck and watched the balloons float into the sky. I felt so euphoric because I knew that my life was going to change forever. I just knew we were ready for this baby. It was such a beautiful moment, one that I will always treasure.

*O*nce Gia was born in 2001 (she was absolutely perfect and I fell in love the minute I saw her!), both my mom and Joe's mom warned me about the *malocchio*—the evil eye (pronounced *maloik*). They had talked about it all the time, but now that I had her, they were afraid someone could do it to her. When I was a teenager, I used to get the worst headaches. My mom took me to see this old lady she knew to find out if the headaches were caused by the *malocchio*. I watched as she put drops of olive oil in a bowl of water. If the drops got big, that meant someone had given you the *malocchio* and she would say prayers to break it. It worked. My headaches went away. I remember the lady would yawn from saying the prayers, which meant the *malocchio* was gone. The bigger and longer the yawn, the worse the *malocchio* was. The lady yawned for a long time, which meant mine was very bad.

My family took the *malocchio* seriously. When I was growing up, my mom and dad told me that it could actually kill you. To protect myself from people I felt were giving me the *malocchio*, my mother would always tell me to make the sign of the horn with my hand: You put up your index finger and pinky while holding your middle and ring fingers with your thumb. I did that when those girls in high school were jealous of me and my crush. Some of them had no idea what I was doing and thought I was weird. That's why Italians always wear horns around their necks—to ward off someone who looks at them with envy. (Joe wore one when he started doing really well in business later on. It didn't seem to work, though, given what happened to us. Now he wears a huge horn around his neck that his mother got him in Italy and was blessed by priests.)

My mother-in-law told me that sometimes people can give you the *malocchio* without even meaning to do it. So I always had Gia wear a fourteen-karat-gold pin with the Italian horn on her little outfits, just in case.

Before I had Gia, I had planned on going back to work. But I couldn't bear the thought of being away from her for more than twelve hours a day. I just couldn't leave her. Joe's businesses were doing well, so I was lucky enough to be able to stay home and take care of her full-time.

We were still living in Joe's apartment when we had Gia. We turned the second bedroom I used as my closet into her nursery, so we were pretty cramped in there. We needed to move into a house. When we were dating, we'd bought a piece of property around the corner from where we lived, so we could build on it. But in 2000, a friend of Joe's showed him a fantastic property in Montville, which is where we live now. As soon as we saw it, we fell in love with it. Even though it already had a 5,500-square-foot house on it, we were going to expand it and make it into our dream house. The yard was huge—and so private.

Since we knew we were going to remodel, we started out with only the furniture from Joe's apartment so we wouldn't waste money. It took years—and a lot of hard work, time, and sacrifice— to get the house to look the way it does now. I was happy we moved to a house because our little family expanded quite a bit after Gabriella was born in 2004, followed by Milania sixteen months later in 2006, and then Audriana, in 2009.

We lived in the Montville house for a few years, then moved out for a few years while Joe and some of his construction crew added on to it and changed the roof. We were still finishing our house when I started *Real Housewives*. The one I had to say goodbye to the night I left for prison. That house is the heart and soul of the family. Joe helped build it with his own two hands. My girls grew up there. We celebrated birthdays and holidays under that roof. It's where I sang my babies to sleep and snuggled with my husband. Saying goodbye to the home I had known for so many years tore my heart into a million pieces, just like saying goodbye to my husband and daughters did.

$\mathscr{I}$ have made a point of teaching all my daughters to be strong, independent, and hardworking. My parents, in-laws, Joe, and I have always worked hard, and the girls truly see that. My daughters constantly help me do laundry, wash the floors, and clean the bathrooms. They all clean their rooms and put their own laundry away, except for little Audriana, of course.

My oldest daughter, Gia, is an amazing, intelligent, grounded, beautiful girl. She is a gifted student and wants to be a criminal defense lawyer when she grows up because she has seen what Joe and I have been through and wants to help people like us—and moms like me, with kids who need them.

In the days after I left, Joe told me how Gia tried to be so stoic about everything and carry on like normal, but comforted her sisters when they broke down crying because I had gone away. When Audriana was sobbing the day after I left, saying how much she wanted me there with her, Gia took her in her arms, hugged her, and told her everything was going to be OK. "Mommy is fine and we will talk to her later today or tomorrow." She had Audriana sit with her on the couch while she read her a story to take her mind off of me being gone, even though Gia was trying to cope with my leaving, too.

She helped me so much while I was at Danbury. I would tell her what I needed her to do around the house or for the girls and she always got it done, even when she had been at school all day and at varsity cheerleading practice until 9 p.m. She is a strong young woman and is such a great role model for her sisters. She has such a bright future ahead of her. All my daughters do.

Gabriella is my quiet, sensitive one. She is a bit shy around new people at first, and didn't like the cameras when they were around in the earlier years of *Housewives*, so I never forced her to be on the show. She did start to come out of her shell a little bit and had fun on Season 6.

Gabriella likes everything to be perfect, like her mommy does. She's so neat that sometimes she will sleep on top of her bed, with just a blanket over her, so that it always stays made.

She excels at everything she does. She has always gotten top grades at school and *loves* playing soccer. She lives and breathes it and plays on a club team. Growing up, I always thought soccer was for boys, but now I love the sport. Seeing how passionate Gabriella is about the game makes me love it even more.

When I was at Danbury, Gabriella also helped me with the younger girls, which made me cry. I was so grateful for how she and all the girls stepped up when I was gone. She would wake up Milania and Audriana each morning and help get them ready for school, like I used to do.

I like to call Milania "my spicy one." If you've ever seen her on the show, you know why. She definitely steals the spotlight and loves to ham it up when she is on camera. She's come out with some doozies over the years on the show. I mean, this is the girl who once said on the show, "I love being a diva!"

When she was four, they were filming us getting our hair done together. She kept telling the guy doing her hair that it hurt. Finally she yelled, "I want the jerk out!"

Here are some of Milania's best:

*"You're not a cooker, you're a hooker!"* said to Gia. (She says she *still* doesn't know what the word "hooker" means and doesn't understand why everyone laughs at that line . . .)

*"You better not come up here, you stupid little mouse!"* said to a mouse trying to climb up a slide she was on.

*"Oh my God . . . holy! Look how strong you are! You're like a dragon!"* said to Joe . . .

But then there was: *"You're a big poop!"* also said to poor Joe . . .

Some of the things she says really shock me, which you have probably seen by the look on my face. But other things are just so funny, it's really hard not to laugh. Joe and I don't want to egg her on, but when she said, "I'm into older men," it was really hard not to burst out laughing.

Milania has been like this from the get-go. She needs *a lot* of attention and I always give it to her. Anytime there's yelling or drama going on in the house, Milania is almost always involved. She used to love walking around my bedroom in my bras and high heels. She always gave me *agita*, an Italian-American term for angst, when she slid down the banister in our foyer.

What people don't know about Milania is that she is always worried about everyone else. When she knows someone is sad or upset about something, she's the first one to ask, "Are you OK?" Whenever I came down with a cold or a headache, Milania would come in and ask me how I was feeling, get me a glass of water and medicine, and lie down with me to keep me company, stroking my hair to make me feel better. If one of her sisters was upset because a playdate got canceled, she would offer to play with them so they wouldn't feel lonely. Milania is like me. Whenever someone in my family or one of my friends is having a hard time, I am texting them or on the phone with them every day, asking what they need and checking up on them to make sure they are OK.

Then of course, there's my baby, Audriana, who is the sweetest, most precious little girl. All I want to do to her is hug and squeeze her so tight. When Audriana came to see me at Danbury, we would play tic-tac-toe and she always let me win. What little girl lets you win? She wanted me to be happy. Once, Milania fell off a ladder in the garage when she was trying to get our Halloween decorations down off a shelf, and Audriana rushed to her side to make sure her sister was OK. I love her for that.

I told Audriana I had to go away to work on my book. Of course I am going to tell her the truth when she gets older and can understand what happened.

Saying goodbye to my girls after they had visited me in prison ripped my heart out of my chest. Seeing them so upset? I know this may sound dramatic, but I would rather have had someone cut both my arms off instead.

I have to say, while I was working on this book, I couldn't help but cry when I wrote about my daughters. They are my everything. The ones who kept me going through one of the hardest times of my life. I will always be thankful to them for that and for growing up to be such lovely girls and young women. God bless you, my babies. I'm so proud of you and I love, love, love, love you so much.

# 3

## HOUSEWIVES—JERSEY STYLE

By 2007, life was good. More than good. We were really happy. Joe and I were redoing the Montville house, which we were excited about. I was busy taking care of Gia, Gabriella, and Milania, who were six, three, and almost two at the time.

Joe and I kept busy with friends and family, inviting them over or going to their houses. In the summer, we went to our house on the Jersey shore as much as we could—just the five of us or with good friends and family, including our parents, Joe's sister and brother and their families, Joey and Melissa, my cousin Kathy, her husband Richie and their kids. We loved taking everyone out on the boat we had at the time, spending the day out on the water. We were so lucky to have such carefree, amazing, fun summers.

I had a big group of girlfriends I hung out with, including Dina Manzo, who I had been friends with for a long time. We had met years ago through our mutual friend, Jackie, and clicked. She felt like the sister I never had because she understood me so well. She could tell by the sound of my voice whether I was on cloud nine or frustrated beyond belief. We were always very close. I met Jacqueline Laurita through Dina, when I ran into the pair of them at a food market in 2002. Jacqueline is married to Dina's brother, Chris Laurita. She had just moved to Jersey from Las Vegas and was pregnant with her first child with Chris, their son, CJ (she also has a daughter, Ashley Holmes, from her first marriage and later on, had another son, Nicholas, with Chris).

I didn't see Jacqueline again for a while, until I ran into her at a Christmas party at Dina's older sister, Caroline Manzo's house a few years later. We totally connected and felt like we had known each other forever. She was the first one to pop a bottle of champagne, grab my hand, and yank me onto the dance floor. We would always laugh our heads off over something silly—and called each other Lucy and Ethel. Jacqueline, Dina, and I were inseparable. We hung out at each other's houses or would go out to dinner or for drinks with the girls or with our husbands. At the time, I truly loved Jacqueline like a sister, like Dina.

That same year, a production company called Sirens Media was scouting locations and casting for a new Bravo show that was initially called *Jersey Moms*. Bravo had hit the jackpot in 2006 when it premiered a similar show, *The Real Housewives of Orange County*, about the day-to-day lives of five gorgeous women in Southern California who lived lavishly.

Following the success of Orange County, Bravo immediately created two other *Real Housewives* series (because who wouldn't?): one set in New York and the other in Atlanta. It goes without saying that these two locales pulled incredible ratings also—and the rest is history.

Now they were looking to shoot their newest show in Franklin Lakes, an upscale Jersey town, which, like the other locations in the series, was the perfect setting. Like the women on the other shows, the ladies in Franklin Lakes lived in unbelievable houses, drove Range Rovers and Mercedes, loved to shop, and of course, looked good at all times.

While the producers were looking for cast members for the new show, they stopped by the Chateau Salon in Franklin Lakes, where *everyone* got their hair done. They asked the Chateau's owner, Victor Castro, if he could recommend any clients with over-the-top lifestyles—complete with the big house, the fancy cars, the bling, and the clothes—and who were interesting, glamorous, and gorgeous.

Jacqueline and Dina were among those who immediately came to Victor's mind, and so he recommended them. Predictably, Jacqueline loved the idea and said she wanted to do it. She always said her life was an open book. At first, Dina was on the fence about life in the limelight, but eventually she agreed to do the show. She told me she wanted to do it to get exposure for Project Ladybug, a nonprofit she founded to help children with life-threatening medical issues. Dina's like that—openhearted and open-minded. I think it was the combination of the two, and the thought that she'd be able to help even more families and children, that really convinced her to do the show.

Jacqueline told Dina about another regular at the salon, Danielle Staub, who she thought might be good for the show, too. I think Dina said something like, "Let's get to know her first." But Jacqueline went ahead and told the producers about her. They interviewed Danielle, who was newly divorced, and thought she would fit in well with the show they had in mind.

When another friend of Jacqueline's turned down an offer to do the show, she and Dina recommended Dina's sister, Caroline. (Caroline and Dina married two brothers, Al and Tommy Manzo—now Dina's ex-husband—who own the Brownstone, the catering hall that was the setting for many a blowup.)

Dina also told the producers about me. They called and asked if they could come speak to me. I was shocked, to say the least. Since I was so busy raising three little ones, I never watched much TV and didn't really know what a reality show was. The world of reality TV as we know it today was just starting to rev up, so I didn't have much to use as a reference. I never read the tabloids or celebrity magazines because I was always so busy being a mom (and because my parents never had them lying around the house when I was growing up), so I didn't know if they even wrote about reality TV stars. That didn't even cross my mind. I didn't watch any of the *Real Housewives* shows, either—just the Disney Channel with the girls, or the History Channel with Joe.

Even after speaking to the producers, I wondered if it was a scam. I remember thinking, *Why would anyone want to do a show about regular wives and moms like us and document our day-to-day lives?* Even though my fantasy was to become a movie star when I was little, I was now a mom with three young daughters, so becoming a star was no longer on my radar and not part of my decision-making process at all. But Jacqueline was going on and on about it and kept saying it would be fun for us to do, so I thought I would at least listen to what they had to say.

When the producers came to see me, I was still skeptical. We talked outside of our house in Montville, which was under construction. I introduced them to my three girls and answered their questions about what my life was like. Joe was busy working on the house, so he said hi and that was it. The producers told me they loved me and wanted me to be on the show just from that initial meeting. They sent me a contract, but I still wasn't sure about this. My friends and family didn't know much about being on a TV show, either, but told me to think about it carefully. So for me, this was stepping into the unknown.

It took eleven months for me to agree to do it. The producers would call me regularly to check in, saying how perfect I would be for the show. I took so long to decide because I really wasn't sure about what I would be getting myself into. I asked Joe about it. He said, "It's up to you, honey. I will support you in your decision, but I really don't want to be on TV. You can be on there with your friends." Of course, he did end up being involved with the show, but at the time we didn't think that would happen.

Toward the end of those eleven months, I met Jacqueline for lunch at this Chinese place we liked in Franklin Lakes. She and all the other ladies had signed their contracts long before. She brought a blank contract—a contract meant for me—and said, "Are you going to sign it, already? If you're not going to do the show, then I'm not going to do it either."

She was like, "Come on, do it with us."

Maybe it was peer pressure or maybe I was feeling spontaneous, but I bit the bullet and signed the contract right then and there—without a lawyer to look it over. Jacqueline took it and immediately mailed it, so I couldn't back out.

In the end, I said yes because I figured it would be fun. They were just going to follow us around and film what we did every day: going out for lunch or dinner together, or just hanging out with each other and our families. Honestly, what went through my mind was the amazing memories we'd have—I pictured it being a televised home video of my daughters.

I definitely didn't do the show for the money or the glamour. I didn't get paid much for the first season, and for the most part, we did our own hair and makeup! I remember trying to get ready for a scene and doing my makeup with my daughters right there, Velcroed to my side, as I tried to keep my hand steady to put on lip gloss and liquid eyeliner. They were asking me questions right and left, trying on my blush and mascara, and running around with the energy only kids have.

I ended up spending that season's salary on show-related expenses including pricey dresses, shoes, and handbags for the various parties and events. I had to put aside money for taxes, so in the end, I didn't make anything that season. But again, I was just doing it for fun. I remember thinking, *What possible harm could it bring?* I truly had no idea that being in the limelight meant that everything you did or said would be scrutinized and would bring on a jealousy I had never seen before, from strangers, friends, and family alike. Talk about *malocchio*.

Looking back, it was so easy to just sign a piece of paper. I had no idea it would change my life forever—for good and for bad. I never thought a show about regular moms shopping and just doing their thing would blow up into what it became—or that it would bring so much drama to my family. Or should I say, I never thought my family would come on the show and cause all the drama that they did.

The first season centered around Dina, Caroline, Jacqueline, and their families. I was kind of like the fun friend. The sidekick. People always ask me when I was my "most real" on the show, and I always tell them that you saw the real me in the first two seasons. (As the seasons went on, people would say I was mean and vengeful. But it was because of the situations I faced on camera. I'm actually pretty laid-back, low-key, and have had drama-free friendships for decades. No yelling, screaming, accusing, backstabbing . . . just normal. But that's not always what you saw on the show.)

After I signed the contract, we met with the producers, who gave us a rundown about how everything would work, and then a few weeks later, we started filming. Just like that. I was nervous that first day. After a while, though, I forgot the cameras were even there, which, as you can imagine was good and, sometimes, as I later found out, not so good. In one of my first scenes, Gia, Gabriella, Milania, and I visited Joe at his office, which was his first time on TV. He did great. He just goes with the flow. When we were doing the show, he didn't feel the need to be on camera all the time. It just wasn't his thing. He was busy running his businesses and respected the fact that the show was my thing. He was fine not being involved in every scene.

While we were filming the show, which they later renamed *The Real Housewives of New Jersey*, we had no idea what would appear in the actual episodes, because they would always film so much more than what you saw on TV. The episodes also aired long after we finished shooting. Of course, this was all new to me. The producers would ask us what we were up to, and if they were interested, they would come along and film us. They liked when we did things together, so we could be filmed talking about the drama of the day while we were out and about somewhere.

When I joined the show, Joe's businesses were doing well and we definitely lived comfortably, but it wasn't like we had cash growing on the fruit trees in our backyard—though some people told me that's what it looked like. When Joe and I moved into the Mont-ville house, we used the furniture Joe had in his apartment and the baby furniture we had for Gia. I never splurged on big things for the house because we wanted to wait until after the remodel was done to redo everything. Joe worked on the house for a long time. Although we added on to the house, it *looked* like we built it from ground up, but we didn't. I tried to be smart about what we bought and to not spend money frivolously.

While I was close friends with Dina and Jacqueline, I didn't know Caroline that well. I only knew her as Dina's older sister. I thought she was nice and a good mother and respected her because she was one of my best friend's sisters.

I met Caroline when Dina was living with her after Dina's first divorce and would invite me over. Caroline started inviting me to her yearly all-girl Christmas party (one year they had male strip-pers there, dressed in Santa hats . . . it was hilarious). I would see Caroline at meetings and fund-raisers for Project Ladybug. When we started working together on the show, we became closer.

I didn't know Danielle at all. When I first met her, I liked her, too. She was the first to speak her mind when the going got tough. She was so open and honest from the get-go that I thought I could trust her. That said, I've definitely learned my lesson: meeting new people is exciting in the beginning, so I let my guard down much too early—before I get a chance to see their true colors.

Things between Danielle and me were fine at first. I stood back and watched as she and Dina started getting into it. Danielle was upset, too, accusing Dina of spreading rumors about her past by sharing *Cop Without a Badge*, Danielle's ex-husband's book, with people in town. Then of course, Caroline started questioning Jacqueline's friendship with Danielle. Let's just say there was *lots* of drama! But at this point, I was still on the periphery—an outsider watching it all unfold.

As the season wore on, Danielle found herself in the hot seat again and again with Dina and Caroline. It all came to a head in the season finale, when we got together at a dinner I hosted. There we were, chatting away, when Danielle decided to pull out a copy of *Cop Without a Badge*. She went on to tell us that while two facts in the book were correct—that she did change her name and that she was arrested—the rest of it was filled with lies, and that she wasn't happy that certain people were spreading those lies around town. By certain people, she meant Dina. Danielle said she was miffed because she had heard that Dina had shown the book to people at the Chateau. I was just sitting there listening, but was thinking, *This dinner is getting real tense, real quick.*

I was starting to get mad. I had had a few cocktails and wasn't happy that Danielle kept going after Dina, who is not a fighter. I felt bad for her. I was upset that Danielle was going after someone who she knew wouldn't fight back. All of this was racing through my head like a runaway freight train.

You have to understand, loyalty is *the* most important thing to me—and when I see someone attacking somebody I care about, I get worked up beyond belief. Admittedly, it's a fault of mine—but it's a fault that stems from love.

Danielle said she wanted to clarify things in the book and wished certain people hadn't brought the past into the present by showing the book to people in Franklin Lakes. Dina said she didn't show the book to anyone. I tried to deflect attention from Dina and defend her when I asked—on camera, no less—"So why did your ex-husband write that friggin' book?" Then I said, "Obviously *something* in that book has to be true."

Danielle swiveled her head around at me and, with eyes blazing, ripped my head off, saying, "Two things are written that are true: Name change. I got arrested. Pay attention—*puh-leeze*!"

Oh boy. Anyone who knows me well knows I do *not* like when people talk down to me, and in such a harsh tone. Danielle *drop-kicked* me over the edge by disrespecting me in front of my family and friends—and the cameras.

I exploded.

"I am paying attention!" I screamed. "Obviously there has to be something else! It's just not name change and arrested!"

My blood was boiling. All I could see was red. I started shaking the table. And then came those now-infamous words: "Prostitution whore! You were fucking engaged nineteen times?!"

And then, as you all know, I flipped the table. Wine-filled glasses, silverware, napkins, and plates went flying. Caroline said she started laughing because she was so nervous and in total disbelief. Joe pulled me out of the room as I continued to shriek. He calmed me down, because he knows as well as I do that whenever I get that mad, I'm literally in another zone. But I rarely, if ever, get that angry, though it may not appear so on TV. Dina and Jacqueline told me later—and also said on camera—that in all the years they had known me, they had never even seen me get mad. That was true. I do have a long fuse, but once in a while, someone lights it with a blowtorch. (And that, of course, is what they always seem to capture while filming . . .)

When I came back into the dining room and sat back down again, I was still pissed. How dare she insult me like that, after she had pounded poor Dina into the ground.

Truth be told, I was mortified. This was not my proudest moment—and I did it while cameras were rolling. *OMG.* I just remember saying to myself, over and over after it happened, *I cannot believe I did that.*

I cringed when that episode aired. I think I watched it with one eye open. I was hoping that people would watch the table-flip scene and forget all about it. It ended up making headlines around the world. *Madonna mia!*

So many people called the house that night, saying, "Oh my God, Teresa!" Some were laughing their heads off while others were asking what the heck happened because they had never seen me like that. But then, people started coming up to me left and right when I was out, telling me how much they loved that scene! I can't tell you how many people told me they wished they could do the same thing. They even showed a clip of that scene at the Grammy Awards that year. I almost fell off the couch.

I regretted flipping the table at first. I couldn't believe I let my temper get the best of me like that. I went way too far, even for me. But at the same time, I felt like I was defending myself, even if I didn't do it in the best way possible. (But I did get my point across . . .) I was relieved to find out that some people out there—especially my fans—understood that I reacted that way because I was pushed beyond the limit. I remember thinking, *They get it. They get me.* I am feisty. I can be fiery. But my temper has caused me problems since then, which is why, when I got to prison and had time to really think about how I react when I'm angry, I set out to try to change that.

While I was mortified at my "I-can't-believe-I-did-that" table-flipping moment, what I didn't realize at the time was that it's actually what helped put me on the road to stardom. When the season aired, people kept saying I stole the show with my funny antics, my unending love for "Juicy Joe," the way I doted on my adorable girls, my over-the-top lifestyle, and my carefree attitude toward life. But this put me in a whole new stratosphere. It's just not the way I had ever wanted to get there.

When we finished shooting and the show first aired, we had no idea that the first season would become as popular as it did. As I said, I just did it for fun and didn't give much thought to what was going to come after people started seeing us on TV.

Right before the first episode aired, we went to New York City to meet with Bravo executives, who prepped us for the publicity we would be doing, like going on talk shows and appearing at events. This sounded so exciting, so I thought, *This is going to be a blast!* And it was.

But at the same time, doing publicity was a lot of work. This was all new to me, too. You needed to prep before you went on TV, especially because you were judged by whatever came out of your mouth during an interview. I found it very stressful. Sometimes after an interview, I would go over it again and again in my head and ask myself if I answered the right way, wondering if it came off the way I wanted it to. That happened while we were filming the show. I would lose sleep over something I said or did and would get mad at myself sometimes for reacting a certain way.

While we were filming the first season, before it aired, no one paid attention to me when I was out shopping or taking the girls somewhere. Why would they? To them, I was just another harried mom with three young, energetic kids. Once in a while I would run into someone who had heard I was doing the show, and I would just say, "It's been a lot of fun! I hope you tune in!" and leave it at that.

I didn't say too much about it because I figured, *OK. Maybe a few people will watch it.* I mean, it was a reality TV show about a bunch of moms. I had never seen the other *Housewives* shows or read about how wildly successful they were. So I thought, *How many people will really care?* I truly had no idea the craziness this show would bring. After all, I was just a normal wife and mom who was thrust into the limelight with little preparation for what was to come.

After the Season 1 finale aired, life as I knew it began to change. I would be walking somewhere, thinking of what I had to do next or trying to keep track of the girls, and would hear people calling my name. Sometimes I didn't even hear them because I wasn't used to it. Then there were the people who got *really* excited when they saw me. I was talking on the phone in the grocery store once, when a woman in the next aisle overheard me and yelled, "Teresa! Is that you?" She came running and, when she saw that it really was me, shrieked, "I *knew* it was you from your voice!" I laughed because I didn't understand what all the fuss was about, but she was sweet and I enjoyed meeting her. While all of this was flattering, I never let it go to my head. I honestly still felt like the same person I always was.

One of the biggest pluses about doing the show was that I started to work again. I'd always enjoyed working, and this job was perfect for me, since the filming schedule was conducive to having kids, and I could bring them with me most of the time. After the first season, all I was thinking about was making money to save for college for the girls. I wanted to help provide for my daughters and give them the best life possible. So I was happy to be contributing to the household. It is a pretty fun job, too. I love working on the show. I love the producers and the folks at Bravo. Andy Cohen, who is an executive producer of *The Real Housewives* franchise, and of course, the host and executive producer of Bravo's late night talk show, *Watch What*

*Happens: Live,* is the best. And the show is what I've come to know. The show has become a part of my life now. A big part, and I would never, ever go back.

Other than being stopped by people for pictures and going back to work, my life pretty much stayed the same after the first season aired. Since I had such young children, I didn't go to parties or red carpet events in the city that much, if at all. I still took care of the girls, went to all their school events, drove them everywhere, cooked and cleaned my own house (later on, when things got a lot busier, I had a cleaning lady come in once a week to help me). Joe and I continued hanging out with our friends and family. At this point, I was happy with my decision to join the show. Everything was working out well.

*O*f course, nothing stays the same. During Season 2, I ended up getting into it again with Danielle when I chased after her at a country club to find out *who* had told her my house was in foreclosure, when it wasn't. We had another tussle at the reunion, with me jumping off the couch to confront her, pushing Andy back in his seat when he tried to stop me. He later said, "You're strong!" I didn't mean to push him, but he was in my way and my fiery Italian temper came out in full force. (If you're Italian, you know exactly what I'm talking about . . .) Andy and I laughed about it later and have since become close. But he wasn't laughing about it that night.

People ask me whatever happened with me and Danielle and if I've seen her over the years. I really haven't and was surprised when she wrote on Twitter after my sentencing in 2014, "dontcha frigin LOVE karma baby!!!!!!! Yup . . ."

She changed her tune, though, on *Access Hollywood Live* six days later, when she said that while we hadn't made amends, "I don't believe you kick somebody when they are down . . . I'm genuinely reaching out to her and giving her support. This is a very hard time she is going through."

While I didn't like what she tweeted when I got sentenced, I appreciated what she said on *Access Hollywood*. She and I didn't exactly see eye to eye on a lot of things, but after the dust settled and I was able to look at everything objectively, I realized that she wasn't the kind of person who would try to hurt me or my family. I don't hold a grudge against her, either. When I found out in prison that she got engaged, I said, "Good for her!" and I meant it. Though I don't ever see a day where we will be BFFs, I wish her well. Holding on to negativity doesn't do anything for anyone.

WATCHING A RERUN OF YOU guessed it REAL HOUSEWIVES OF New Jersey, How is it that everyone IN HERE gets ALONG But WE COULDN'T. It MAKES ME SAD to see ALL OF US fighting ON Television, WHEN WE SHOULD of BEEN lAUGHINg.

*Throughout the book you will see scans of the diary I kept while I was an inmate. I started keeping a diary as soon as I got to prison because I wanted to remember every detail of my experiences there—and because it helped me cope.*

My brother and I were always very close, as kids and teenagers and in our twenties. Best friends. Since we don't have a lot of family here in America, my parents, Joey, and I relied on each other for everything. My parents also raised us to honor and respect each other. As Joey's older sister, I always looked out for him. He's my blood and that's what family is all about to me. People would tell us how blessed we were to have such a tight bond, which I thought was a little strange because I thought every brother and sister got along as well as we did.

As young kids, of course, we played a lot together, but we also had our fights, the way all siblings do, like the time I got mad at him and threw all his toys out the window. But despite our childhood squabbles, which lessened with time, Joey and I always had fun together, especially as we got older. I loved hanging out with him. From the time we were little, we would always spend New Year's Eve as a family with my parents. As we got older, he would bring his girlfriend and I would bring my boyfriend. We would get all dressed up and go to a fancy catering hall. We would double-date, and go to the Jersey shore with our friends. Some of my favorite memories are spending days at the beach with him and hitting the clubs at night in Seaside Heights (where *Jersey Shore* was filmed). After I got married, my brother would come over for dinner all the time. He and Joe, who had known each other their whole lives, loved spending time with one another.

Most importantly, my brother and I were always there for each other, no matter what. When the weather was bad, I would call him and tell him to be careful driving home—and he would do the same for me. Little things like that. We also confided in each other about everything. If he had a problem with one his girlfriends or something going on at school or work, he would talk to me about it and I would give him my best advice. He returned the favor. If I needed advice, I would always call Joey. While we were both close to our parents, sometimes we needed to talk to someone our own age who understood things better than they did. It was just nice to know I had such an amazing, caring brother. Someone I could always count on.

I never imagined in my wildest dreams that my bond with my brother would ever be broken. We would even talk about other siblings we knew who weren't getting along, and we wondered how they could have let that happen. Everything with us was fine, until I did the show. I never thought fame and money could ruin a family until it ruined mine. I hate to even talk about what happened with my family, but I want people to understand how I was feeling at the time and why I reacted the way I did. The bottom line is that so many things happened off camera that led to some of the big blowups that were filmed. Sadly, that's just how it was. Anyone who knows me well knows that I have a good heart and that I am very loyal. But when I'm fired upon, I react by firing back—something I am trying to change.

Joey and Melissa met in the fall of 2003, got engaged that spring, and were married in August 2004. When Joey married Melissa, I welcomed her with open arms to our family. I was hoping she would be the sister I'd always wished I'd had. We all spent a lot of time together. Joey and Melissa would come to our house in Montville for birthdays, get-togethers, and holidays. We would go to each other's shore house. We always had the best time together, which is exactly what I imagined it would be like when my brother and I each had families of our own.

Many people told me that my relationship with my brother would change when he got married, since that sadly often happens. I didn't believe them, but things between us did become a bit more tense once he married Melissa. We had never argued before that. Ever. But after Melissa came into the picture, our relationship seemed different. Whenever she had an issue with me, she would tell my brother about it, rather than talking directly to me. He would get mad at me because he was only hearing her side of things. I respect the way he treats her as a wife, but sometimes I felt like it got to be a little too much. I get it. I'm married and am loyal to my husband. But his refusal to hear me out still hurt.

Before Melissa married Joey, I used to call her every morning to talk, like I did with Jacqueline. But after a few months into their marriage, I didn't hear back from her as much, if at all. I wasn't sure what was going on. I was confused where our relationship was headed.

Before I started doing the show, I was also close to my cousins Kathy and Rosie. They were among the only family I had here in America. They have three brothers, but the boys are older, so I never saw them much. But Kathy and Rosie were at my Sweet 16. They came to our wedding. Just like with Joey and Melissa, we always had the best time. For years, we invited Kathy and Richie on our boat and to the shore house, spending holidays together and even going on vacation one year. This is what I thought family was supposed to be like.

When I started doing *Housewives*, my life became a whirlwind with filming, interviews, meetings, and appearances. I also wrote my first cookbook, *Skinny Italian*, in 2010, so I was busy doing book signings and traveling for a book tour while raising three young girls and running my household. I was overwhelmed, to be honest. This was a whole new world to me and it was more than demanding, but I loved what I was doing. Being on the show was my job and I was taking it very seriously. That said, I simply wasn't around as much as I used to be. Later on, Joey and Melissa said they were upset because they hadn't seen me in two years. Of course I still saw them—at holidays, family get-togethers, and the Sunday family dinners I used to host, just not as much as before. I thought they understood how busy I was as a working mom with three young daughters and, after the first season, a baby. Joey also told me he couldn't believe I hadn't asked him and Melissa to be in any of the scenes I had filmed on the show in the two years I had been doing it. I explained that it wasn't my decision. I told him that the show, at that point, was about the five housewives interacting with each other. I was shocked that my brother asked me about being on the show because he and Melissa had never told me they wanted to be on it before this, and that was just the way I saw it. This was my job.

I will never forget when I was getting ready to shoot Season 3 and got a phone call from Andy telling me that my sister-in-law and cousin were going to be joining the show as the newest housewives. I wasn't even sure I'd heard him right. I was absolutely shocked. I said, "Are you kidding me?" Here I was, always telling them what was going on with the show, yet they never said one word to me about wanting to come on it as full-time cast members. As far as I knew, they only wanted to make the occasional cameo here or there.

I wish they had gone about everything differently. If Melissa and Kathy had told me they wanted to join the show as cast members and had been open about it, I wouldn't have gotten upset. My feeling is we could have shown America what a beautiful family we were. I think people would have loved seeing how much fun we always had together. But since they kept everything a secret, I was upset with them. Every family has its ups and downs, but they usually keep their differences out of the public eye. Reality shows are all about drama, so I knew where this was headed.

*N*ow, if you saw the show, you know what happened from Season 3 on. If you didn't, let's just say that while there were no more table flips, there was drama in spades: everything from a huge fight at Joey's son's christening (where people got knocked down, pushed, and punched) to Joey charging my husband at a "healing" retreat we had gone to so that the family could learn to communicate better and get past our differences. (That went well . . .)

Here's the bottom line. I'm not going to rehash it all. It's all in the past. There's no sense strolling down *that* memory lane. Let's just say there were a lot of fireworks.

But here's the thing. While all these arguments, squabbles, battles, and brawls may play out on national TV and make for juicy viewing, at the end of the day, this was also my life people were seeing. In our worst moments, I wasn't thinking about the cameras, or the fame, or the exposure and shame this would bring to my family. I was thinking about how broken we were, and was reeling from the fact that people I cared about could say those words to me. Absolute shock took over: Who had we become? What happened to our tight-knit family?

I'll be honest. When I first got to prison, I was still mad at a lot of friends and family. It was all still fresh in my mind. But once I was there, I had a lot of time to think. I had time to go back and relive things in my own head. In fact, I had nothing but time.

But then there's that saying: absence makes the heart grow fonder. It definitely applied to my husband and me. Like many husbands and wives, I think sometimes we took each other for granted. But once we were apart, we really saw how much we meant to each other—and how much we did for each other.

It was the same with Joey and me. When I sat in my prison dorm room, alone, missing my girls, Joe, and my parents, I also missed my brother. I thought back to all the good times we had shared. How much we used to laugh! I thought about how he really was there for me so many times when it counted—like the time he asked someone who disliked me to leave a party he had thrown when she came uninvited. Why? Because he is my brother. It made me cry then and it makes me cry now, because it showed me that even though we had gone through some rocky times, he still loved me no matter what. The more I thought about it all, the more I realized that so many times we react in anger because we are hurt. We come off as nasty, with biting words (that we later regret) because we are in pain. We are trying to protect ourselves—defending ourselves to the end. So many times it's more about being right than anything else, or trying so hard to get others to understand our point of view without understanding where they are really coming from. We hear their words, but because we are in defense mode, we really aren't listening. But in the end, who are we really hurting? Not just people we care about so much, but ourselves, too.

Here's the thing—it all comes back to family for me. I need to get back to my roots and where I came from. *That* is what gave me my strength in life. My confidence. Knowing that my parents and Joey were there for me no matter what was what made me the woman I am today. I was confident because I knew I had backup. I knew that if anyone bugged or bothered me, my brother would be right there for me. And of course I would be there for him. And if something amazing happened? I knew my parents and my brother would be there to share in my joy—and I in theirs—even when our little family unit changed, which is inevitable.

Joey and I had a loving, warm childhood, and then we grew up. We got married. We now have our own families. Of course things changed. They always do. Life is all about change. But what I may have forgotten along the way is that we also have to change how we view things once that happens. In my heart of hearts, I would love for things to go back to the way they were between me and Joey and Melissa, and others I have grown apart from.

I remember being at Danbury early on and seeing fight after fight in there. Girls hurling the worst insults you've ever heard in your life at each other—and even going so far as to punch each other so hard that they ended up with bloody faces and bruises all over their bodies. Why? Over something one of them heard that the other said, or because one of them had cut the other in the line for the phone.

I thought, *These women look ridiculous.* For a split second, I wondered, *Is this how I come across?* While I have never given anyone a bloody nose, I have nailed people with some verbal zingers. Words I knew would nuke their hearts. Why? Because my heart got broken, so I fired back. But when I stepped back, I thought, *This is not how I want to come across. There has to be a better way.*

My faith helped me to find a better path. My belief in God helped me get through the legal hurdles I faced and the many long months I spent in prison. I remember one chilly springtime afternoon in my weekly prayer group, we all had to pick promises in the Bible we wanted to read and I chose one about forgiveness. I felt like I had to learn about forgiveness in order to move on. While we were discussing the promises, I thought about how the most important parts of the Lord's Prayer, which I have known since I was a little girl and still recite every night to myself before I go to bed, says,

> *forgive us our trespasses,*
> *as we forgive those who trespass against us . . .*

Forgive those who trespass against us. Such a simple message, yet so hard to do in real life.

I didn't say too much during the prayer group. But I thought about how hurt I had felt by some of the cutting remarks my brother, sister-in-law, cousins, aunt, and others had said to me along the way.

But when I heard that other women in there had forgiven people for setting them up so they would end up in prison, physically abusing them or their loved ones when they were little, sexually molesting them, and other things that stood my hair on end, I thought—*What did my family and close friends do that was so terrible?* Yes, their words and actions caused me pain, but not like this. I'm not trying to minimize what they did, but at the same time, I thought, *If these women could forgive—and I mean really forgive—why couldn't I?*

I remember tucking my Bible under my arm and heading back to my room to think about what we had just talked about. I lay down on my bed and stared at the ceiling. Forgiving is *hard*, I thought. It's easy to say, "I forgive so and so," but then when you start to think about the pain that person caused you, and things that happened as a result, it can make you upset all over again and then you aren't feeling so forgiving.

Holding on to anger only makes us bitter. Forgiving takes time. While I'd like to think forgiveness is a two-way street, in reality it isn't always. Sometimes you have to forgive knowing that other people you hurt may not see things the way you now see them. And that's OK.

In prison, I also became more accepting and tolerant of others (because you had to!). Spending a year away from my family gave me the chance to think about how I interact with other people, and to learn to react with humility and empathy. That's something I hoped to do when I got back home and started dealing with people in my life I have hurt and who have hurt me. It wouldn't be easy, but at least I am aware of it.

My closest friends, who, besides Dina, are not on the show, have told me that one of the things they love best about me is how much I am there for them when they are in need, no matter how big or small it is. That I am the one they know they can count on. That's how I have always been, but when I get angry at people in my family or close friends I made along the way, I often forget about that simple trait of mine. Sometimes all it really does take is a caring phone call to check in on people when they are going through something difficult, even if you are mad at them. Sometimes it is putting your pride aside and really listening to what people are telling you—not just hearing their words, getting defensive, and thinking about what you can say to show that you are right and they are wrong.

It takes a big person to do that. It takes a strong person to do that. It takes someone with a lot of heart. I am striving to be that person, especially when it comes to my family, because at the end of the day, that's who will always be there for us. My family and friends showed me that they were there for me during my darkest days. I will always keep their love in my mind and heart.

Now, while so much of what I dealt with on *RHONJ* was painful for me and resulted in arguments, I had plenty of happy moments during the show, too, which I also thought about a lot in prison.

I was so happy that they filmed us during holiday gatherings, big events like Audriana's christening, and trips to Joe's family's house in upstate New York and our shore house. I am so glad that we have my parents and Joe's parents on film, especially since we lost Joe's father in 2014. We love looking back at those happy moments with him. Our parents came with us when we filmed that episode in Sala Consilina, which was such a special trip for all of us. They also filmed us taking formal portraits with more than fifty members of Joe's family, including his father and grandmother. These are all moments we would only have in our memories if it weren't for the show. I wouldn't trade that in for anything.

I loved seeing the girls grow up on the show! When I said yes to doing *Housewives,* I wanted it to be like my own televised series of home movies of the girls—and it has been! I love going back and watching those first episodes when Gia was so little (and still such a mature, well-spoken, sensitive girl), when I would take her on auditions; the few episodes where Gabriella makes a rare appearance; reliving the best one-liners from Milania; and of course, watching my baby, Audriana, literally being filmed during her birth and seeing her blossom before my eyes.

While I was filming, I also had so much fun going to appearances, book signings, and events with my beloved hairstylist David Antunes and my makeup artist Priscilla Distasio. I laugh about the days when Priscilla and I were on the go from early morning till the wee hours while doing QVC appearances for my products and books. Since we would get to our hotel room at almost midnight and had to be up at 4:30 or 5 a.m. (sometimes earlier, depending on the airtime), she would do most of my makeup before we went to bed. She would laugh when I went to sleep like an Egyptian mummy, totally tucked into the bed with the sheets and blankets wrapped around me so tight that I couldn't move, and my hair spread out to the side on my pillow so I wouldn't mess it up. Crazy!

One night, after a long day in Philadelphia, we decided that we just couldn't leave the city without running up the stairs of the Museum of Art like Rocky. So there we were, in heels, pretending to run in slow motion up to the top, then raising our arms high in the air in triumph, like he did in the movie, and collapsing into hysterical laughter. We did things like that all the time, which made those grueling days and nights a lot easier.

Being on the show gave me the chance to do so many amazing new things, too, that I probably wouldn't otherwise have done. Joe and I were able to renew our vows in a fairy-tale second wedding at Oheka Castle on Long Island for a photo shoot we did for *In Touch* magazine. I loved that the girls were able to see Mommy and Daddy get married again. The looks on their faces were priceless. I got to wear a gorgeous wedding gown. Joe looked so handsome in his tuxedo. My daughters, who were our flower girls, looked so beautiful. It was so much fun, and it really was like being in a fairy tale, especially when we all rode in a horse and carriage. At the end of the wedding, Joe told me he loved me more than anything on earth. I told him we were blessed to have each other in our lives and that I loved him so much, too. It was one of the best days of my life.

One of the biggest opportunities that came my way was competing on *The Celebrity Apprentice* 5, which aired in 2012. I was thrilled to be on a show that helped me raise money for The NephCure Foundation, which supports continuing research to find a cure for a rare kidney disease called FSGS—focal segmental glomerulosclerosis. I got involved with NephCure when I met an adorable kid named Matthew Levine and his family at an Eric Trump Foundation charity event in New York City for the St. Jude Children's Research Hospital, months before I was asked to be on *Celebrity Apprentice*. (Like his father, Eric is one of the nicest people I have ever met. I love his big heart and how he has helped so many children over the years.) I told Matthew's mother that her children were beautiful, and after she thanked me, she added, "My son is beautiful on the outside, but inside he is very sick." She went on to tell me that he was taking fifteen pills a day because of his illness. I was so taken aback because he was only a child when I met him, and one of my daughters was the same age at the time. I couldn't imagine how this woman felt. Her family's story really touched my heart, and stayed with me long after our first meeting.

I was over the moon when I was first asked to be on *Celebrity Apprentice*, but I was nervous, too. I knew it was an intense show, and I didn't want to leave my daughters for a long time (you have to live at Trump SoHo while it's filming). I had never been away from my daughters before. But when I agreed to do it, they asked me which charity I had chosen to support. I was going to pick Project Ladybug, but I immediately thought of the little boy I had met at the St. Jude event and wanted to fight for NephCure.

I loved doing the show, but hated being away from Joe and the girls, so we made the best of the situation. They came to see me on the weekends and we had the best time seeing Broadway shows, going out to fun restaurants, sightseeing, and just walking around the city, taking it all in.

Though I lost my first challenge by twelve dollars to Dee Snider, I had so much fun on *Celebrity Apprentice* and hung in there almost to the end. It was a lot of work! We had to be up super-early and work late into the night. It was weird staying in a room at the Trump SoHo all by myself, because I'd never lived alone before. I made it to the final five, but got "fired" two weeks before the season finale.

When I got axed, I said, "I don't think Mr. Trump fired the right person, but I'm proud of myself that I made it this far. I wanted to prove to people that I'm not just a housewife, that there's more to me than that."

Even though I got fired, Arsenio Hall, one of the contestants who was still in the running, asked me to help him on the finale, so I was on the show until the end. I was thrilled that I raised seventy thousand dollars for NephCure. I wish I could have won more money for them. I tried my best, though. Everyone who competed was an amazingly hard worker, and each and every one of us was passionate about raising money for our charities.

One of the best things about being on *Celebrity Apprentice*, besides raising money for NephCure, was that people got to see a whole other side of me—the real side—calm, focused, and professional. "Everyone will see me in a different light as a businesswoman and, of course, it's for charity," I told *Naughty but Nice* columnist Rob Shuter on the set of *New York Live* at the time.

I absolutely loved working with Donald Trump. He's such a great guy. He was always so nice to me and he loved my husband. When Joe and I met with him in his office before I did the show, the two of them hit it off right away. Whenever we were in the boardroom, before the cameras started to roll, he would always ask me, "How is Joe doing?" Joe, of course, thought he was fantastic.

I am happy to say that I am in a good place now. I'm not happy about some of the things I have done in the past. Does that mean I will never lose my temper again if I am pushed to the limit or that I will let people walk all over me? No. But I've learned to look at things differently—and am trying to find ways to channel the anger

I sometimes feel in a more positive way. (For example, when I got upset about something in prison, I did yoga, meditated, or hit the gym. Hard. I got out my frustrations, thought things through, and *then* reacted.) I can't always do that going forward, especially if I am filming a scene, but just know that I am trying.

I know better days are ahead. I just don't want things to go back to where they were.

THE PAST IS THE PAST, TOMORROW IS A NEW DAY AND EACH NEW DAY IS A BLESSING FROM GOD. GOD TELLS US TO FORGIVE AND I FORGIVE THOSE WHO HAVE WRONGED ME AND WHEN I COME HOME I WILL SEEK FORGIVENESS FOR ANYONE that I MAY HAVE WRONGED. WHILE I FORGIVE I WILL NEVER FORGET.

# 4

## MY NEW REALITY

*A*ll the fighting, feuding, backstabbing, bickering, pain, and drama I dealt with on the show was nothing compared to the legal nightmare Joe and I faced in 2013 and 2014. The world watched on CNN, MSNBC, Fox News, and other outlets, as well as on *Real Housewives* at the end of Season 5 and through Season 6—as the life we had crumbled around us. These past three years have been the hardest of my life—and I had to endure it all in the public eye. While this part of my life has been more than trying—and still is—I have done my best to hold my head high, walk with grace, put my life in God's hands, and stay strong, even when it almost became too much.

In 2013, the glamorous, fun and drama-filled life I led on the show intersected with stone-cold reality. We had spoken about our bankruptcy on camera here and there over the years. But at the end of the Season 5 finale, viewers were shown a clip of Matt Lauer reporting on *Today* that on July 29, 2013, the U.S. Attorney was indicting us on thirty-nine counts of federal fraud, including charges of bankruptcy fraud and conspiracy to commit mail and wire fraud.

The most terrifying part of all this? Initially, we faced up to fifty years in prison if we were found guilty. Most days, the thought just didn't seem within the realm of possibility. I felt like my world was spinning out of control . . . but I also couldn't grasp what this *really* could mean for our family.

We went to the federal courthouse in Newark the day after the indictment was announced, to face our charges. This was so surreal to me. I had never been in trouble in my life—and now this? On the car ride over, I felt sick to my stomach. I looked at Joe, who seemed very stoic and strong. He kept telling me everything was going to be OK. I couldn't believe we were going to court. I had no idea what to expect.

When we got out of the car, the media pounced. Helicopters buzzed overhead as reporters and photographers surrounded us, shoving their cameras, microphones, and tape recorders at us as we walked into the federal courthouse, pushing into us and yelling question after question. I felt beyond overwhelmed when I saw all those camerapeople and reporters there. I got upset when someone shoved a camera right in Joe's face. On a stressful day like this, it seemed totally unnecessary. I couldn't believe how many people were waiting for *us*, especially at a moment like this. It was insane. This kind of pushing and shoving was something I had seen on TV and in the movies, but I was actually living it and it all felt like a bad dream.

I held on tight to Joe's hand as we walked toward the front doors. I hoped my girls wouldn't see this on TV later on and that no one in school would tell them about it. I didn't want to worry our parents, either. I thought the stress from all of this would just be too much for them. My parents didn't know the full extent of what was going on. I just told them that everything was going to be OK. They told me that they knew who their daughter was—someone honest and with good values—and that's what mattered. Looking back, I wish that was all that truly counted in court.

After we surrendered to the federal government for the indictment and were processed, we were each released on a five-hundred-thousand-dollar bond. We had to hand over our passports and were not allowed to leave New Jersey or New York without permission from the federal government. When we left the courthouse, we were greeted once again by the media circus waiting outside for us. I held my head high as I made my way through the crowd to our car, getting jostled along the way, but staying quiet. Joe and I didn't say a word to anyone, even though they kept shouting questions at us. I wanted to cry, but I stayed strong. I had to. I knew this was just the beginning of a long, hard, scary road. I had to keep it together, especially for my girls and my parents.

When we got home, I went about my day as usual, even though I couldn't stop thinking about what had happened earlier. My children didn't know where we had been that day, because they were in school. I was home when they got home. Everything was good. I helped them with their homework, took them to their activities, came home and made dinner for them, and got them ready for bed.

After the girls fell asleep, I wanted to go to bed, too. It was maybe 10 p.m. and I was exhausted, but I couldn't stop thinking about the indictment, much as I tried to forget it. My mind was going a thousand miles an hour. I couldn't remember when I had last been this stressed, if ever. I could barely eat because my stomach was tied up in knots. As tired as I was, I couldn't sleep because I was so worried about the nightmare swirling around us. I am a worrier and all

I could think about was what would happen to Joe and my parents and, most of all, my precious daughters. I put up a strong front for my girls and didn't say a word to them about what was going on. My babies are my world and I didn't want them to know how terrified I really was. I had put on a stone face many a time on the show to hide my true feelings, and now I was doing it at home. I had no choice. I didn't want to scare them, but the reality of it all was overwhelming.

I had told *People* magazine in 2012 that the hardest part of being famous was "being scrutinized. It's hard being judged when people don't really know you." With everything going on with our case, I felt this was truer than ever. I felt that people were making assumptions about me based on what they had seen and read about me. So many stories that had been written about me were untrue—and the way I was portrayed on the show was not the real me at all, just me at some of my worst moments. But that's what people saw.

People asked me if Joe and I were treated differently after the indictment, but we weren't, thank God. Not by the people we were close to, who knew we were good people and loved us no matter what. We were lucky to have that support from people close to us, including the girls' teachers and their friends' parents. They would tell us they were praying for us, which really touched my heart. Even strangers in stores would come up to me and tell me they were rooting for us.

Not everyone was so open-minded. The indictment was killing my businesses. While the liquor stores that sold Fabellini continued to do so, new stores wouldn't take it. They said they needed to see what happened first. The same thing happened with BJ's and Costco, which were going to carry my dessert line and my specialty food line including pasta, olive oil, olives, and marinara sauce. They wanted to wait, too. I was supposed to go on HSN to sell my hair care line, but they told me that now wasn't a good time. The indictment torpedoed that deal, too. I had spent so much time and energy building my businesses, and now they were almost dead in the water.

Since I wasn't running around to business meetings or events anymore, I was spending most of my time with Joe and my daughters, trying to maintain my normal routine as best I could. That was hard, though, when I kept seeing stories about our ordeal in magazines, newspapers, and on the Internet and TV. I would be standing in line at the grocery store and glance at the magazine rack—and there I was! It was also difficult to forget what was going on since we had to meet with our lawyers so much. The whole thing sent ice through my veins, and avoidance was the only real way I could cope.

On August 14, 2013, we returned to court for our arraignment and entered our pleas: not guilty. Our trial was set for October 8. I was scared about what would happen in court, but kept praying that everything would be OK and stayed strong. I knew I couldn't fold, because my daughters and my parents were depending on me. So Joe and I did our best to keep things as normal as possible at home. I kept up a brave front because I had to. If you didn't know me or know about all the legal problems Joe and I were facing, you wouldn't have thought that anything was going on with me. I just kept life the way it always was with my family.

We continued to film Season 6, though the case was weighing heavily on us. I just tried to stay as positive as possible and go on about my life. We celebrated our anniversary that year by going to dinner and keeping the conversation light. We talked about what the kids were up to, some funny thing Milania said that made us laugh, and how our parents were doing. We tried not to think about everything we were facing, but it was always in the back of our minds. Until you are in a situation like this, you just don't understand how much it weighs on you every single moment of every single day.

On November 18, 2013, our situation grew even more serious when we were indicted on two more charges—bank fraud and loan application fraud. Two days later, we pleaded not guilty to those charges. Now I was feeling more anxious than ever. At that point, our trial had been moved to February 14, 2014. What a *fantastic* way to spend Valentine's Day.

By the good grace of God, along the way, thirty-two of the thirty-six counts against me in the indictment were dropped. Around this time, Joe and I met with our lawyers, who advised us to enter a plea deal that the government had offered us. On March 4, 2014, we went to court, where I pleaded guilty to the remaining charges: one count of conspiracy to commit mail and wire fraud and three counts of bankruptcy fraud for concealment, false oaths, and false declarations.

The scariest part was learning that Joe could be sent to prison for three to four years, and that I could go away for two years. I was hoping I would get probation or home confinement. The thought of leaving my girls killed me. They were my life and they needed their mother.

We were all dealt another huge blow when Joe's dad passed away unexpectedly on June 18, 2014. Joe was devastated—and so was I. I still can't believe he is gone. He had so much energy and he was such a vibrant man—always happy and full of life. He would always be the first one on the dance floor at any party and entertain the crowd by doing a split in the middle of the action, laughing the whole time. I have a picture of him and Gia dancing on New Year's Eve. She was already trying to wrap her mind around the legal trouble we were in, so the loss of her grandfather was a lot for a thirteen-year-old to handle.

We were grateful, though, that we had gotten to spend Father's Day with him just two days earlier. He wanted the entire family at his house. He was happy because he was able to make pizzas for us for the first time in his new brick oven outside. He ran around taking selfies with everyone. Thank God we took a lot of pictures that day.

My father-in-law was at our house the week he died, building a rabbit coop in our yard for bunnies he and Joe were going to get the girls. June 18 was a busy day for us. It was the last day of school for Gia, Gabriella, and Milania. Audriana was also graduating from preschool, so I was running around buying her flowers to give to her at her graduation. When the other girls got home, the three young-est girls and I headed to Milania's friend's house to go swimming in her pool.

While we were there, I called the assistant at Joe's attorney's office to ask him something. He told me he had just spoken to Joe, who sounded seriously upset about something having to do with his father. With shaking fingers I hung up the phone and called Joe right away, praying everything was OK. It wasn't.

Joe told me that his father had died—outside of our house. Joe was working outside in the front yard and only saw his father's truck parked on the side of the house when he went to get some tools in our garage. He called for his father, and when he walked around to the side of the house, he found him lying facedown on the ground next to his truck. Joe called 911 before he knelt down, trying as hard as he could to revive his dad by splashing water on his face and push-ing on his chest. He said he was crying and yelling for his father to open his eyes. But he didn't.

When Joe told me he found his father on the ground, I started screaming and crying into the phone. I told Joe I would be right home. My daughters heard me and came running over, asking, "Mommy—what's wrong?" I said, "I think something happened to Nonno Franco." I hugged the girls and left them with Milania's friend's mom, who was kind enough to watch them, because I didn't want them to see what was going on at home. I had my friend John, who was also there, drive me to my house because I was so hysterical.

When we got there, the driveway was packed with cop cars and an ambulance. When I got out of the car, I ran past the yellow police tape and over to Joe, in tears. He buried his head in my shoulder as we both stood there, hugging each other and sobbing. He was crying, "My dad, my dad . . ." over and over. It felt like my heart had been ripped out of my chest. His father was so important to us. We loved him so much, and now he was gone when we needed him the most. Suddenly, nothing else mattered. What mattered was that one of our loved ones was gone, forever.

Little by little the whole family started to come over. This was the worst day of my life—it was the first time someone who was so dear to my heart had died. I had never been to a funeral home to make arrangements for someone so close to me, but I went with Joe and his family to arrange it all. My heart was broken for my husband and my daughters, who had never lost a close relative before either. They adored their Nonno. I had no idea why this had happened—at a time that was already so tough.

Joe found his father around 5 p.m. but thinks he had been there for several hours. Gia was inside when Joe found his dad, and he told her not to come outside. The strange thing is that we didn't even know my father-in-law was coming over that day. He never told me or Joe. He parked his truck on the side of the garage, way in the back. In the summer our yard gets very lush, and the green-

ery grows high on the side of the garage, so neither of us saw his
truck or even knew he was back there. We don't even know when
he got there. I feel like God wanted his father to be with Joe and that
that's where his father wanted to be. I also think God didn't want me
there, because we usually never go to friends' houses after school.
God knew that, at this point in my life, I was not strong enough to
see my father-in-law like that.

At his wake, Gia stood by her dad during the entire afternoon
and evening sessions, as he stood vigil by the casket. She is an amazing daughter. I couldn't believe how strong she was. She told me she
wanted to be there for her dad. My husband and father-in-law were
only twenty years apart and so close, and as his death was sudden, it
really was a new level of grief for all of us.

I'm crying even as I am writing this. Joe's father was there for
us through everything—the good and the bad. He came to court to
support us and put up the money for Joe's bond. He was truly like a
second dad to me. I love him so much. We all do.

That summer, we mourned the loss of Joe's father while we just
kept trying to put one foot in front of the other. I started filming
again in the fall, which was good, although I didn't like it when some
of my fellow cast members brought up our case on the show. I didn't
want to think about it, let alone talk about it to anyone except Joe,
my parents, my closest friends, and my lawyer. I didn't want to share
my worst fears with people I barely knew, let alone on TV.

When sentencing day arrived, I did everything I could to stay
strong, but those were, of course, some of the most terrifying hours
of my life. Joe and I walked hand in hand into the federal courthouse
in Newark as reporters and photographers rushed us once again.
Even though I had put on a brave front all these months, my nerves
at this point were totally shot. I hadn't been eating or sleeping much.

My mind just kept whirling. But as I walked through the courthouse doors, I just tried to keep it all together. I was determined to get through this horrible day as best I could.

The sentencing started at 10 a.m. Joe went first. A U.S. District Court judge sentenced him to forty-one months in prison on four counts plus twelve months on another count, which he would serve concurrently. Joe was also ordered to pay $414,000 in restitution to Wells Fargo bank, plus $10,000 in fines. He also got two years' probation.

When he was sentenced, I literally felt a knife go through my heart. I couldn't breathe. All I could think of was, *This is the man I have loved my entire life.* I never thought it would actually happen, but here we were. My mind, my body, and my soul were overwhelmed.

When it was my turn to go before the judge, I stood up at the table where I had been sitting, trying not to cry as I read a letter to the court, telling the judge, in part, how much my daughters meant to me.

The judge listened quietly to my statement. Then my world came crashing down. She said she had thought about giving me probation. But then she said, "My gut says Teresa Giudice deserves to be in jail for a period of time. I have hope and I have faith that you have learned your lesson."

She sentenced me to fifteen months in prison and ordered me to pay the $414,000 in restitution along with Joe. I was allowed to spend the holidays with my family, but had to turn myself in to prison on January 5, 2015. I was also given two years of supervised release after serving my prison sentence.

When I heard the word "prison," my heart started racing. I felt like I had a tornado rushing through my head. I thought I was going to black out. My fingers froze and I couldn't move my hands.

I couldn't breathe. It took everything I had to stand there and be strong. But it felt like another knife—a bigger and sharper one than ever before—had just been plunged into my stomach. I stood there, blinking and confused. I heard the word "prison" but it just didn't register that I was actually going away.

One of the good things that came out of that horrible day was that the judge staggered our sentences, allowing me to serve my time first, before Joe began serving his, so our daughters would always have one parent at home with them. But I didn't even hear her say that because my head felt like it was going to explode. When I processed it later, though, I was relieved and grateful that she allowed us that leeway.

She also gave me a lighter sentence than what the prosecutors wanted me to get. I was originally facing twenty-one to twenty-seven months in prison, but the judge said she gave me fifteen months because I had expressed "genuine remorse" in court and because I had no criminal history, paid my taxes, cared for my parents, and worked for various charities. She also said that she understood just how much I love my girls, which was perhaps the largest factor in her decision. At one point, she said, "I've got to say, you're a devoted mother . . . There is a bond between these girls and their mother. I have to consider these girls, and their bond [with you]." She also said, "This doesn't define you as a mom." I appreciated that she saw that, and I started crying again, because all I could think of were my babies and how they were going to fare when I went to prison. We also learned the government would probably garnish our earnings going forward (and they did).

I hated seeing the media waiting for us when we left court. I was shaken to the core and in my own world at that point. I just wanted to get home to my family. When we got in the car, I broke down on the way home, sobbing into Joe's shoulder. We were both stunned. Neither of us could believe that we were going to prison. We held each other for a long time. I told him I loved him more than anything in the world—and he told me the same. We rode in silence for the rest of the trip home. All I kept thinking was that when this first started, I thought that the judge would see the truth about everything and that it was all going to work out. But here's the bottom line: I never thought I was going to end up in prison.

By the time I got home, I felt like a truck had run me over. I felt like I had been beaten up. I was so drained and just numb. We had been in court from 10 a.m. until 5 p.m. with only a ten-minute break. When we walked into the house, my parents, Joe's family, and some of our closest friends were waiting for us. There were so many people over—especially Joe's family, which is huge—that it reminded me of when my father-in-law passed away and everyone was at our house. The difference was that everyone was crying when Joe's father died. When we got home, everyone was upset, but tried to be strong for Joe and me. I don't even like to compare the two moments, but it just seemed like that other horrible day in our lives.

I didn't say much to Gabriella, Milania, and Audriana, but Gia knew what had happened. She broke down crying when we walked through the door. I took her in my arms and held her, trying hard not to cry. I hugged the other girls for what seemed like an eternity. I just didn't want to let them go.

Milania wanted to know why so many people were at our house—and why everyone seemed upset. I didn't know what to say. I was already so shell-shocked and couldn't think straight. Someone jumped in and said that we were there for a memorial for Nonno, who had passed away three months before.

I went upstairs and told my mom to come into my bedroom. I

told her what had happened. She started crying and she was saying, "Why you? You are always such a good girl. You do not deserve this." I started crying and said, as my voice cracked, "There's a reason why. They thought I broke the law." I asked her not to get upset. I said, "I need you and I don't want you to get sick over this." I hugged her, and said, "I will be fine. Please don't worry." It broke my heart to see my mom upset like that. I really didn't say too much to my dad. I just hugged him and kissed him. He asked me, "How long?" I told him fifteen months. I also told him what I had told my mom—that I would be fine. He said, "Yes, you will be fine. Don't worry about anything." What he meant was, don't worry about my daughters. I knew exactly what he was saying—that he and my mom would be there to help Joe take care of them. All he had to do was look at me and I understood him clearly. We just have that kind of connection. I stood there and looked back at the man with the strong hands who had protected me my whole life, who couldn't do anything to help me right now except comfort me with his words. "OK," I said. "I love you, Papà." I hugged him again and tried not to cry.

I had told my parents what had happened, which was hard enough, and now I had to figure out what to tell the girls. I honestly didn't know. How do you tell three little girls that their mommy is going to prison? Maybe Gabriella and Milania would understand it, but little Audriana wouldn't. I needed some time to think about how I was going to handle this.

My brother called in the midst of this. He was crying hysterically and said he couldn't believe what had happened. My voice was shaking, and I tried not to cry because I wanted to be strong for him. I told him I would be fine. It broke my heart to hear him crying like that on the phone. He told me he loved me and would be there for me no matter what. I told him I loved him, too. I hung up and broke

down in tears. All of the tension in our relationship and all the angst
we had gone through together just didn't matter—I loved Joey so
much and hated to see him hurting like this. His call told me for sure
that no matter what we had been through, we had an unbreakable
bond.

All I asked of Joe now was that he take care of our daughters.
I did everything for them and now he had to take over. I also told
him what Gia had said about taking care of her sisters when I left
for prison, which breaks my heart to this day, but makes me love her
even more. She said, "Mommy, don't worry about it. I'll be there. I'll
help Daddy with the girls." She said, "That'll prepare me for when
I'm a mom." As a mother, what more could you ask for?

$\mathcal{F}$rom the moment I got sentenced until the night I had to leave
to turn myself in to prison, I vowed to enjoy every moment with
my family. Gabriella's tenth birthday was on October 4, just two
days after the sentencing. I wasn't moping around or feeling sorry
for myself. We celebrated like we always did. We had a party with
her friends at Coastal Sports, a sports facility in Fairfield, New Jersey, and had a wonderful time. I enjoyed planning her party, getting everything ready, and watching her blow out the candles on
her cake. I was savoring every minute of times I may have taken for
granted before. I just tried not to think about what I would have to
face a few months down the road. My three youngest daughters still
didn't know I was going to prison.

The following day, I put on a glittery gold gown and filmed the
Season 6 reunion. I didn't back out. I wasn't in the best of moods,
but I showed up and did my job because I am a professional. I apologized to my fans for letting them down and said my goodbyes. As

much I don't like the reunion shows, I felt sad walking off the set that night. I was leaving what was familiar and was now facing an uncertain future.

I made the most of my next three months home. If you look at my Instagram account from that time, you will see that I did something fun with my daughters every weekend. We went horseback riding, to a hockey game, and skiing at Mountain Creek in Vernon, New Jersey.

We also spent the weekend in New York City with our friend Lisa G. We went ice skating in Rockefeller Center, visited the top of the Empire State Building, took a horse and carriage ride in Central Park, had lunch at the Plaza Hotel, and went to the unbelievable toy store, FAO Schwarz. We tried to enjoy life as much as possible—and though each memory is wonderful, it's also tinged with pain, because I was counting down the seconds until we were apart.

In a weird way, I felt like I was dying, because I knew I had such limited days with them. I just felt like I wanted to build special memories for them, which they could look back on when I went away. This was important for me to do for all my girls, but especially for Audriana because she was only five at the time. I never thought I would be away from one of my daughters at that age. But God was giving me a challenge. I didn't know why at the time, but I took comfort in putting one foot in front of the other. At this time in my life, it was better to be a little robotic (while I tried to keep our household as normal as possible) than to be the alternative: a sobbing, inconsolable mess.

*I* didn't know it then, but someone was about to come into my life and help turn things around for me in a big way. In early December,

I was busy preparing for Christmas, which was always a big deal in our house. But this year, it was different because I was going away after New Year's, and that cast a dark shadow on the holiday I had always associated with happy times. Even when I tried to put prison out of my mind, I couldn't.

I had about a month left before I had to turn myself in, and I still had a lot to take care of before I surrendered. We had paid $200,000 of the $414,000 in restitution the judge ordered us to pay, but we still owed $214,000 and the government wanted its money.

In the coming weeks, I had to go to the U.S. Attorney's Office in Newark for a series of meetings to figure out how we were going to pay the rest of the restitution back. Joe and I were going to do everything we could to pay them back as soon as possible.

But I didn't have a lawyer, because I had parted ways with the ones I had in the past. One night, while I was getting ready to drive the girls to all their activities, Joe told me that a friend of his was bringing a new lawyer to our house. He said he thought this guy might actually be able to help us. I thought, *Yeah, right, I've heard that one before.*

Joe's friend told him that this lawyer had helped him out and that he was a great criminal defense lawyer who worked very hard for his clients. *Great*, I thought. *Where was this lawyer when I really needed him?* When I got home, Joe was sitting at the kitchen table with his friend and the new guy. Joe introduced him to me and said, "Tre, meet your new lawyer. His name is James Leonard."

I asked him to come with me into the living room so we could talk privately. "Teresa," he said, leaning in close, "all these problems that you and Joe are going through, they too are going to pass. You'll see. Brighter days are coming." There was something about the way he said it that made me think he truly believed that. "You do know I am going to prison in a month . . ." I said. He smiled. "You're going to be fine in there. Don't be afraid of that." That made me stop for a moment. Since Joe and I had gotten sentenced, no one had ever told me that I was going to be fine. Everyone was saying things like, "I'm so sorry," and "Oh my God, I can't believe it." But here was this guy sitting on my couch, saying, "You're going to be OK. Don't worry." I don't know exactly why, but I started to cry. Maybe it was because it hit me that I was *really* going to prison in a month. But maybe it was the fact that I was relieved that this lawyer seemed so confident that everything was going to turn out all right for me and Joe, despite everything we were going through. I decided to follow Joe's friend's suggestion and hired Jim on the spot. I'd finally found a lawyer I could count on and trust.

We had a low-key Christmas that year with our family. This was our first Christmas without my father-in-law, so it was tough for all of us. Joe's sister, Maria, hosted our Christmas Eve festivities. We toasted their dad at dinner and said a prayer for him, asking God to protect him.

On Christmas Day, we opened our gifts in the morning before we went to church. Audriana, Gabriella, and Milania were so excited that Santa had come—and had eaten the cookies we left out for him the night before. I loved seeing Gia so relaxed and happy, since like me, Christmas is one of her favorite holidays. These were the moments I treasured and would carry with me in the coming year.

When we got home, I started cooking up a storm because Joe's family was coming over for Christmas Day. I made all kinds of *delizioso* dishes, like stuffed mushrooms, lasagna, prime rib, ham, and broccoli rabe. For a second, I felt like my life was normal again. We didn't talk about prison at all.

When it came to celebrating New Year's Eve, in years past, we would all go to a catering hall with Joe's family, but this year, my sister-in-law Sheila and Joe's brother, Pete, held a low-key New Year's Eve party at their house. It was very emotional, especially at midnight. We were crying because we missed my father-in-law so much. Joe and I were also upset because we knew we had a tough year ahead of us. At the stroke of midnight, I kissed Joe, just like we did when we were kids, and hugged him a little tighter than usual. I said a prayer asking God to protect me and my family in the upcoming year and to give me strength to get through it all.

The days leading up to my surrender date were quiet. On New Year's Day, we went to Maria's house for dinner to celebrate my mother-in-law's birthday. The next day, we took down our Christmas tree and put away all our decorations and relaxed at home. On January 3, the Saturday before I had to turn myself in, we took the girls skiing. When I got into bed that night, I looked around my room. This was the last time I would be sleeping in my own bed for a long time, since I would be leaving for prison the following night. I said another prayer, thanking God for all the good in my life—my children, my husband, my parents, family, and friends. I asked God once more to protect us all and give me strength. I was going to need it.

When I woke up, I looked over at Joe, who was still sleeping, and immediately thought, *Today is the day I lose my freedom.* In less than twenty-four hours, I would be leaving for prison so I could turn myself in during the early hours of January 5. I got out of bed, brushed my teeth, and went downstairs to make my coffee and get breakfast going. These were the last scrambled eggs and toast I would be making for my family for a very long time.

Joe and I took the girls to church at the Cathedral Basilica of the Sacred Heart in Newark, where we had gotten married. I also wanted some quiet moments to reflect on everything that had happened, pray to God to give me and my family strength over the next year, and spend some quality time with Joe and the girls. I had always prayed a lot, but now I was relying on God and my faith even more, to get me through the next year.

When we parked the car, I told the girls they had to be quiet and behave in church. That's when I saw the first photographer. And then the next. And the next. A pack of paparazzi was taking pictures of us going into the church. I started to get mad. *Is nothing sacred?* I thought. But this is the price you pay for fame. It has a very steep price, as I'd come to learn in the last six years. Steeper than I ever could have imagined.

We had a busy day planned. Gia's fourteenth birthday was in four days, on January 8. I wouldn't be there to celebrate with her, since I was beginning my sentence on January 5, so we decided to throw her a party the Sunday afternoon before I left. I let everyone know that this was in no way, shape, or form a goodbye party for me.

As soon as we got home from church, I headed straight to the kitchen to cook for the party. I made my baked ziti (which the girls love), meatballs, braciole, chicken cutlets, a big salad, and cookies. I love to cook. It relaxes me. It calms me down. And I love having my family over to the house. So I was happy.

At around two o'clock, my parents and Joe's family showed up. We sat and ate. We laughed. We all sang "Happy Birthday" to Gia, who blew out the candles on a huge cake adorned with purple and pink flowers that I had gotten her. Nobody cried. Nobody was walking around like the world was coming to an end. It was a happy day, just the way I wanted it.

Everybody was gone by 6 p.m. Again, there were no tears. Just hugs and kisses goodbye. They told me everything would be okay and that they loved me. I told them I loved them back. It felt good to have them all there. I was sad, though, because I wasn't sure when I would be seeing them next. But I was happy to have good memories of my last day at home with all of them—my beautiful family.

Then came time for the toughest goodbyes of all. Joe and I went upstairs with the girls. We all lay down on the big bed in my room. All six of us.

I told the girls, "Mommy has to leave."

"When?" asked Milania,

"Tonight," I told them.

Gabriella, who was ten at the time, got so hysterical, she couldn't even breathe. She usually held her feelings inside, but now she was inconsolable. When Joe's father died, all the girls had gotten very emotional. They love their grandparents so much. We are all very close. They cried a lot. But this was ten times worse than that. I held Gabriella and told her it was going to be okay—even though I knew it might not be. What else could I do?

Audriana, my baby, who was only five at the time, started to cry. Huge, heaving sobs. Then Milania, who was eight at the time, started up, followed by Gia, then finally, me and Joe. We lay there, a tangled mess of arms and legs, hugging each other and crying. Me,

Joe, and Gia, bless her heart, tried to calm the little ones down as best we could. This was tearing my heart out, but I didn't let them see that. I couldn't. I had to be strong for them. They were my focus— not me. In true Milania fashion, she wiped her tears on my sleeve and we all laughed.

But as I held my girls and kissed them on their cheeks and on their foreheads, I started to get mad. Instead of having more time with my babies, I had to leave for prison in the middle of the night while they were sleeping—because of the paparazzi. This is how bad things had gotten. This whole thing was totally out of control. How had it come to this?

At that moment, I knew things had to change. That I would use my time in prison to rethink things. I was going to come out of prison a better person and try to make things right again in my life.

We lay there for about an hour and a half. Then I knew it was time to start putting the girls to bed and say my goodbyes. This was going to be hardest part of all. I had dreaded this moment for months. And now it was here.

$\mathcal{I}$ got up off the bed and told each of the girls to go to her room, because I wanted to spend time with each one of them. The first room I went to was Audriana's—my littlest sweetheart.

We snuggled into her bed, pulling the covers over us. I held her very, very tight as I read her one of her favorite books, *Goodnight Moon*.

We said a prayer in Italian together—one we say all the time.

*"Gesù mio, fai stare bene a mia mamma, mio papa, Gia, Gabriella, Milania, Audriana, tutta la famiglia e tutto il mondo."*

*"My Jesus, please take good care of my mommy, my daddy, Gia, Gabriella, Milania, Audriana, the whole family and the whole world."*

Then we did the sign of the cross and her drowsy little eyelids started to close. I love hearing her sweet, soft, little girl voice say that prayer. I tried not to cry when I thought that I wouldn't hear her say that prayer with me in her bed for a long, long time. I stayed there with her and held her. I wouldn't leave her until she fell asleep. I love all of my girls the same, but Audriana is my baby. I am her mommy. Her whole world. All I could think about was how she was going to wake up in the morning and I wouldn't be there. I sat there with her in my arms crying softly to myself as I watched her drift off to sleep.

This sounds weird, but I worried that she would forget about me while I was in there, because she was so little. I also wanted to make sure she knew I wasn't abandoning her. These are the strange thoughts you have when you are going to be away from your family like I was.

Then I went to Gabriella's room. I think the reason Gabriella was so hysterical was because my leaving was throwing off the order in her entire world. I realized that she wasn't ready to handle this at all. But I had to go. I had no choice. I got into bed with Gabriella. I was holding her. We were hugging and crying.

Gabriella started asking me why I had to leave. My baby, Audriana, thought I had to leave because Mommy was going to work and writing a book. I told Milania and Gabriella the same thing—adding that I was writing about prison and had to live there because of that.

Gabriella was sobbing again. She couldn't catch her breath. Now she was saying, "I don't understand. You go to work all the time, but you always come home."

I held her tight and kissed her on the forehead and said, "You will be able to call and visit. I will be able to email you."

I just lay there with her, thinking, *I am going to prison. Holy hell.*

We prayed together. We said a different prayer than the one I said with Audriana—one in English this time. I calmed Gabriella down enough so that she could relax and go to sleep. When she finally fell asleep in my arms, I kissed her on the forehead again and whispered to her that I loved her.

Then I went to Milania's room. I read Milania one of her favorite books, *Olivia*, about a very independent little pig who loves to wear red. She always loves that one. I have read it to her more than a hundred times, I think. I probably know all the words by heart at this point.

We were crying as I snuggled in bed with her. "While I am away, you need to be a good girl," I told her.

Milania can be a handful. She is super-independent and speaks her mind, as you know. I still can't believe the things that come out of her mouth. But she's also so adorable and affectionate and, like Audriana, needs her mommy. Quietly, she asked, "Are you going to be able to call home?"

I said yes, I would.

Then, out of nowhere, Milania looked me dead in the eye and said, "I hate that this is happening to you."

I realized that she knew more than I'd thought she did. It was very surreal. In that moment, Milania stopped being the one I was consoling. Milania was now the one consoling me. She held me tight and said, "Don't worry, Mommy. I will be a good girl. I will take care of Daddy and my sisters."

At that point, I realized just how strong my girls are—that we raised them to be strong. That's how I was raised. If I had been in a situation like that, I would have said the same thing to my parents.

Milania wasn't asleep when I left her. She lay quietly in her bed.

I hugged and kissed her. We said a prayer together. When I left her room, she was staring off into the distance. She seemed content.

All this time, Gia was holding it all together and helping Joe and me with the girls. She was the only one who knew where I was going and why. I have to say, I am so proud of the strength and maturity she has shown throughout this whole nightmare. But now it was just the two of us in her room. Gia broke down. She was hysterical. I got into bed with her. We were hugging and holding each other. I tried to calm her down. I told her I loved her so much and that I was so proud to be her mother. After a while, I said, "I really need you to look after your sisters and help Daddy. I need you to step up and do this for me while I'm gone."

Gia stopped crying. She knew she had a job to do, and from that moment on, she tried to be strong and focus on her job, and her job alone. I cannot tell you how much that means to me. I love her for all the help she gave me while I was at Danbury—and for the sensible, intelligent, grounded young woman she is becoming.

While I was upstairs with the girls, Joe was downstairs, sitting at the kitchen table, crying and trying to cope with everything going on. The kitchen table is the heart of our home. It's where we have shared all our meals together—in good times and bad. Over the doorway to the family room is a message I had stenciled on there that says, GIVE MUCH * GATHER OFTEN * GREET MANY. That has summed up so many wonderful memories we created there.

While I was talking to Gia, Joe came into her room. He had tears in his eyes and then started crying again. He sat down on the bed with us. We all held each other and just hugged. We didn't say anything. Milania made her way in there, too.

Joe looked at her and said, "It will be OK . . . it will all be OK. Daddy will fill Mommy's shoes now."

"I want Mommy, not you!" said Milania, never one to mince words. She didn't say it in a mean way. She was matter-of-fact about it. Joe made some wisecrack joke and we all laughed. Leave it to Milania to give us a good icebreaker when we needed one most.

As tough and independent as she might seem, Milania likes me to snuggle with her until she falls asleep. So does Audriana. (I would often fall asleep in their beds with them.) I wasn't sure how both girls were going to deal with me not being there to help them go to sleep while I was gone.

Now that the girls were settled in, I had to get ready to leave. It was getting late. I looked at my phone to see what time it was. It was just before midnight. I had to hurry up.

I stared at my reflection in the gold leaf mirror over the sink in my master bathroom. This was the same mirror I had sat in front of when Priscilla, my makeup artist, and David, my hairstylist, came to my house to get me ready for TV appearances, red carpet events, galas, speaking engagements, and book signings.

Now I was getting ready for prison. I took off my hair extensions. I knew I wouldn't need them in there. Jim was on his way to my house to pick me up and drive me to the federal prison in Danbury, where I would be locked up. I still couldn't believe this was really happening. Teresa Giudice, star of *The Real Housewives of New Jersey*, *New York Times* best-selling cookbook author, and constant tabloid sensation, was going to prison. But so was the real Teresa—Teresa the wife, the daughter, the sister and, most importantly, Teresa, the mother of four daughters who are my whole world. Having to leave them was tearing my heart apart. I would be leaving a part of myself behind when I walked through those prison doors. The hugest part there is.

I walked over to the tub and glanced out the window. It was pitch-black outside. I couldn't see a thing. I had no idea that a group of die-hard reporters, photographers, and fans was standing across the street from the security gate leading to my house, waiting for me to leave. I knew they would show up at some point. I just didn't realize they would be there so early. Over the past six years, I had gotten used to the paparazzi staking me out—at the worst times possible.

I got dressed and was getting some things together when I heard a car pull into the driveway. I knew it was Jim and Mike, the retired FBI agent he brought with him for protection. I thought, *Here we go . . .* They rang the doorbell, and Joe let them in and invited them into the kitchen, where they sat around the kitchen table, waiting for me to come downstairs. Joe had a glass and a bottle of his homemade red wine in front of him on the table. He got up and handed Jim and Mike each a glass. I heard Jim say he couldn't drink because he had to drive. Jim told me later that Joe shot him a look like, "Pal, you are gonna need this."

Joe sat back down at the kitchen table, wiping his eyes, with tears still running down his cheeks. Almost as though he was talking to no one in particular, Joe looked up at the ceiling and said, "I can't believe this is happening.

"Teresa saying goodbye to the girls is just gut-wrenching," Joe said.

Gut-wrenching doesn't even begin to cover it. What had happened in the last six hours was probably the most painful, most excruciating time of my entire life.

After I finished getting ready, I knew I had to leave. I went back to each of the girls' rooms. Audriana looked like a little angel sleeping. I kissed her and said a prayer over her and did the sign of the

My father, Giacinto Gorga, and my mother, Antonia Gorga, at their wedding reception in Sala Consilina, Italy, on December 27, 1969. They were so in love and still are. I think I got my love of hats from my mother.

Joey and I when we were 8 and 10, standing on the lawn of our house in Paterson, New Jersey, where we used to play for hours.

Having fun on a trip to South Beach with my friends in my early twenties. I love it there!

Here I am in second grade at St. Mary's School in Paterson, about a year before I started liking Joe and would find any excuse to go to the bathroom so I could walk by his classroom!

*Photos are courtesy of the author unless otherwise noted.*

Joe and I leaving the Cathedral Basilica of the Sacred Heart in Newark, New Jersey, after saying our "I do's" on October 23, 1999. I was so happy to be married to Joe! *(Photo by Abbey Photographers of Palisades Park, New Jersey)*

Joe and I with Joe's parents on our wedding day. God bless you, and may you rest in peace, Nonno Franco . . . *(Photo by Abbey Photographers of Palisades Park, New Jersey)*

I went all out for my senior prom! I wanted to wear a color that no one else would have, with dyed shoes to match.

Joe and I on a romantic picnic when we first started dating. I still feel about him now the way I did then.

Gia and I in our matching leopard print bikinis on our boat at the Jersey shore in 2003.

Halloween 2007: Joe went as Hugh Hefner and I dressed up as a cowgirl. We were celebrating at SPACE in Englewood, New Jersey.

Joe and I jet skiing in the Bahamas. We had just gone for a ride and the waves were huge. I remember holding on to him and feeling so safe.

Much-needed family time during a vacation to Punta Cana in the Dominican Republic in March 2013. We went there for our cousin's wedding.
*(Photo by Dave Kotinsky/Getty Images)*

Gabriella's tenth birthday party at a sports facility in Fairfield, New Jersey, which she loved. Her birthday was two days after Joe's and my sentencing. We had a fun time, but it was also bittersweet because I knew my time with my daughters and husband was limited.

Hanging out with my family on a lazy July day. I am a total summer girl!

Joe and my daughters celebrating his birthday while I was at Danbury. He took such good care of the girls while I was away. I know it wasn't easy!

Joey and I at the launch of my hair care line at Stone House at Stirling Ridge in Warren, New Jersey, in February 2013.
*(Photo by Dave Kotinsky/Getty Images)*

My girls and I at the beach at the Jersey shore. This is one of my favorite pictures of us together. I had it blown up and hung it on the wall of my shore house. (I love when we all match!) *(Photo by Andrew Coppa)*

My beautiful daughters—Gia, Milania, Audriana, and Gabriella, posing at the Rockefeller Center Ice Rink in December 2014, just two weeks before I went to Danbury. *(Photo by Lisa Giammarino)*

The girls having fun—and then some—with Joe at our Montville house. (God bless you, Joe, for being such a great and patient dad!) *(Photo by Andrew Coppa)*

My mother, Antonia, and Audriana at a Mother's Day celebration at Audriana's kindergarten class in May 2015, when I was away. I was sad that I couldn't be there with Audriana, but so happy that my mother was able to go in my place. *(Photo by Lisa Giammarino)*

LEFT: The outside of the men's prison at the Federal Correctional Institution at Danbury, Connecticut, which is what I first saw when I arrived there in the early hours of January 5, 2015, to turn myself in. *(Photo by J. Leonard Jr.)*

RIGHT: My daughters and I relaxing on the grounds of the camp during a Mother's Day celebration. We ran races and did arts and crafts that day. We had so much fun, but it was hard to say goodbye to them.

Posing with some of the friends I made while I served time at Danbury. We went through a lot together, and I will never forget them.

Sitting on a rock on the prison's beautiful grounds. I spent a lot of time outside, by myself, doing a lot of thinking. That helped ground me and keep me sane in there.

My beautiful family during one of their many visits. I couldn't wait to see them every time they came to see me. I loved when we were allowed to go outside together.

My family loved seeing me with curly hair! This is the first time they had seen me wear my hair like this in years.

Hanging with some of my favorite ladies in Danbury. Life wasn't always easy there, but we made each other laugh and had some good times that I will always treasure.

cross. When I turned to leave the room, that's when everything hit me. I had wondered and worried about this moment for months and now it was here. I couldn't help but cry, but I didn't lose it. I wouldn't allow myself to go to that deep, dark place. All I could think of was my four girls and being strong for them. I vowed to myself that I would come back stronger and better from this than before, God willing. I had to stay positive. I had no choice.

I pulled myself together and went to check on Gabriella, giving her a kiss and saying one last prayer for her, before I went back to Gia's room. Milania was in there, snuggled up to Gia in her bed. I lay down with them one more time and we said more prayers. We talked a little bit more and cried. I gave them one more hug and kiss and said good night. When I left, I saw Gia cradling Milania in her arms, and I couldn't help but cry again. I turned and walked toward my bedroom. I didn't want them to see the tears rolling down my face.

When I walked into the kitchen, I asked Jim, Joe, and Mike, "Do you need anything? Are you OK?"

Jim told me later that he and Mike looked at each other like, "She's getting ready to go to prison and she's asking us if *we* need anything!"

While Joe was talking to Jim and Mike, I started wiping down the kitchen counters as I had done so many times before, in happier times. I wanted to leave my house spotless. Nobody cleans my house as well as I do.

I had spent the last few months I had left organizing the whole house—especially the girls' closets and all their things, so that everything would be in order for them, like I was still there. I reminded

Joe about the year's worth of tomato sauce the two of us had made and stored in the garage for him and the girls.

My mom is a great cook and so is Joe's mom. Our moms were going to be cooking a lot for Joe and the kids while I was gone. But since my kids love everything I make, I wanted them to have my sauce anytime they wanted it. I didn't want them to have to go without even that.

I took off my jewelry and decided to leave my wedding band at home, even though we were allowed to wear one. I didn't want to lose it. I didn't need to prove to anyone that I'm married because I figured everyone knew that already.

I handed Jim an envelope with a piece of paper in it for him to give to the prison officials. On it were the handwritten phone numbers, email addresses, and mailing addresses of the people I wanted to put on my phone, email, and mail lists for approval. I also put two hundred dollars in cash in there to start an account so I could buy phone time, toiletries, and other things I would need in there. What was missing in that envelope was photographs. I wasn't allowed to bring pictures with me. People would have to mail them to me.

I told Jim I had taken my extensions out, which he had told me to do, since they weren't allowed in prison.

"I didn't even notice," he said. "It doesn't look any different."

Such a typical man, I thought, laughing to myself, knowing that all my girlfriends would have noticed.

"What were you expecting?" I asked.

"I thought your hair would look like Joe's!" he said.

I made a face at him and we laughed.

That's when he stood up and gave me a rosary and two medals: one of St. Christopher and one of St. Teresa, my patron saint. I tried not to cry as he clasped them around my neck.

• • •

As the time to leave drew near, I saw Jim nod to Mike, like, "Let's leave them alone."

"Teresa," Jim called to me as he was walking toward the front door. "We'll be outside. Whenever you're ready . . ."

Joe and I stood in the kitchen, looking into each other's eyes. We didn't need to say anything at all. We had said everything that needed to be said, before this moment.

"I love you, Tre," he said, hugging me tight.

"I love you, too, honey."

I kissed him and walked through the foyer. As I was about to leave, Milania and Gia came downstairs. I hugged and kissed them and walked through the door, making sure I had a smile on my face to show them I was being positive about everything happening to us in that moment, even though I wanted to throw up. I felt like my heart was being ripped out of my chest, but I didn't want to let them know that.

I turned back to Joe and the girls and said, "I'll call you as soon as I can. And I'll see you all soon."

This was the last time I saw them before I became Inmate Number 65703-050.

We got to Danbury an hour earlier than expected, so Jim suggested we stop at a local diner he had seen on the way, to kill time. The place was pretty empty since it was about 2 a.m. I slid into a booth next to Mike and ordered coffee. I didn't want to eat anything, because it was so late and I was trying to be healthy, but Jim said, "Oh, come on . . ." so I ended up ordering a greasy bacon and egg sandwich.

When the waitress put it down in front of me, I smiled and said to Jim and Mike, "I'm not going to be eating anything like this for a long time . . ."

Ten minutes or so later, a group of people sat down in the booth across from us. I was nervous that they would recognize me. But they were talking in Spanish and never even looked in our direction, which was good. The next morning, though, Jim learned that they had somehow taken pictures of me eating—and sold them to the media, which ran the pictures hours later. Absolutely unbelievable . . . though looking back, that photo was like a *Real Housewives* version of *The Last Supper*.

When we were finished eating, the three of us headed back to the Denali. When I slid into the backseat, I asked Jim if I could smoke in his wife's car. I don't smoke, but I'd brought an electronic cigarette with me, to calm my nerves.

We got to the prison and Jim parked the Denali. As we walked toward the building, he put his arm around me and said, "You're going to be fine. Don't be nervous." I looked at him and tried not to cry. "It's not me I'm worried about," I said. "It's my girls."

After I said goodbye to Jim and Mike, I turned to the guards and said, "I'm ready."

And I was. I was as ready as I would ever be.

5

---

## ORANGE IS THE NEW . . . NIGHTMARE

*B*y the time I got to bed that first night, it was four-thirty in the morning. I needed about ten hours of sleep or more after being up for so long, but I was woken up two hours later when some of my new roommates got up to get ready for their jobs. I wouldn't be getting my job assignment for a week or two, so I could do what I wanted at this point. I was exhausted and wanted to sleep more, but I got up and said hi to the girls in my room. There were three bunks crammed in there, so I had five roommates. They were really nice and all said hi back, introduced themselves to me, and welcomed me to "the camp."

"You're going to do just fine in here, Mami," said Heaven, a pretty Dominican in her early thirties who was in there for drugs.

"Yeah—you be OK," said a tall woman with long dreadlocks and a thick Jamaican accent, who was also in there for drugs. "We heard you were coming."

Heaven handed me a long, detailed printed list of what I could buy at the commissary, the prison store where I could pick up the things I needed that the prison didn't provide us. They only gave you toilet paper and maxi pads, which might not sound like much, but I later learned that other prisons don't give you any of that stuff, so we really were lucky in the grand scheme of things.

They actually call the commissary "Walmart" at Danbury. You could buy Suave, Infusium, or Pantene shampoo and conditioner, toothpaste, soap, deodorant, soda, makeup, tweezers, nail clippers, Noxema, Oil of Olay, ChapStick, food and snacks like rice cakes or raw almonds, aspirin, Tums, reading glasses, a book light, notebooks, air fresheners, alarm clocks, fans, earbuds, towels, washcloths, radios, and even scissors, which surprised me. You could also buy sunglasses for just $5.20! Such a far cry from the glam $350 Tom Ford shades I used to wear before I went away. I didn't see Chanel or Lancôme on the list, but hey—at least I could get some things I would need in my new home away from home.

We weren't allowed to carry cash, so I set up an account with the two hundred dollars I brought from home. Since I got there on a Monday and commissary day was on Tuesday, I had to wait to get the things I needed for those first couple days. Thankfully, a sweet woman named Nikki, who was in there for financial stuff, brought me a bag of things I would need until I could get to the commissary. Nikki looked like a slightly older version of Jennifer Garner. She had all-American good looks: shoulder-length, chestnut-brown hair, which she swept up into a neat ponytail; pretty brown eyes made even more beautiful with a little mascara and navy blue eyeliner, and pale pink lipstick. She was in great shape and I could understand why: she told me she worked out every day. What I liked most about her was her upbeat attitude. She was really friendly and reminded me of some of the girls back home who were there for me when I needed them. I thanked her for being so nice. She got me everything I would need for the first two days: Pantene shampoo and conditioner, Tone soap, Colgate toothpaste, St. Ives body lotion, shower shoes, body wash, a razor, deodorant—everything except food and clothes. I was really touched and relieved because I had heard horror stories about the way new inmates are treated. So Nikki made me feel a little better by welcoming me in (kind of like my real-life Morello from the Netflix adaptation of *Orange Is the New Black*).

She also gave me Vaseline so I could take my makeup off . . . and told me to use a maxi pad to remove it. *What?!* Here I was, used to Lancôme makeup remover, and now I was wiping off my face with a feminine hygiene product. When I went into the bathroom to take it off, I said to no one in particular, "I can't believe I'm taking my makeup off with a friggin' maxi pad." When Heaven heard me complaining, she said, "Hon, we use maxi pads for everything in here . . ." Once I got over the initial shock of using a sanitary napkin to take my makeup off, I realized that it actually worked really well. Who knew? But oh, *Madonna mia* . . .

I would come to find that everyday items could be used for so many things. Take the humble maxi pad, for instance, which I was already using to remove makeup. As time went on, I learned that you could use the pads as slippers and shower shoes, shoe cushions, pedicure shoes, soothing eye pads, face masks to prevent you from getting sick, a sponge to wash plastic containers if you were using the microwave in the common areas to make food, facial hair remover (you use the adhesive on the other side to pull the hair out), and cleaning rags. Who knew they were just as good as a Swiffer Sweeper? I laughed the first time I wiped down the floor and then my locker with a maxi pad. I couldn't help but think, *If only everyone could see me now* . . .

• • •

$\mathcal{D}$espite what some people think, Danbury is *not* a country club, though sometimes I led my husband and children to believe it was like one. Better for them to think I was in a posh prison, rather than suffering. But the reality of it was that being there was like being in hell. I felt like I was buried alive. I felt like so much was happening on the outside and I wasn't a part of anything. I felt trapped—like I'd lost all my freedom and there was nothing I could do about it. While I met a lot of great women in prison, it's still full of depressed, frustrated, bitter, and toxic people who like to start trouble just for fun. (Sound familiar?)

I felt helpless in there when my friends and family needed me. I couldn't do anything for them except call them or email them because I was totally cut off from everything. I hated being away from my daughters. Prison felt like a mental institution, an old people's home, and a military base all rolled into one. The guards are in charge of literally everything you do. The hardest thing is being away from your family and not being able to talk to them whenever you want and for as long as you want. They only give you three hundred minutes a month to talk on the phone, which was not enough time for me, since I had to talk to five people—my husband and the four girls—and only got a few minutes with each one. Fifteen minutes flies by faster than I ever realized. All I wanted was to spend time with my family. Friends and family could only visit us twice a week, which was not enough time, either. During visiting hours, I couldn't always hold Joe's hand or touch him. I could only kiss him when he came and when he left. But I was grateful that I did get to see them, even if it wasn't for the amount of time I would have liked.

I am a very positive person and tried to stay strong in front of my family when I spoke to them on the phone or saw them at visitation. As strong as I am, I had many moments when I just broke down. I have never cried so much in my life. Even at the end of my stay there, I was still crying all the time because I missed my family so much and just wanted to be home with them. During the first few months there, I would wake up pretty much every morning and think to myself, *Am I really here, in prison? Why, God, am I even here?* As the months went on, I got used to being in there, but I would still wake up once in a while and wonder if I was just having a bad dream. I wasn't. This was now my life. While I wanted to be home with my family so bad, I also thought to myself, *I can do this.* I took Jim's words and ran with them: I was a fighter. A warrior. I had to remind myself of that every single day.

The camp where we lived was very dirty and old. "Down the hill" there was a low-security prison where about a thousand men were held, which was built in 1932 and opened in 1940. Though the camp where we lived wasn't nearly as old, one of the inmates told me that some of the Watergate criminals spent time here. That sent a shudder through my spine . . . I was being held in a facility that once housed the most notorious white-collar criminals of our time. *So why was I here?*

When I first got there, I was so grossed out that I didn't want to touch anything. But like anything else in this life, you get used to it and you adjust. But it did make me appreciate all that I have that much more. The inmates who are on the cleaning detail try their best to make it look shiny and new, but it's really an impossible job. It's hard to keep it clean with more than two hundred women living there, especially when many of them are messy. No matter how vigorously the cleanup crew scrubbed everything, it still looked the same. The pipes in the ceiling were covered with inches of dust, and we were constantly inhaling that debris. When it rained, the dining room and other areas of the camp got flooded. In the bathrooms, you needed to put your hands underneath the faucets in the sinks for water to come out, but they shut off after a few seconds. So I would jump from sink to sink to have running water for more than a few seconds. There were only six sinks in each bathroom, and only four worked, even though there were fifty women in my dorm. The sinks usually had food or garbage in them. The water in the showers was freezing cold, so we asked other inmates to flush the toilets, which would trigger the hot water to come on in the showers, even for just a few minutes. The water there was hard, and bad for our skin, but honestly, that was the least of my worries.

Living in a prison dorm is like living in an unfinished, cement basement. Our rooms were like dark, dreary, cold dungeons, which had very little space. It got so hot in the summer that I thought I was going to suffocate. All we could do was either take ice-cold showers or soak the hard, scratchy paper towels they had in the bathroom in cold water and put them on our faces and necks. In the fall, it was freezing because the heat didn't get turned on until the middle of October. It was so cold that my bones ached at night. I slept in long johns, sweatpants, a T-shirt, a fleece top, and socks with two blankets over me just to keep warm.

When I say prison was like being in the military, it's because there are rules and regulations you have to follow for *everything*. They told us when to wake up and when to go to sleep, when to eat and when to stand still for head count, which is a routine where the guards check to make sure no one has escaped. (I heard that if you tried to escape, you would get an extra five years in prison.) For the first month or so of my stay there, I felt so demeaned when I had to stand there while they counted us—like we were sheep or some-

## JAIL LINGO

RANCID - FILTHY DIRTY GETTO, LOW DOWN MESSY AS IN DIRTY EVIL NASTY, SCUMY.

WASH MY ASS - MEANS taking a shower BUT NO say going to take a shower you say to go to wash my ass.

GAY for the stay - you are really not gay but you need some lovin, or you are actually maybe or straight on the outside relation for convenience.

## JAIL LINGO

① Inspection - every Friday - floors need to perfect beds made military style. only bible or locker. You are only allowed to have 4 hangers hanging, but they sell you 60 at COMMISSARY.

thing. They could raid your room anytime they wanted to, make a mess of it, and take whatever they wanted. A lot of women would get in trouble for taking fruit from the cafeteria to eat later on, because you weren't allowed to bring food back to your room. You could only bring food back that you bought from the commissary. They didn't sell fresh fruit—or fresh anything—there.

I hated the food. They served hot dogs and sauerkraut and hamburgers and French fries a lot. Women should not be eating like this. There was no nutritional value in most of the food they gave us, but I tried my best to eat as healthy as I could while I was there. Believe me, the food wasn't giving us the strength we needed to fight off sickness . . . and you'd better not catch anything, because it took days and sometimes longer to get the medicine you needed, if you ever got any.

Then there were the TV rooms. The chairs in the TV rooms were made of hard plastic. They were horrible and killed my back and ass. Everyone was constantly fighting over the TV because there just weren't enough sets for all of us. We constantly had to wait in long lines for everything—the phone, the dining room, the showers, the sinks, and on and on. I swear, I spent 50 percent of my time in prison standing in line. Airport security will never again seem like a hassle.

When I first went into the bathroom, I gagged. It smelled like a porta-potty that hadn't been cleaned out in months. It was filthy. Soggy clumps of toilet paper and paper towels were lying on the floor, which collected stagnant water in the sinking tiles. Women tossed their used sanitary napkins and tampons right on top of the garbage, for all to see, and in the toilets. When I looked up, I saw that the ceiling was missing in spots. I saw exposed pipes and, stuck to the ceiling, dried balls of toilet paper that some of the inmates had tossed up there. Why? I have no idea. Boredom, I guess. The sinks were lined with a brown layer of scum and mold, plus the garbage and discarded food. I wanted to throw up. I didn't want to touch a thing. All I could do was stand there and cringe. The first time I saw that bathroom, I closed my eyes and tried to block it all out.

*I can't believe I'm in here . . .*

What's funny about that first, skin-crawling trip to the bathroom is that about ten days or so into my stay at Chez Danbury, one of my friends emailed me some stupid story she read online that said I became the talk of the prison because I sat directly on a toilet seat in my cell. The story said we had stainless steel toilets with no seats in our prison cells, and that no one sat on them because they were so disgusting. Are you kidding me? Whoever wrote that might have been watching too many episodes of *Lockup* on MSNBC. First of all, we didn't have toilets in our cells, because we weren't in cells. We lived in rooms or cubicles, in what they called dorms, and shared bathrooms in the areas where we lived. What I want to know is: who *saw me* on the toilet in a stall? I'd rather die than sit directly on a public toilet seat, let alone on a *prison* toilet seat. *Madonna mia . . .*

That first day, I took inventory of my new room. Three metal bunk beds were packed into a small space. They had hard bars supporting the thin, stained mattresses. There was a big, dirty window, concrete walls, and a scuffed-up tile floor—like one you might see in a public school. No more walk-in closet for me. We were all given a locker in our rooms to keep our things secure. My locker was tan, about three feet high and maybe three feet wide, with three rickety, rusted shelves on each side. After I thoroughly cleaned the shelves, I put the clothes I had been given on the left-hand shelves. On the top right-hand shelf, I stored my legal folder with all my important papers in it. On the second shelf were my vitamins and toiletries, and as time went on, instant coffee, rice cakes, bottles of water, peanut butter, cereal, and oatmeal. We weren't allowed to tape pictures to the walls, but were allowed to hang pictures inside our lockers. Later on, I taped pictures of me, Joe, and the girls in happier times, as well as pictures of them that I had cut out of magazines or that my fans had printed out from my Instagram page and sent me, which was so thoughtful. I smiled every time I opened my locker and saw my family smiling back at me.

When I thought back to my bedroom at home, I wanted to cry. My bedroom was almost half the size of the whole block I was in. I had a massive, super-king-sized canopy bed with elegant draping around it, a chaise lounge, a fireplace, doors that opened to a balcony, and cathedral ceilings. I used to love to lie on one of the plush, fluffy cream-colored carpets in my bedroom and talk on the phone or tickle the girls. My walk-in closet was twice the size of my new room. But I had to stop myself from thinking about that—and about the fun memories I had with Joe and the girls there. I had to be strong and get through this—one long hour at a time. Pitying myself wasn't going to help. I'd never been that way and wasn't planning on starting now.

As I began getting situated in my little area of the room, a parade of inmates started coming in to say hi to me or to just walk by the room to get a glimpse of me. The last famous person in here had been singer Lauryn Hill, in 2013. (Piper Kerman became famous after she left. Inmates who knew her said she was always helpful, funny, and really nice.) Now that I was the new celebrity inmate, I seemed to be causing quite a stir. My roommates said they had never seen so many people inside or outside their room. The hall was packed with inmates, waiting to get in there. Most of the women were really friendly. A lot of them told me they watched me on the show. Others told me they couldn't believe they were really meeting me because they were such big fans. Some of them told me about all the things you could do there, like the workout classes, which sounded great to me because one of my goals was to get into the most amazing shape of my life while I was at Danbury. Some of them, I later found out, were jockeying to get me to be their friend because that was considered prestigious. But I did get a few menacing stares, too, from some of the women who just walked by my room in the "streets," which is what they called the hallways outside the rooms. They would turn their heads, glance in, give you a strong look, and keep going. I called them the "drive-bys." They made me nervous because I had heard some of the women in there were *tough*. I kept my guard up in case I got hassled or jumped or something. I had to be ready for anything. But I knew I could handle whatever came my way. I am one tough Italian cookie, after all . . .

The other thing I was on red alert for was people trying to get my picture in prison. I had heard that the tabloids were willing to pay top dollar for a photograph— or information about me. I heard that Lauryn Hill made friends with a woman who ended up selling information about her to the rags. They were the hunters and I was their prey, so I needed to be careful about what I did and said because I knew I was a target. I couldn't stop worrying about the media, even in there.

Even though I had a lot of things that I wanted to do to organize my area, so many people still kept coming by that my roommates started to get mad. I felt bad. But it wasn't my fault that all these people wanted to gawk at me. I was used to people staring at me because I'm on TV, but even I was starting to feel like a caged animal at the zoo.

Breakfast was from 6:15 to 7:15 a.m., but on that first day I skipped it. I wanted to fill out my paperwork so I could get Joe, the girls, and my parents on my visitors' list, so they could come see me as soon as possible. Getting approved for visitation takes a few weeks to a month in some cases, because they have to do background checks on everyone. Since Joe was a codefendant with me in our case, he had limited visiting time—just one day a month, which got changed to two days a month later on, thank goodness, even though that still didn't seem like enough time.

I had this constant gnawing in my stomach because I couldn't stop thinking about Joe and the girls, especially after our heartwrenching goodbye the night I left. I turned on my side and faced the wall so the two girls in the room couldn't see me crying. I tried hard not to make a noise or sniffle. I just wiped the tears from my eyes with my shirt while I finished filling out the papers.

I really wanted to talk to my family and let them know I was OK. I missed them so much and hadn't even been there for twenty-four hours yet. I felt like I was dying inside, but I tried not to show it. Around 9 a.m., I headed to the computer room so I could email them. But I wasn't set up to use CORRLINCS, the prison's email system. Another thing I had to wait for.

One of the things I thought I'd be able to do in prison was surf the Internet during computer time. That thought kept me from truly feeling I was absolutely cut off from the outside world. I soon found out that the computers were for email—and email only. You had to press your thumbprint onto an electronic pad to even get into the computer room and the commissary. So I had no access to what was going on in the world at all, unless someone let me know or I happened to see it on TV. I soon found out that you had to watch what you emailed, too, because the officers read everything that came in and out. Same with snail mail. The officers opened all your mail and read and inspected it before you heard your last name yelled out to come get it at mail call. But people could send you a limited number of books and magazines, which was great. I definitely wanted to grow my reading list while I was there.

I decided to take my first prison shower, which I had been dreading after I saw the bathroom. I put on the shower shoes Nikki had given me and brought a tiny, worn towel (that looked worse than some of the rags I used to clean my house), a threadbare washcloth, and some of Nikki's donated bath supplies to the shower area. All eyes were on me when I got there. I could see some of them whispering to each other and looking at me, like, "There's Teresa!" Some of the ladies in there came up to me and said hi. A couple of them looked me up and down or gave me a side eye. I heard one of them say to her friend, "This bitch better not think she's better than us . . ." I just looked away and pretended like I didn't see or hear a thing.

Since I seemed to be the newest victim of the prison spotlight, I didn't want anyone to get a glimpse of *anything*, so I went into the shower stall with my T-shirt and sweatpants on, took them off behind the curtain, and hung them up outside the shower stall on a hook, draping the thin, scratchy towel over my clothes. The curtain didn't cover the opening of the shower stall all the way, which of course made me nervous. I tried to stand directly behind the protection of the curtain while I was in there, which is pretty difficult in a tiny little shower stall (especially when you don't want your body to rub up against the tiled walls or the slimy curtain). I would come to find that other women were like me—they got undressed behind the safety of the curtain. But others didn't seem to care who saw them *au naturel*. A bunch of them were walking around naked, strutting around like proud peacocks, talking and laughing. I didn't want to get an eyeful of that, especially since many of these ladies were not into bikini waxes at all, if you know what I mean . . .

I was looking forward to a long, hot shower, but of course, I was horribly mistaken. You had to keep a button pressed to keep the water running, which was a pain. Parts of the shower walls and floor were moldy or covered with a thin layer of brown slime. I took one of the fastest showers of my life because I totally skeeved the sight of this bathroom. God knows what was growing on that floor. It was like one big prison petri dish.

I found out that I wasn't far off with thinking that way. When I first got to prison, all the inmates were worried about catching MRSA or another kind of staph infection, because one of the inmates had come down with it. Then I heard that another one had shingles. So I was not about to touch the walls or the floors in the shower at all. I was scared I'd need any sort of medical attention—and God knows if I'd even get it.

When I was done, I grabbed the towel on the hook, dried off behind the curtain, and put my clothes back on in the stall before I stepped out of the shower. All eyes were on me again, but I was thinking to myself, *Sorry ladies! No peep show from me today!*

After I put my shower things back in my locker, I had a mandatory meeting with my counselor, my case manager, and the on-site psychologist, who were all really nice and told me to come to them with any questions or concerns I had. I went back to my room and chatted with the woman in the bunk under mine. She was in her early sixties, was married with grown kids, and carried a heavy fourteen-year sentence for drug-related crimes. She said she was an addict in her former life who sold drugs, and that her "asshole husband" ratted her out, which is how she ended up locked up. I could barely cope with the fact that I had to be in there for a year. I had no idea how she dealt with the thought of being in there for so long.

I was straightening out my locker when a woman from down the hall brought me a notebook, which I began using as a diary. Before that, I just wrote on any scrap of paper I could find. It's so funny because I kept hearing reports that I was keeping this diary while I was in there and that tons of people wanted to know what was in it. I guarded it with my life. When I was done writing in it each day, I always made sure to lock it up. (This turned out to be a very good thing because later on in my stay, someone told me that some of the ladies tried to break into my locker to steal my ID card with my picture on it and the diary I kept in there. Someone told me they thought the diary was worth millions . . . which made me laugh.)

After the lady who brought me the notebook left, my room-mates protectively gathered around me and shared some of the most important advice I'd ever hear in prison. They told me not to take *anything* from anyone. I felt like an orphaned baby cub, surrounded by mama lions in the jungle, who were just trying to keep me safe. Before Jim dropped me off, he had said the same thing to me: do not trust anyone inside, and keep your eyes and ears open at all times.

"Some people may just want to help you, but you never know," said one of my roommates, Matilda, talking very softly and lean-ing close in to my face. "You don't want to have to owe nothing to nobody down the line."

"It happened to me when I first got in here," said Teeny, who, at twenty-one, was the youngest one in our room. "Someone gave me some tuna packets and spices on my first or second day, then jacked me up in the hallway a week later and said I hadn't paid her back yet. She wanted a whole bunch of stuff from the commissary from me. I had no idea what was going on."

*Oh my God . . .* I was starting to get overwhelmed, if I hadn't been before. I'd had to watch my back with many of the *Real House-wives* ladies, but never anything like this.

Lunch was at 11 a.m., but I decided not to go. They were serving hot dogs and tater tots. No, thanks. I don't think I had eaten anything like that since I was in third grade. I also wanted to avoid eating beef or any fatty meats when I was in there. I just wanted to eat as clean as I could, if that was possible. As I was sitting on my bed, wondering what to do next, Nikki, who worked in the kitchen, came into my room with a salad she'd had someone make for me— mixed greens, peppers, carrots, broccoli, cucumbers, cauliflower, and cheese, tossed with vinaigrette. I thought about what my roommates had said, but this salad looked incredible and I was hungry, so how could I say no?

"I thought you might like this," Nikki said.

I wanted to jump off the bed and give her a big hug, but I didn't. I wasn't sure if I should do something like that so soon after meeting her. I had to get the lay of the land first.

"Oh my God, thank you so much! This is exactly what I wanted. Hot dogs and tater tots aren't really my thing."

"Me, neither!" she said, laughing.

When I got here everyone was very welcoming, it is like a family everyone sticks together and tries to help each other get through the days. It is called syevival so you can get home to your family.

I know my roommates told me to be careful about taking anything from anyone, but there was something about Nikki that made me feel good about her the minute I met her. As it turned out, I was right. She and I became good friends and hung out the entire time I was at Danbury. Like me, she loved to exercise. We worked out all the time together. She even taught some of the exercise classes, which was great, and let me help lead some of the classes when there were too many ladies there. All in all, I was just happy to have made a new friend.

After she left, I finished the salad and started thinking about my family, and started crying again. It was only 12:50 p.m. and the day was *dragging* by. It was so noisy in there because the ladies would talk and laugh really loud, yell, sing, gossip, and argue in the streets all day long. I had zero privacy and just felt like I couldn't escape. Even though I had mopped the floor and cleaned the room, it still looked dirty. I still couldn't believe my mattress was stained with urine or blood. At least that's what I *hoped* it was, compared to the dozens of alternatives. I could literally *see* the dust blowing out of the air vents in my room. And honestly, I was still a little scared about being in there. I didn't know what to expect. Even though a lot of people were being really nice to me, I didn't trust anyone yet. I was a little worried about the scarier-looking inmates who kept shooting me those dirty looks. At this point, I didn't know if people there got violent, and if so, how violent, so I was watching out for that, too. I thought back to the time I was almost jumped in high school . . . I didn't see that coming. But I held my own back then and knew I would here, too, but still, I wanted to keep my eyes wide open, just like Jim and my roomies told me to.

More than anything, though, I felt lonely. All I wanted to do was talk to my family. But I found out that I wouldn't be able to call them until the next day. As a new inmate, I had to wait twenty-four hours before I could make my first call. I don't know why they had this rule in there, but it seemed so harsh. I was so upset. It was killing me not to be able to talk to them.

Although dinner was at 4, you could go at 3 p.m. They called that the short line. I liked that better because it was beyond crowded when everyone from the camp packed into the dining room for the main mealtimes—like Times Square in New York City during the holidays. A woman named Liz invited me to go to dinner with her on my first day. She was in her mid-sixties, with a blond bob, who always wore pink lipstick with fuchsia lip liner.

I was wary of Liz at first. When she first approached me, she told me she knew a lawyer who had reached out to me. I already had a great lawyer I loved, so I didn't need another one. I was standoffish, because my roommates had told me to be careful of anyone who tried to help me in any way. But then, other girls started telling me that she was OK. So when I ran into her again, I told her I was sorry for acting the way I did.

"I was feeling a little overwhelmed by everything when I first met you," I told her.

"I've been there," she said. "I get it."

So we headed to dinner—at 3 p.m.—the prison's early bird special. I had my first meal in the dining room: chicken salad, beef soup, and an orange, which was surprisingly good. While we ate, she told me that she was a former paralegal who liked to help other inmates file motions and other legal paperwork. She said she didn't ask for anything in return because she just wanted to help. I found out later on that there were women in there who were attorneys—but they charged inmates for their services. Of course, you're not supposed to charge anyone for anything there, but a lot of people did anyway.

Even though I was new at the camp, I was relieved to see that my schedule was already starting to fill up fast—I was one step closer to keeping busy. I planned to take a workout class every day at 5:30 p.m. and head to the gym after that. What I liked about Danbury was that even though they told you when to eat, sleep, and work, you could pretty much do whatever you wanted the rest of the time. You had to be in your room for head count at 4 p.m. and 9 p.m. (except on weekends, when head count started at 10 a.m.), show up for your job, go see your counselor here and there, and attend six mandatory educational classes. Other than that, you could do arts and crafts, go to exercise classes, work out in the gym, knit or crochet, play cards, watch TV or movies, email on the computer—or just hang out "in the streets."

When I got to that first workout class, there were too many women in there so I walked out. I went out a back door in the camp and walked down a huge flight of stairs to the little gym near the track and did my own thing for that hour. And no surprise: the gym was disgusting. Nothing like the place where I work out at home. Most of the equipment was rusty and run-down. The walls and floor were scuffed-up. It looked like a gym someone had set up in their garage. But it had a stationary bike, a spinning bike, weights, and an elliptical machine, so I was happy. I made sure to wipe down the handles and the seat before I got on the stationary bike, which made me feel better. And the session on the bike got rid of a little of the stress from the day before, and made that terrible gnawing feeling in my stomach go away—at least for the moment.

I was so tired by the time I got back to my room that evening because I had only gotten two hours of sleep the night before. I told my roommates how upset I was that I couldn't call my family, trying so hard not to break down in tears. I did not want them to think I was weak. I went to bed early, because I was determined to get up at the 5:30 a.m. wake-up call so I could get to the computer room at 6 a.m. and register my home phone number in the system and finally call home. That's all I could think about. The only thing more valuable in prison than weekend visits with your family is being able to speak to them on the phone.

When I curled up in bed, I started thinking about Joe and the girls again. I cried myself to sleep that night, thinking about how badly I ached for them. I tried to be quiet and muffled my sobs in my pillow. I hoped my roommates couldn't hear me sniffling. Finally, I went to sleep—where everything was blissfully empty.

The next morning, I learned the hard way that wake-up call was not always at 5:30 a.m., as I had originally thought. Sometimes there was no wake-up call whatsoever; it all depended on which guard was working. At the beginning of my stay, we happened to have an officer on duty in the mornings who didn't do wake-up calls at all (later on, though, we got a female officer who would walk into your room at 6 a.m., flip on the lights, and say, "Time to wake up!" If someone shut them off again, she would come back in and yell.)

Even if there was no wake-up call, at 7:30 a.m., an officer would call the inmates over the loudspeaker to go to work. Thank goodness Matilda woke me up that second day around 6:15. She knew how upset I was about not being able to call my family. I literally jumped out of bed, threw on my uniform, grabbed my paperwork, and raced to the computer room to register my home number. I couldn't wait to hear their voices.

The officer there told me I had to wait an hour or so to get approved. I had never waited so long to make a call in my life. I wanted to scream but kept my cool. I headed to breakfast—my first one there—and had cereal, an orange, and a banana nut muffin, which was good (and would become a staple of my prison diet). I headed back to the computer room to add more phone numbers and email addresses to my contact list so I could start communicating with my family and friends. But I still couldn't use the computer because *that* had to be approved. *This is ridiculous*, I thought. Life in prison, I was discovering, is nothing but one big, long waiting game. But then again, all I had was time . . . and lots of it. Life there was the exact opposite of life at home for me.

It was laundry day, so at 7 a.m., I brought a small pile of dirty clothes to the laundry room. I didn't have much at this point, but I wanted as many clean clothes as I could get. Now, this was interesting to me because I used to do *all* our laundry at home. With four girls in so many different activities and a husband in construction, there was *a lot* to wash. So I loved that they did your laundry for you! You did have to fold it when you got back to your room, which was no problem for me, because I like to do that. I found out later that you could pay someone to fold it for you, if you wanted. Some people even paid to get their clothes ironed. I didn't need to do that, though, with T-shirts, sweats, and shorts. My clothes looked fine after I folded them. But sometimes when I went to pick my things up, the laundry lady had already folded everything for me, because she and I had become friends. Again, just so nice and not what I had expected when I first got here, at all. Later on, I would be accused of getting "special treatment," when all my friend wanted to do was give me a hand. *Whatever*, I thought. I was used to people thinking things about me that weren't true at all. (In fact, while I was in there, I felt like I was watched even more closely than others because of who I am.)

While I waited for my approvals, I walked right out the front door of the camp and headed over to the commissary, a boxy, glass-fronted building that was a hop, skip, and jump from where we lived. When I first got to the prison, I thought the commissary was the visitors' center because it was so close to the building where inmates were housed (of course, there wasn't even a true visitors' center). I couldn't believe we were allowed to go outside like that, but since this was a minimum-security camp, we were allowed outside the main building. I'm sure more than a few inmates before me had thought of escaping, but you had to walk—or run—a really long way, on 348 acres of open land, before you hit the street. After seeing the guards standing on the hill near the commissary and riding around the grounds in small white pickup trucks all day long, crisscrossing the property, I couldn't imagine anyone would even try. If you did and were caught? You would most likely be immediately shipped out of the camp to the Federal Metropolitan Detention Center in Brooklyn. From what I heard about the MDC, it was a much rougher place, with all different kinds of inmates who were in there for serious offenses—so you definitely did not want to get sent that way.

I walked through the doors and waited in yet another line. I went to one of the windows, pressed my thumbprint on the electronic pad, and handed the clerk behind the counter the list of items I had checked off on the commissary list. I peeked in there while she went to get my order. The commissary was small but carried a lot of things. I couldn't believe how much they packed into one little room. I bought Pantene shampoo and conditioner, a bar of Tone soap, Colgate toothpaste and a toothbrush, sweats, a T-shirt, hair ties, Queen Helene hair gel, and St. Ives body lotion. I bought some of the same things Nikki had given me so I could give them back to her.

The only kind of makeup they sold was Wet n Wild—the supercheap stuff you get at the drugstore. I bought eyeliner, lip gloss, foundation, and mascara (but no false eyelashes . . . they definitely didn't carry those, and who knows if they would have gotten ripped out, anyway . . .). What a blast from the past. I used to buy Wet n Wild lip liner in fuchsia when I first started wearing makeup in high school. *What a small world*, I thought. Everything had come full circle.

The commissary had pretty much everything I needed, except for Clairol Nice 'n Easy hair color—and raisins. They were out of the hair dye and wouldn't be able to get it for me for a couple weeks. I was OK with not being able to do my roots for that time, but the one thing I cannot live without? My raisins. I eat them with my oatmeal. I can't eat oatmeal without them.

When I was walking back from the commissary, I asked one of the guards, "Why don't they sell raisins?"

"Raisins are considered contraband," she said.

I looked at her like she was crazy.

"Raisins?! Why?!"

She explained that a lot of the ladies hoarded them, fermented them, and turned them into prison-style moonshine! You would need a lot of raisins to do that, but somehow, some of the women managed to make raisin-flavored alcohol, which they call hooch. This was definitely a new one for me. Joe likes to make homemade wine. Maybe I should let him know about this one . . .

A few hours later, I was in my room organizing my locker, when this petite Hispanic woman with a huge bun on her head and tattoos all over her neck came up to me from behind and shoved two boxes of the exact hair color I needed—medium brown—and a paper bag full of raisins into my hands.

"Here! Take this," she whispered. "Hurry up and put it in your locker, before anyone sees."

I wasn't quite sure what to say, since I had been warned not to take anything from anyone.

"Come see me if you need anything else."

Then she was gone. After she hightailed it out of my room, Dreadlocks came walking in. "Oh, I see you met Magic. She is a literal magician who can get you anything you want. And I mean *anything* . . ."

(I loved the names they had for each other in there. I found out later on in my stay that some of the ladies called me Hollywood . . . Hey, I could get used to that.)

She told me Magic was considered the camp's contraband queen. There were others, of course, who sold illicit items, but she was one of the best. If you wanted something? She either had it or could get it. I don't know how she did it. She sold everything from loosies—loose cigarettes—to Nair hair removal cream, which I guess was in high demand there. So were diet pills because everyone wanted to lose weight *fast*. But Magic sold everything at a huge markup. *Huge*. One cigarette cost ten dollars and a pack cost one hundred and forty.

That's when I started getting nervous. I thought, *Oh*, Madonna mia. *Now I'm gonna owe her for the hair color and the raisins. What is she gonna want in return? Shit*. Another problem I didn't need that just fell into my lap. I couldn't get her out of my head that whole night because I'm such a worrier. So when I saw her by the phones the next day, I went up to her, thanked her, and said, "That was really nice of you, but what do I owe you?"

"Don't worry about that," she said, leaning up against the wall. "That was a gift. What you can do for me is watch my back in here and I'll watch yours. Deal?"

She put her hand out. We shook on it and she left. It was so bizarre. I felt like I was a character on *The Sopranos*, doing some secret underworld deal, where I swore omertà, even though all I was getting was hair color and friggin' raisins. But thanks to Magic, from that day on, there wasn't a day that went by when I didn't have my oatmeal with raisins . . . my Magic raisins . . . (but not enough to make moonshine!).

Now I had to deal with my new wardrobe. When I first got there, they gave me six pairs of white cotton granny panties, three uncomfortable sports bras that didn't fit me well at all, six pairs of socks, four T-shirts, four uniforms (the olive-green shirts and matching pants), and a pair of steel-toed boots. The olive-colored T-shirts they gave me were all size large. They only give out size large and up, so the shirts were swimming on me. When I got to the commissary, I was able to buy some comfy gray sweats and some gray T-shirts in size small, which made me happy. I was definitely learning that it *is* the little things in life that are important, especially somewhere like prison.

I bought some dark-gray-and-black Adidas sneakers, too, but they had to order them for me, so it took a few weeks to get those. Nikki let me borrow a pair of her sneakers until I got mine. Thank God for her because I started working out the first day I got there.

I have to say, I met a lot of generous people when I first got to Danbury. That first night, I slept in that green top and pants they had given me because I got to my bunk so late. That's the same top I wore in my ID photo. Since I wasn't able to get to the commissary on that first day, Heaven gave me prison-style pajamas to sleep in for that second night—a T-shirt and sweatpants. It really was nice of her. That's what women did in there. When someone was new, the other women tried to offer support by giving her the stuff she needed until she could get to the commissary. So if you got there on a Wednesday? You were screwed unless someone helped you out, since you couldn't go to the commissary until the following Tuesday. I was lucky I got there on a Monday—and that my two hundred dollars went right into my account. Some of the inmates told me they'd had to wait a week or two before they could buy anything.

Before I got to prison, I would never even think of wearing anyone else's clothes, let alone their shoes. But once you're locked up, things are different. When you're in there, you don't discount your blessings—even if, in your previous life, you would have done so. You're just grateful for what people give you, and you do what you have to do to survive. And of course, the other women would make sure the clothes were washed and that the shoes were clean before they gave them to you. Again, not what I'd expected at all.

I learned to pay it forward in there, too. I was so grateful for all the people who helped me that I wanted to help the newbies out, as well. When people finally got out of there, they usually left stuff behind that other people could use. A woman I became friendly with gave me her boat shoes when she left. I loved them because they were different—they were a little piece of the outside world. To me, they were like Louboutins. I wore them when my daughters came to visit because I didn't want them to see me in the black boots. So way before I left, I told this other girl that they would be hers when I bid goodbye to that place. I had to. She's a Jersey girl, too, and God knows we watch out for each other!

After my prison shopping spree, I went back to my room, put my new things away, and attempted to clean. I washed the floor and dusted the fan and the windowsill. And the best part: I cleaned off all of the gunk and grime from the huge window, so finally, some light shone through. I definitely counted that big window as a blessing. I had a bird's-eye view of the prison grounds from my top bunk. The prison sits high up on a hill, on acres of empty land—pretty, rolling hills, with greenery that turned to gorgeous red, orange, and yellow hues come fall. I liked to look out the window whenever I could. At least I could *see* the outside world, even if I wasn't in it.

*F*inally, the officers told me I could call home! I raced to the phone bank and waited impatiently in line. Earlier, when I was setting up my phone privileges, I had stated my name for the recording that came on when our friends and family got calls from us, telling them this was Teresa Giudice and that they were getting a call from a federal prison. Again, just surreal.

I also came to learn that you had to yell out to the crowd waiting there, "Who's last in line?!" when you got there, because everyone stood all over the place. I hated that. When I finally got a phone, I was so happy I started tearing up. I was even shaking a little bit. What if they weren't home? When I heard Joe come on the line, I broke down. It was so comforting to hear his voice. He asked how I was doing, and I barely squeaked out an "OK." I got a grip on myself and told him I was doing fine. That it wasn't so bad in here and that I was settling in. He said he started crying because he couldn't believe I had really gone to prison and wasn't coming back for a long time. I lost it and hoped no one was watching me sob into the phone. I calmed down but started crying again when each of the girls came on the line. Oh God, how I missed them already. I loved hearing their sweet voices. I told them what I had done so far and that I missed them so very much. They told me what they were up to that day and said they missed me, too. We exchanged "I love you's." I could have listened to them all day long. Milania had started telling me about school, when the call ended. At first I thought something had gone wrong. Did I not pay for my minutes after all? Were the phones down? Did Milania hang up? One of the inmates next to me filled me in: when you reach the fifteen-minute limit, the phone shuts off and you have to wait a half hour before you could call them back. I could have talked to them for hours. All that waiting . . . for fifteen minutes. But at least I got to talk to them, which was a victory in and of itself.

I was happy. Floating-on-air happy. I tried to call my mom and dad, but realized that in my sleep-deprived state I hadn't added their phone number to my list. I raced back to the computer room to add them to the list and then, yes, wait for approval. I emailed my honey and told him I loved him and then finally got to talk to my parents. I was lucky a phone was free. I cried when I talked to them, too.

When I went back to my room, Nikki stopped by again with another amazing salad! I thanked her and chatted with her a bit before she had to leave. I was throwing the last of the salad away when an officer stopped me.

"You can't eat that in your room. You can only eat it in the lunchroom."

He said he wouldn't tell the lieutenant—this time—because I was new and didn't know the rules yet. Thank God. I didn't want to be punished on my first day there.

"I had no idea you couldn't eat in your room," I replied, trying not to shake. "I'll never do it again."

"OK," he said, turning on his heel and walking back down the hallway.

This was the first of many lessons—big and small—I would learn about the official and unofficial rules in there.

Later that day, I met this really great woman named Tonya, who was in there for financial stuff, too. She had long brown hair, gorgeous hazel eyes and, like me, was a total girly and glamour girl, so I was immediately drawn to her. She had lived a nice life before she was sent to Danbury, so we seemed to have a lot in common.

She told me not to ask anyone any questions. Nothing. She also told me not to trust anyone in there because most of them were criminals.

She told me that you could find whatever you needed in prison, if they didn't sell it in the commissary. What's that saying? Neurology is the mother of invention? (Just kidding . . .) I mean, necessity is the mother of invention? In there, it sure was. She told me that the more creative types made and sold sleeping masks, curlers out of toilet paper, and dildos by wrapping a maxi pad around a toothbrush or two, taping them together, and sticking that in a rubber glove they got from the kitchen. If you wanted a thicker dildo, you just used more maxi pads. I was like, "*WHAT?!*" I, for one, would *not* be buying a homemade dildo, thank you very much.

But she also said that if you got caught with one of these "inventions," you would be given what they called a "shot," a formal write-up documenting your bad behavior. If you were unlucky enough to get a shot, you would get punished in some way. You could have your free time, your calls, and your emailing privileges taken away, and in worst-case scenarios, your visiting hours. If you got caught with something really bad, like a gun or knife, you could be shipped out to Brooklyn. Even though people may not have snuck these things inside the prison, they were still considered contraband because they weren't allowed. The biggies—cigarettes, drugs, weapons, and pills—were obviously illegal. But I was surprised to learn that stamps were, too. *Stamps?* At first, I couldn't figure out why, but I found out later that people could stick drugs, like heroin, on the backs of the stamps and smuggle that into the prison. I don't know if that's true or not, but wow—that's something I wouldn't have thought of in a million years. Chewing gum was also considered contraband because inmates could stick it in the locks to prevent the officers from getting in—or out.

Even though contraband was off-limits, it didn't stop the women from bringing it in. Another thing I learned during my stay was that women would hide taboo items like drugs, cigarettes, dildos, and other sex toys in all kinds of nooks and crannies in the building. If you were really bored, I guess you could go on a contraband scavenger hunt . . . God only knows what you would find.

I found out that the officers listened in on all of your calls. I also learned that if you really did something bad in there, they could either send you to Brooklyn or put you in the hole—aka the Special Housing Unit, which they called the SHU. When you go to the hole, you are in a cell, by yourself, for twenty-four hours straight, unless they give you an hour a day to exercise or take a shower. You eat in your cell. You go to the bathroom in your cell. Usually there's no TV or radio in there. You may get to read a book. Maybe not, depending on what you did. Again, I made sure to follow *every* rule because I wanted to keep my privileges and be able to leave in December 2015, when I had heard I was scheduled to be released to home confinement. Plus, I had this weird feeling that *if* I did anything wrong, it would somehow make news in the outside world. It was that pressure that kept me walking the straight and narrow in prison. The proverbial knife edge my father was always warning me about.

I couldn't wait to go to sleep that night because I was really tired and drained from all the new information, people, and situations coming at me. I changed into the T-shirt and sweats I had bought to wear to bed, climbed up to my bunk, and settled in for the night. I shut my eyes, said my prayers, doing the sign of the cross before and after, and had started to fall asleep, when I smelled something fishy. I thought, "Who's cooking in their room at this hour? That's weird."

The smell got stronger and then I heard some kind of muffled sound. At first, I thought it was the heating system. I wasn't sure. It was really dark in the room, but as my eyes adjusted to the blackness, I could see two women on top of one of the two other bunks, writhing around on the bed. They were totally going at it.

*Oh my God* . . . I flipped over, faced the other way, and pulled the blanket over my head.

*I cannot believe this is happening!*

I don't want to sound naïve, but I did live a pretty sheltered life before I got there. I had heard that this goes on in men's prisons, but for whatever reason, I had no idea this went on with women. I didn't say a word, though, and just let them do their thing.

It was just my second night in there, sleeping in my "home away from home." *Well, Teresa, you're here,* I thought to myself. *Welcome to prison.*

The next morning, I didn't say anything to anyone about the live porn show I'd seen in my room the night before. But I couldn't get that gross image—or that strong *smell*—out of my head. I found out later that one of my roommates was a lesbian—who had a girlfriend also serving time at Danbury—and that another one, although she was married and had a bunch of kids, was what they call "gay for the stay." Her girlfriend was called a bulldagger—a butch lesbian who turns a straight woman gay (at least that's what I think it means). I love sex and all, but I didn't miss it enough to find a lesbian playmate while I was there. Nooooo way—that's just not my thing.

I saw women disappear into the woods together near the track to frolic with each other alfresco. I remember walking into the shower area many times and seeing four legs behind a curtain with sound effects, like grunting, and shouting out words I'd rather not write here in case my daughters or parents read this. (And I always saw crazy things going on when I went to the bathroom in the middle of the night. One time I saw this girl holding a dildo in her right hand. I guess I interrupted her. She looked at me like, "Get the fuck out of here . . .")

I feel like I am staying at a low budget spa. There are a lot of lesbians in here. It is called gay for the stay. Last night I woke up in the middle of the night and two women were in a bed directly across from me and they were going to town on each other, down town :

God I miss my Juicy Joe! 😢

Another time, one of the inmates was showering with the curtain open in front of her girlfriend, who was sitting on a chair watching her lather herself up, let's just say. I looked the other way and just went about my business. But *Madonna mia* . . . I did a silent sign of the cross in my head when I saw that. All I could think of was how my dad wouldn't let me wear a cheerleader skirt—and here these two were acting like they were at home, in the privacy of their bedroom . . . I just kept walking *real fast* . . .

I have nothing against gays, lesbians, bisexuals, or transgender people. I have a lot of friends who are gay. I saw Caitlyn Jenner on the cover of *Vanity Fair* and then on the ESPY Awards on TV and thought she looked absolutely beautiful. But having sex with another woman? I'm just not into that. My feeling was *Hey, go for it.* It's none of my business—unless it's happening a couple feet away, in my own bedroom, when I'm trying to sleep! Let's put it this way: I would feel uncomfortable if a guy and a girl were having sex in the bunk next to me. That said, I still wasn't going to say squat about any of this because (a) that's not my style and (b) I was starting to learn what happened if people thought you were a rat and (c) I still had to live with these women for months and months and months.

The ladies in my dorm had their quirks, for sure, and could be territorial over some things. If you accidentally sat in "their" seat in the lunchroom, they would let you know about it. Or if you used the computer they liked to use? They would snap at you and give you some lip. Not the biggest deal. But if you were a snitch? Watch out. That's when you could get the shit beaten out of you or have the whole camp hating you and tripping you up every chance they got. So I stayed quiet. And humble. If you know me, you know that I'm really down-to-earth. I have no airs about me. I'm a girl's girl. But a lot of people only know me from TV and the stuff they read in the tabloids. If other inmates thought I was a stuck-up bitch at Danbury, I was truly done for. I had to be careful about that, too.

My feeling was this: no matter where these ladies came from, we were all in this together. For all of us, it was about survival—getting through each day so we could get back to our families and our lives. So why cause trouble? I didn't like to be the target of drama and

I didn't want to do that to anyone else, either. But not everybody thought the same way I did.

As much as I tried to fly under the radar and avoid having a drama target on my back, I couldn't, because of my pals in the media. We used to get all the magazines in there. We laughed when we saw stories in the tabloids about me being a diva while in prison. So untrue. And that I had other inmates doing things for me at my beck and call. Again, not true. And lastly, that I got special treatment. No way. Hey, I wish I did.

At the beginning of my stay, there was a story that said I feared for my life. We laughed at that, too, because that was so far from the truth. I didn't fear for my life, but I *was* watching out for people who gave me nasty looks, the people I knew wanted something from me or wanted to cash in on me in some way. It's like celebrity radar. I was glad, though, that other people were starting to see *all* the lies that are written about me . . . and that yes, I am decent, kind, and laid-back. I found out later that a lot of the inmates in the men's prison—the massive building at the bottom of the hill with all the scary fences around it—read the story, thought it was true, and were worried about me. Especially the Italians and the mob guys. They sent a message up the hill to some of the inmates that said, *"Make sure nothing happens to Teresa."*

This was only my third day, and I was really starting to get into a little routine. I woke up at 6:30 a.m. for breakfast. I had pancakes and bran cereal that a sunny cafeteria lady in her late sixties served to me from behind a counter. I don't know how she could be so upbeat in the morning, but I was happy to see her.

"Good morning, Miss Teresa," she would say.

So far, everyone in there had called me Giudice because they usually called you by your last name—and mispronounced it (but I'm used to that by now).

"You know my name?"

"Of course. You are so sweet and so beautiful. How could I forget you? Have a nice breakfast and a wonderful day."

I usually sat alone at breakfast because it was pretty empty there in the morning. Just the early risers—some of the older ladies and me. I liked mornings there, too, because it was *quiet*. When everyone started getting up, it got so noisy, sometimes I couldn't even think straight. It got really crazy there at night, when all I wanted was to go to sleep. Some of my roommates were night owls and social butterflies who were practically throwing block parties in our room. I was hoping I could get moved to a quieter area at some point, because it was hard to concentrate when I was reading or writing in my diary—or when I was just trying to fall asleep sometimes.

I was still tired from the night before, because I learned about another fun thing they do in prison: shine a flashlight in your eyes during a 5 a.m. head count to make sure you are still there and didn't escape. I bolted upright in bed when the officer shined the bright light in my eyes.

"Oh my God! What happened?" I shouted. I thought someone had turned on the lights and that we had to run out of there because of a fire or something. "Nobody told you about this?" said the officer, a sweet woman in her late forties. "We just do this to make sure no one decided to take a walk—a long walk—outta here. Go back to sleep, hon."

Of course, I couldn't. I was still shaking from that rude awakening. That morning, I tried to keep my eyes open during my mandatory appointments with the prison dentist and the prison doctor, who gave me a physical. They wanted to make sure you were healthy when you arrived. If you weren't, they would either keep you in the infirmary or house you in a room with other inmates who were sick or ailing in some way. The dentist said my teeth looked good, and I got a clean bill of health from the doctor. *Buona!*

After calling my family and checking emails each morning after breakfast, I started heading to the gym right after that so I could do the bike and some weights. I went to lunch at ten-thirty. It was pouring out and the ceiling was leaking, so they had buckets all over the place to catch all the water coming in. Someone told me part of the ceiling had actually collapsed at one point because of all the rain. The whole place really needed a huge makeover. The only bathroom that was halfway decent was the one near the computer room. It looked a little newer and maybe that's why it looked cleaner. I tried to use that one whenever I could.

After lunch, I ran into Tonya, who invited me to go watch TV with another girl. We went into one of the TV rooms to watch *Sex and the City*. It was the first time I had watched TV in prison—not that I watched much at home, anyway. It was nice to actually sit and watch an adult TV show because all that's on at my house is the Disney Channel . . . hour after hour after hour.

After the show ended, Tonya, her friend, and I talked a bit. They were asking me how it was going. I said everything was fine and that I missed Joe and the girls so much. But I was still thinking about the sexcapade in my room the night before. I was dying to talk to someone about it, but I thought, *I'd better not. Not just yet* . . . I was still feeling my way in there and didn't know who I could really trust, so I kept these things to myself. I didn't want to get the reputation as a rat, even if I was just venting.

Before I knew it, it was dinnertime! It was at 3 p.m. sharp if you were short-lining it like I did. So early! They served turkey ham, which I refused to eat. I think one of the bulldaggers named it dick meat because it was gross and inedible (believe me, I was laughing hard at that one). I couldn't agree more. It was a grayish pink and looked like it was going to slither off the plate. No, thanks. I opted for the sweet potato and beans, instead. I skipped the greens, too, because they looked slimy. Not the best dinner on the planet, but at least I got something to eat.

After I checked my emails and wrote back to Joe, the girls, and a few other people, I took a shower and washed my hair for the first time. I didn't wash it when I took my first shower because I wanted to keep my blowout intact as long as I could. Rinsing all the shampoo out was hard because I have so much hair and I had to keep pressing the button to keep the wonderfully cold water running. At this point, I hadn't yet discovered the prison hairdresser, so when I got out of the shower, I let my hair air dry. This was the first time in more than five years that I wore it naturally curly! I always had it blown out, along with my extensions. I looked in the mirror and thought, *I don't even look like myself.*

I know this is silly—but that's really when it all hit me. I was looking into the mirror, and of course, my own eyes were staring back at me. But I didn't feel like myself. Not really. It felt like a dream, like a nightmare I couldn't wake up from. There were so many times I'd squeeze my eyes shut, if only for a second, and think of Dorothy in *The Wizard of Oz.*

*There's no place like home.*

# 6

---

# DRAMA QUEENS,
# DRESSED IN GREENS

*I*f you thought the women on *Real Housewives* argued, bickered, and battled, well, that was nothing compared to all the drama I saw and experienced in prison. I mean, when more than two hundred women have to eat, sleep, shower, and get through the day in one building together, there are bound to be fireworks. And there were.

I witnessed my first fight soon after I got there. I had just gotten back from the gym and was sitting on my bed reading Ellen Degeneres's book, *Seriously . . . I'm Kidding*, when I heard arguing in the "streets." A sweet, sometimes shy woman named Letizia was in a big fight with her girlfriend. Letizia was going home to her husband and three kids in a few days, and her girlfriend, who still had six years to go in there, was fit to be tied.

"You are *my* wife, not his! If I find out you touched him, I'm gonna break out of here and kick your ass—and *his*!"

Letizia started yelling back, which surprised me because she always seemed so meek. "I am so sick of your shit! You don't own me! I'm *glad* I'm leaving so I don't have to see your ugly-ass face anymore!"

The angry lover stormed back to her room, gathered up a bunch of things Letizia had given her over the years, and dumped them on the floor in front of her doorway. "Fine—then here's all the shit back that you gave me."

Letizia started crying and was swearing out loud to herself and shut her door. When the other woman saw her do that, she raced back down the hallway and flung the door open. "Who do you think you are? *Don't* you shut *me* out!"

After hearing all the commotion, I climbed down off my bunk and was peeking out our doorway, with some of my roommates, to see what was going on.

"This is better than TV!" one of them said.

And I thought a table flip was bad . . .

Matilda, who looked out for me, told me to just stay in the room. "Don't go out there, even if you have to go to the bathroom," she said. "Just wait. Things can get pretty crazy and you don't want to be dragged into it."

"I wasn't planning on it," I said. "But thanks."

Another inmate came over and yelled at the ladies to stop fighting. They were lucky that none of the officers caught wind of their dustup. After everything died down, I climbed back up to my bunk, but my roommates were all fired up from the fight, so they all started talking about how they'd landed in there. They told me they had seen what had happened to me on TV.

"Everybody was mad that the judge sent a mother of four to prison for nothing," said Dreadlocks.

"But that's what they do," said Heaven. "They don't give a shit about nobody. They just want to get you in and out of their court. Like, '*Next!*'"

At this point it was about 10 p.m. and I was ready to go to sleep. I was so tired. I am a morning girl. But they were still going on and on (one inmate told me they call that "monkey mouth" in there) about how unfair the judicial system is toward women. I was just listening at this point and had gotten under the covers, ready to go to bed.

Then, out of nowhere, Teeny asked me if I washed my "chucky."

I was literally dumbfounded and at a loss for words. No one had ever asked me that in my life. Not even my gynecologist.

"Do you use soap on the outside *and* the inside?"

I tried hard not to look shocked. It took me a few seconds to answer.

"Yes," I said. "Of course."

Apparently she liked my answer, because she said, "Good." Then she started going off on one of the inmates in the "streets," saying she didn't have the best, um, personal hygiene habits.

"She doesn't wash the inside so she smells. A lot."

*Madonna mia . . .*

I went to my first party the first week I was there. I had no idea they threw parties in prison. This one was for a woman who was finally leaving after seven years. Her sentence had gotten extended because she was selling contraband cigarettes and got caught when someone gave her up. They held a special dinner for her: turkey with rice, cabbage, salad, and a chocolate cake. She got up in the dining room and gave a speech, telling everyone how much they meant to her, how they had made these past seven years a lot easier and how much she would miss them.

"May God bless you all," she said. "God has a special place in his heart for all of you . . . Thank you for being there for me when I needed it most . . ."

I found out later that some of the women were mad that I got invited to the party and they didn't. Really? This was high school drama. No, elementary school drama. You're not going to get invited to every single party in there—or in real life. I was like, "Get over it."

After the party, I called home to say good night to the girls. Joe told me he had gotten my clothes in the mail from the prison—the ones I had handed over to the guard that first night. He said when he opened the package, he held my clothes and could smell me and my perfume on them. I couldn't help but break down. Then Milania got on the phone and kept asking me, "When are you coming home?" That broke my heart. I love her and all my girls so much. She has a tough exterior sometimes, and gets revved up for the cameras, but she's really just a sweet little girl who missed her mommy. She was still a baby to me. I told her I would be here for a while, working on my book, but that I loved her so much. When the call ended, I leaned up against the wall, put my face in my hands, and because no one was around, started sobbing. *Why was I in here?*

(She did make me laugh, though, months later, when I asked her why she didn't email me that much. She wrote back, "I'm busy, Mom! But I love you to the moon and back!" That's my Milania!)

When I got back to my room, I found one of my roommates in bed with her girlfriend, under a sheet, kissing and fooling around. They didn't even seem to notice me.

*Here we go again . . .*

I climbed up to my bunk and started writing in my diary. I wondered if they sold earplugs in the commissary. If not, I would have to see if anyone "made" them. If not, I would need to figure out how to make my own, so I could block out the noise coming from the lovebirds next to me, and their "smoochy, smoochy" session.

I was offered some kind of contraband or illegal "invention" almost on a daily basis. I always said no, because you never knew if someone was doing it to trick you so they could turn you in. I was still very new at this point—and a lot of eyes were watching me—so I had to be extra careful. Aside from the few people I trusted, I didn't know who really liked me or who had it in for me. I took that stuff from Magic, who seemed to keep up her end of the deal. She wasn't gonna rat me out because if she did, she would get in trouble, too. More trouble than I would. But I decided to avoid buying or taking anything more.

One inmate, though, offered me loosies—loose cigarettes—for seven dollars, which was cheaper than what Magic charged. I said no. Except for that one electronic cigarette I smoked before I turned myself in, I didn't smoke. I wasn't about to start, either, because I didn't want to get in trouble. Another inmate told me I could get pills if I wanted them and who to go to if I did. No, thanks. I had never done drugs before and I certainly wasn't going to start now. But I knew other girls did buy them, because one of the inmates told me that if you paid attention, you would notice huge mood swings in certain women. One day they would be totally fine and then the next? Either super-hyper or just plain out of it, with glazed, red eyes.

When I saw other inmates acting funny, I just steered clear of them. God knows what they could do or say. Who knows? Maybe in their drug-fueled stupor they would say that I gave them their pills or whatever they were on. Again, I wanted to avoid any and all trouble.

On my second trip to the commissary, I bought a radio and headphones, which was great because now I could listen to music while I worked out. You needed them to watch TV, too, because it got so loud in the TV rooms that you couldn't hear the sound without them. While I was tuning in to various stations, I heard that TMZ, Radar Online, and others were trying to get information about me while I was in there. *Get a life*, I thought.

I went to lunch and skipped the spaghetti. I was trying to eat as low carb as possible and wasn't sure about the tomato sauce. (You know how I love my tomato sauce just right! I am Italian, after all! But I did tell one of my friends how to make potato and macaroni salads the way I do, which is in one of my cookbooks.) So I just had a salad and a banana. Then I went to make my coffee, which had now become my after-lunch ritual. We all drank instant coffee, which we bought at the commissary because the coffee maker in the dining room wasn't working for most of the time that I was there.

I had really gotten into a groove now, schedule-wise. I got up at either six or six-thirty every morning, had breakfast, called home, checked my emails, then went to work out in the gym. I started doing these great workout tapes by Cathe Friedrich that I loved. Then I would head to lunch, check emails again, work out, go to dinner, take an exercise class, jump in the shower, check emails, and watch TV or hang out in my room and write in my diary or read.

A week or so after I got to the camp, I had to go to Admissions & Orientation, which every single newbie before me had attended. It was at 7:15 a.m., so I got up extra early at 5:30, took a shower, ate breakfast, and headed over to the visitation room where the class would be held. The class went on for about eight hours—with a break for lunch. But they told you everything you needed to know while living at the camp. Well, not everything . . . My fellow inmates had already filled me in on some of the unofficial, and arguably the most important, rules to follow.

They went over information in the handbook they gave us—the programs and services available to us, and all the official rules. There were a lot of them. We had to wear our uniforms from 7:30 a.m. to 3:30 p.m. every day. Before and after that, we could wear our T-shirts and sweats. We had to make our beds every day, according to certain regulations. We had to mop and sweep the floors in our rooms (I had that covered already, of course) and keep our lockers neat and organized (check).

All of our clothes had to be put away neatly and our shoes had to be placed under our beds. So far, so good, I thought. They talked about the shakedowns, when the officers searched your room for contraband, and how we couldn't be in the shower during head count. They told us about the mandatory self-improvement classes we had to take, on everything from managing a checkbook to how to write a résumé.

When I called home that day to talk to Joe and the girls, Dina Manzo was there! It was so good to hear her voice. She asked me how I was doing and I said I was fine and that I missed her. She said Joe and the girls were doing great, but that, of course, they missed me.

I felt so uplifted by the time I hung up. I missed Dina a lot, and hearing her lovely voice just brought back so many memories of a great friendship. She and I were always so close and I was glad she was there for Joe and the girls. I waited a half hour and then called my parents. They seemed to be doing well, which made me happy, since I was so worried about them and their health. My mom was coming to see me soon, which was fantastic—but also, of course, made me a little nervous.

After dinner I went to Tonya's room, which was in another section of the camp, in the lower dorms, so she could paint my nails. She could only use clear nail polish because colored polish was considered contraband because they didn't sell it in the commissary. But of course, some inmates had it!

The next day, I was scheduled to have blood drawn, for God knows what, but I refused and just didn't show up. I had had enough blood drawn from me already. I hate needles, but I was also worried that they would be dirty and that I would catch something. Instead, I decided to go outside for the first time to walk around the track. It was about thirty degrees out, but despite it being cold, the walk felt good. They gave us warm jackets, which I was truly thankful for, because it meant I could enjoy the outdoors through fall and winter. Breathing fresh air is just so important to your sanity—and to have that basic privilege restricted is unbelievably hard. Also, the view from the track was gorgeous. Looking at the snow-covered hills surrounding the prison grounds, I felt like I was in Vermont. But this was no cozy ski chalet, that's for sure. What was so interesting to me was that there was no barbed wire fence around the camp, unlike the men's prison at the bottom of the hill. I was so glad I was in a minimum-security facility like this. I may have had my challenges cut out for me, but hey, when the going got tough, at least I had that view.

Things were going well for me so far. I was calling home every day, emailing with family and friends, and trying to fill my day by working out as much as I could. I had made friends, and the women respected me and, for the most part, left me alone.

Or so I thought . . .

I found out that lots of rumors were flying around the camp about me. One rumor? That I had hired a huge black woman with dreadlocks to be my bodyguard. I thought that was hilarious. I didn't hire anyone to be my bodyguard, for God's sake. When I first got here, though, this towering Big Bertha type told me on the sly that she would look out for me. Protect me. Kick anyone's ass who dared to mess with me. I told her she didn't have to do that, but she did it anyway. Wherever I went, she would sit near me and look menacingly at anyone who came near me. Maybe that's where the rumor started?

One of my bunkies, of course, had dreadlocks, so when I told her what I'd heard, we both laughed. Then some people told me that there were rumors flying around that I was "popping pills to stay sane" in there. And that I was eating my stress away by gorging myself on cookies and cake. How did these stupid stories get started? I was barely eating pasta! Then I heard that I was causing trouble at "my job in the laundry room." Oh my God. I hadn't even been assigned a job yet. I had no idea where they were getting this stuff from . . . and I wondered if any of it was leaking to the outside.

Well, it was. Some of earlier stories about me said a woman with long dreads tried to become my bodyguard, but that I ignored her (kind of true). Another said I had found a personal trainer—a woman who taught exercise classes there, so I was working out all the time. (Also kind of true—I did work out a lot with Nikki, but she wasn't my personal trainer. My God! Like you could have one in prison!) Another story said that inmates would leave out magazines with nasty stories about me on the cover, so I could see them and get upset. Not true *at all*. Yet another article said that I was lucky to get a top bunk. Well, dummies, the bottom bunk is the one you want, because it's easier to get in and out of. Usually inmates with seniority get a bottom bunk. So they were wrong about that, too.

I knew people would be writing about me while I was in Danbury. But I didn't like what they were writing and the slant they took—or that some people in the camp believed the things they were hearing. But again, people always love to gossip and make up stories—and from what I've learned, you have to do your best to ignore it.

Since I had no publicist at the time, my lawyer Jim had to field calls from the media—dozens and dozens of them—about everything from the true length of my prison stay to whether I sat on a toilet seat or not. The funny thing was, they weren't reporting on the things that really *were* happening to me—like the nightly sex sessions my bunkies were having in our room with their partners. When I got back to my room at seven-thirty one night, early in my stay, after I had gone to the gym and checked my emails, the lights were out. Weird, I thought. Then I saw not one, but *two* roommates going at it with their girlfriends. I mean, come on. This was getting old. I sighed and climbed up into my bed. But with four women moaning, groaning, and breathing heavily, there was no way I could sleep. Plus, my stomach was killing me—again—from the food I was eating. It had been bugging me for a while. I was trying to eat well, but something in the food was not agreeing with me. At home, I only cooked lean meats, chicken, fish, and tons of vegetables in olive oil. I ate a ton of fruits and nuts. Maybe it was the dinner I'd had? Pasta and chili made out of chopped meat, salad, and bread. I didn't know what was wrong. And I couldn't stand being in the room with these four. So I climbed back down off the bunk and headed to Tonya's room, where she painted my nails again. There's nothing like a little girl time to make you feel better—even in prison.

*I* was working out with Nikki the next day, doing this great Jillian Michaels workout DVD they had in the gym, when a woman with the frizziest hair I have ever seen came up to me to tell me to really be careful of certain inmates.

"There are good people in here, but there are also some really bad people, who want to become your friend for all kinds of reasons," she said. "Don't trust 'em."

She told me that someone in there was leaking stuff about me to the media. I just ignored it because most of what was leaked was untrue. But still, I didn't like being the focus of so many of these women, especially if they thought they could make money off me.

When the inmate left, Nikki said, "Just keep your eyes open at all times."

I tried to shrug all of this off, but I still felt uneasy about it. I felt like everyone was always up in my business, and I was already getting sick of it. So I went to see one of the counselors who oversaw us (and who had processed me the night I got there). I liked her a lot. She was always fair with me, which I appreciated. I asked her if I could move downstairs to A Dorm with Tonya, where it was quieter, more private and there wasn't as much sex going on. (Or so I thought.) I would only have one bunkie down there, which was more my style. I was tired of all the drama where I was living, and everyone having a say about every move I made (kinda reminded me of being on *RHONJ* . . .). She said that some of my roommates who had been there longer would be moved before me and that I would have to wait. No surprise there, I guess.

Just like the real world, prison is all about location, location, location. You wanted the best real estate you could get. I started out in a room in a whole other block, which is where all the newbies go. But then, you could get moved to one of three different dorms: A, B, or C Dorm. I wanted to move to A Dorm, where Tonya lived. Now, everyone wanted to get into A Dorm, because they viewed it as the best one in the place, which is why they called it *bougie*—upper class or pretentious. I originally thought that there wasn't much sex happening there, but later on I learned that there was so much boom boom going on, that they called it Vagina Heights! B Dorm, which is also known as "the Suburbs," is rated as second best. Since there was always a lot of action going on there, it was considered one of the rowdier dorms. I later found out there was a row of girls there who were lesbians or gay for the stay—women who instantly became straight the moment they walked out of the prison doors. C Dorm was considered the worst of the three, which is why they called it the Ghetto. The dorms all looked the same to me, but other inmates viewed it as the difference between getting a room at a flea-bag motel versus The Beverly Hills Hotel. The women there were very into status, and for whatever reason, A Dorm is where everyone wanted to be.

Fridays were room inspection day, just like in the army. You had to clean your room like crazy before the officials came to look over every nook and cranny of your living space. Of course, that wasn't a problem for me since I am beyond organized. I still felt like a little kid whose parents were checking to make sure my room was neat. But you know how it is with some people. They don't care and leave their parts of the room a mess.

Our room failed that first Friday. That means we were now the last ones called to breakfast, lunch, or dinner until we cleaned up our act. I always went to the short line for my meals, when we got to eat earlier than everyone else, so that didn't affect me . . . thank goodness.

While you stood up straight, by the side of your bunk, with your ID card visible, they would evaluate how your bed was made, whether your locker and the plastic bin they gave you were organized, and how clean the room was overall.

We failed because they found dust under two beds. My downstairs bunkie said they found the dust under the other bunks—not ours. I was happy about that because I always kept the floor clean in our room. I swept and washed it a couple times a week. I cleaned the area under my bunk, but now I would have to start doing the other ones, too. Whatever. Of course, they were also looking for contraband, and I had none, so I was good on that score. So far, none of my roommates seemed to have any either, which made me feel better. I didn't want the officers to think I had anything to do with it if they did have something illegal in our room. (I asked one of them later on, "What if someone plants something in my room or locker?" His response? "Just make sure to always lock your locker.")

I got invited to another party that night. I never expected they'd have so many parties in prison! This one was for Zeezee, who was going away to a drug program. They went all out for this party. There was a big spread—things the ladies got from the commissary and that they made themselves. When I worked on my cookbooks, I threw in some recipes that I had made up myself. Well, I found out that the women did the same thing at the camp. One of their favorite concoctions was the "potato log." They would crush up a bag of potato chips, add water to that in a Tupperware container, and then mix that concoction with onions, peppers, cheese, chicken, sausage, or tuna fish, depending on what they had access to at the moment, and cook it in the microwave we shared. It was actually pretty good, though I'm not sure I will be making that at home . . .

I was chatting with a couple of the ladies at the party when a bunch of them started dancing. They were playing songs by Dr. Dre, Jay Z, Nelly, and 2 Chainz—and asked me to come dance. I was nervous to dance because I didn't want that to get out and have it taken the wrong way somehow. I thought it was sad that I couldn't even dance, which I love to do, out of fear that someone would leak it and it would get spun in a bad way, one way or another. It made me mad that I had to watch my every step, even in there. I danced anyway, and the girls there told me later that they loved that I got out there and did my thing (I am a former club girl, after all!). As I said early on, fame was a tremendous blessing—but it could be a big, giant curse at the same time.

LAST NIGHT THEY HAD A GOING AWAY PARTY FOR ONE OF THE GIRLS who was going home AFTER 12 years AWAY FROM HER FAMILY. HALF WAY through the PARTY ONE OF the girls SAID "TERESA CAN'T DANCE." THIS LED TO A TWERKING competition AND THIS WHITE GIRL FROM NEW Jersey WAS BOOTY POPPING WITH THE BEST OF THEM, EVERYONE WAS laughing and SAYING "GO TERESA POP THAT BOOTY." TERESA'S BOOTY WAS HURTING next Day :)

When I was getting ready to leave, some of the ladies came up to me and asked me if I had a good time. One of them said, "I know this isn't what you're used to, but we try our best in here." I told her I had a good time and thanked them all for inviting me. One of the things I truly learned in there was that every inmate is a person who's made bad choices, or who was in the wrong place at the wrong time. Just because they—I mean *we*—were in prison doesn't make us rotten to our core, and it surely doesn't make us immune to emotions. I was just so happy that she'd even think to check in on me. It's the little things that truly matter.

Since the day I got to prison, my stomach had been hurting. I came to learn that a lot of the food there had expired. You could see the freezer burn on the pork chops or the chicken sometimes. So I refused to eat some of the beef, pork, and even chicken, depending on what it looked like. If it looked even remotely bad, I wouldn't touch it. Sometimes the hamburgers looked like hockey pucks. Even some of the food you could buy in the commissary had expired, like the potato chips. One day one of the women told me that the meat they were serving was two years old. I asked one of the officers about it and he said, "That's not true." So I asked my friend who prepared meals in the kitchen.

"Oh, no. It's not two years old. No way. It's one and a half years old!"

We laughed, because if we didn't, we would cry.

Sometimes the food had maggots in it, too, like the rice, for example. To me, that was the worst thing I had ever seen. You didn't want to eat for a couple days after that. That's when I would head to the commissary and buy packets of tuna fish, peanut butter, rice cakes, unsalted peanuts, unsalted almonds, and honey whole wheat pretzels, in case I couldn't bear to lift my fork off the plate in the dining room. I would say it took almost four months for my body to get used to the food there. I felt sick all the time.

The other ladies also taught me to buy mild pepper mix, jalapeño peppers, and Louisiana hot sauce to add to the food that they give us. Anything to make it go down better.

Don't get me wrong. A lot of what they made in there was really good. I loved the ladies in the kitchen. They worked really hard and did a good job. It wasn't them. Just look at what they had to work with.

So we would always inspect our food before we ate it, to see if anything was crawling around in there. Sometimes inmates found green bugs in the salad. One time my friend told me that a piece of her lettuce literally *flew* off her plate!

Although I only had boat shoes and no ruby slippers, I kept telling myself, *"There's no place like home . . . there's no place like home . . ."*

The last time I was in school was when I went to Berkeley College in New Jersey, where I got my associate degree in fashion merchandising and management, so I hadn't gotten a report card in decades. But one of the things I didn't know about prison was that yes, you got report cards in there, too. Midway through my first month at Danbury, I had to go to my first program review. I had no idea what a program review was, but Jim told me it was like your prison report card and that down the road it could help, so he told me to be agreeable and positive. *This should be fun,* I thought to myself, but I went with a smile on my face, just like Jim told me. When I got my first report back, I saw that they had checked off Intellectual Functioning and said that I had no intellectual deficits and that I wasn't mentally ill. Whew, what a relief (as if I didn't know that already).

They recommended that I enroll in personal growth and development training, which I thought couldn't be too bad. They determined that my personal character showed evidence of spirituality, that I examined my actions to see if they reflected my values and that I found meaning in times of hardship. They said that I had excellent personal hygiene and sanitation, and wanted me to enroll in a finance course designed to teach me how to balance a checkbook. When I got the program review I mailed it to Jim to show him that I was doing well. They scheduled the next review for June 30, and by then not only had I completed the personal finance course, I had done the personal growth and development course and a résumé-writing course. My prison report card also noted that I maintained physical fitness through regular exercise and that I had made all scheduled payments toward my restitution. I was thankful that my hard work and desire to better myself were being noticed by my fellow inmates and by those who worked at Danbury.

Toward the end of my first month there, my family got approved to come visit me! I was over the moon because I hadn't seen them since the early hours of January 5, when I left them in the middle of the night. Friends had emailed me with magazine articles that claimed Joe didn't come see me for a few weeks because he didn't care. Again, such nonsense. By this time, though, I was over all of that—I just wanted to see my family.

I had a lot to do to get ready! I wanted to look beautiful for them! The day they visited was Martin Luther King, Jr., Day, and so the lunchroom served a special breakfast: scrambled eggs and potatoes.

Even so, I only had bran cereal, a banana nut muffin, and an apple. I was too nervous and excited to eat anything more.

The night before, I'd had Diamond, another inmate, who ran the prison salon, wrap my hair, so it would be straight. First, she set my hair in rollers and had me sit under a dryer that looked like it belonged in a 1950s beauty salon. After that, she took huge strands of hair and pulled them over to the other side of my head, carefully anchoring them to my scalp with bobby pins. She did the same thing with the other side of my hair, basically giving me a long comb-over and pinning that down. She wrapped one last strand at the crown of my head in a doobie (a big, fat roller). Then she gave me a scarf to put on my head to keep it from frizzing overnight. I felt official now! The next morning, she wrapped it for me the other way. It looked gorgeous!

After my hair was done, Tonya did my makeup. I felt like I was getting ready to film a scene for the show. She did a great job. I told her she should become a makeup artist. After I was ready, I went upstairs and waited by a big window where you could see everyone walking up the hill from the parking lot to the camp. When I saw them, I started crying. I had to go back to my room to pull myself together. When I calmed down, I fixed my makeup and went and stood at the double doors to the visitors' room. They had just signed in. When you enter the visitors' room, the first things you see are a plastic table and a wooden podium for signing various forms: visitors must state their identity, who they are visiting, and sign off on whether or not they are bringing in explosives, weapons, and things like that—kind of like at the security line in the airport, except there was no metal detector. There were a lot of visitors that day, so Joe and the girls had to wait in a long line to get in. When the guards finally called them, they checked Joe and the girls in at a computer. He didn't drive there, but the guards would also take your car keys and hang them on hooks on the wall behind them. You weren't allowed to bring anything with you to the visits.

I could see them through the cracks in the double doors and was waving frantically to my four precious girls and my husband. I had never, ever been so elated in my life. Finally, the guard allowed me to go inside to see them. I made a beeline straight for my family and hugged them all and kissed my honey. Nothing had ever felt so right.

We found six red plastic chairs and sat down. Gabriella told me all about how well soccer was going for her. She just loved it. Gia told me about the cheerleading championship her team had won (and how they dedicated their performance to me, which made me cry . . .). Milania and Audriana kept kissing me and hugging me and telling me how much they loved me. I took turns holding both of them on my lap.

Then came the part where I had to try really hard not to cry in front of them.

"Mommy, when are you coming home?" said Audriana, looking up at me with those big beautiful eyes.

"I will be home as soon as I can . . ." I said.

"Can I stay here with you?"

This was torture.

"Mommy, will you be home for my birthday?" asked Milania.

Milania's ninth birthday was in a couple weeks, on February 2. I had barely made it through Gia's birthday. I knew how much Milania wanted me home for hers. I tried to put on as strong a front as I could.

"I won't be there for your birthday, honey. But you know how much Mommy loves you."

I could see the tears welling up in her eyes. She hugged me a little tighter. This broke my heart.

We went into the chapel/kids' room, which is off of the main visitation room, and sat at a table. Audriana, Milania, and I were coloring pictures for each other. Gabriella and I played a game we made up—"What Do You Want to Be When You Grow Up?" She said she wanted to become a professional soccer player or a model. I loved hearing that. Milania said she wanted to become a nurse—or a movie star. (Of course she did!) I want my girls to shoot for the stars and beyond.

Since Milania and Audriana are the two youngest, they wanted all of Mommy's attention. They were both hanging on me, hugging me, and kissing me on the cheeks and on my nose. It felt so good to put my arms around them.

I was so proud of Gabriella and Gia, who were so poised and so mature. They sat there trying to hold it together for the younger ones, because they knew if they lost it, the little ones would just dissolve into tears. It was so nice sitting there and talking as a family again. They were also strong for Joe, who was having a hard time seeing me in prison.

Before we knew it, it was time for them to leave. Those four hours or so just flew by. When it came time to say goodbye, I didn't think it was going to be as hard as it was. It was just like the night I said goodbye to them when I left to turn myself in, when the six of us were all crying. This time, Audriana started crying, then Milania, which made me lose it. When Gabriella and Gia saw me crying, they started up, too. Joe put his arms around me and sobbed into my shoulder. The last times I'd seen him do that were the night I left—and the day his father died.

"I'm sorry, honey," he said. "It's just so hard to leave you again. I'm going out to the car."

He kissed and hugged me. I could see his shoulders heaving as he walked out the door, wiping his eyes with the back of his hand. By now, Audriana was hysterical, hanging on my neck, saying she didn't want to leave.

"I . . . just want . . . my mommy!" She could hardly get the words out in between sobs. She was hyperventilating, so I kept talking to her in a low, soothing voice. I didn't want her to leave me so upset, but this was killing me.

I knelt down and talked to the girls quietly, telling them how much I loved them. Milania stopped crying, but was still holding on to my arm, as though she would die if she let go. That's kind of how I felt, too, but I didn't want to let them know that. They had no idea that they were the ones who kept me going, day after day. Gia took Audriana in her arms, while we both tried to calm her down.

Gia said Joe had texted her and that they had to leave. It was almost 3 p.m. now, when the visits officially ended.

"Mommy will call you when you get in the car," I told Audriana and Milania, which seemed to make them feel better.

Audriana whispered, "OK, Mommy."

I hugged and kissed them all once more and thanked Gia and Gabriella for being so strong. Gia picked Audriana up and they walked out the door. That was that. It was over.

I started sobbing again. One of the women who was still in the visitors' room and had also said goodbye to her children was crying, too. We looked at each other and gave each other a sad smile, like, "I get it. This is hard."

I went back through the double doors, got patted down for contraband, and headed straight to the phone area. Other women seemed to have the same idea I did, so I had to wait to call Joe and the girls. While I was waiting to talk to them again, I thought about how happy I was that they had come to see me—and that my daughters had seen that Mommy was safe and as joyful as she could be, given the situation, so they wouldn't worry about me. They saw that Mommy had her hair, makeup, and nails done—all markers of my old life that let them know I was doing OK.

When I finally reached them, I asked Joe if Audriana was all right and he said yes. I hate to see my daughters cry, but I always tell them it's good to let their feelings out. (I tell them that because growing up, my dad never wanted to see my brother and me cry, so that's why I don't cry a lot. It takes a lot for me to cry. Not showing too much emotion when I was little has made me a strong person. But I do tell my kids it is OK to cry sometimes because those emotions need to come out.) When I spoke to Audriana, I told her that Daddy would buy her a new Barbie. That made her happy. Gabriella was on her way to soccer practice, and Gia was going to be filming her music video for her girl group 3KT's song "Just 13" at the house. In the video, the camera zooms in on photos of Gia at various stages of her life and of me and Joe with the girls. It ends with a video snippet of me saying, "It's not saying goodbye. It's saying, 'See you soon,' " before saying "MUAH!" and blowing her a kiss. I wanted to blow my daughters kisses and give them hugs forever and ever and ever. Seeing them go was so hard for me—but I knew I had to let them go, because they had to get back to their lives. I didn't want one second of what should be their carefree childhoods ripped away by what Joe and I were going through.

That night, like almost every night, I dreamt of my girls—that they were beautiful, strong, independent, and caring. The best part of waking up from those dreams was realizing that those dreams were my reality. And so, even though saying goodbye at those visits was hard, I knew I was very lucky—I had five people so wonderful that it made those goodbyes extra hard.

One thing the women said over and over was that they had learned their lesson pretty early on, because life at Danbury was not fun, cushy, or like a country club, no matter what people said. They say that people don't need to be locked up for five, ten, fifteen, or twenty years for a nonviolent crime. It's especially hard for women because often they have to leave their children behind. It always really upset me to see children clinging to their mothers and sobbing in the visitors' room, but especially when I knew that those mothers had long sentences. In so many cases, it just wasn't fair.

The day after that first visit, I woke up at 6 a.m. to get in line at the commissary when it opened. When I got there, I realized I wasn't the only one who'd gotten up early. The place was packed and the line was so long. But the smell in there was the worst part! I was practically gagging. I'm not sure if people hadn't brushed their teeth or taken a shower or used deodorant, but the smell was really bad. I started to feel sick to my stomach, so I waited outside. They finally opened the doors at seven-thirty, but I didn't get called until eight-thirty. I tried to breathe through my mouth when I was in there, so I didn't have to inhale the stench. I finally got my sneakers and bought some hair products and French Vanilla Coffee-mate and got out of there as soon as possible.

I headed straight to an appointment with one of my counselors at eight-thirty. He was sitting behind his desk and told me to come in. I put my bag of commissary items on the floor and sat down. I told him I wanted to see if I could go to a halfway house. He asked if that was really what I wanted to do.

"Not really, but if it allows me to see my girls more often, then I'm willing to go."

I had heard scary stories about life at a halfway house, where prisoners can be sent to learn how to reenter society—that they could be dangerous. But my desire to see Joe and the girls outweighed anything else. The counselor said he would look into it for me. I thanked him and left. I had a funny feeling in my gut about going to a halfway house, but I had to do what I had to do.

*I* had been calling home every day, which is what was keeping me going in there. I also spoke to my parents a lot. One cold, sunny morning, about two weeks into my stay there, I got up, had breakfast, and then headed to the phone area. Another line . . . I waited about a half hour or so, then dialed my home number—and a recording came on saying my minutes had expired. I felt like I had been hit in the stomach. I tried to call home again and got the same recording.

I turned to the lady next to me. "My minutes ran out! Already! I've only been here two weeks and I need to call home!"

She could see how frantic I was getting. I mean, Joe and the girls were my lifeline. My everything.

"I need to get more! How do I get more?"

"Hon, you only get three hundred minutes a month," she said to me, rubbing my arm. "Once you run out, you're done."

Now I was getting hysterical. I almost started crying.

"What do you mean? I have to wait?"

I had weathered a few small storms here and there during my first couple weeks at Danbury, but this was like getting hit by a tsunami. At least that's how I felt about it. Of course I found out later that there was a way to keep track of your minutes, but no one had told me that. There was so much to learn in here . . . but this? I was sick to my stomach.

Milania's birthday was on February 2, and I wouldn't get my new minutes until February 6. I had to call her. I have always been there for her—and all my daughters—since they were born. To not be able to speak to her was devastating to me. I went and found Liz. Maybe she would know what to do.

"Why don't you write to the warden and explain the situation," she said. "Ask for extra minutes so you can call your daughter. Sometimes they make exceptions to things."

A bit later, I was called to the camp administration office, where I met with an officer and the assistant warden.

"Have you ever played poker before?" the assistant warden asked.

What kind of question was that?

I said no.

"When you run out of chips? Game over," he said, looking at me with a hard stare.

"But I didn't know I could check my minutes. No one told me about that. I thought I could make as many calls as I wanted."

He just shrugged.

"So now you know you have to keep track of these things."

I wanted to cry.

"I just want to call my daughter and wish her happy birthday—for two minutes. I have never missed her birthday in my life."

"Well, I have had to go without calling my kids on their birthday because I had to work. So you'll just have to deal with it. You're dismissed."

As soon as I left his office, I started crying. Ugly-face crying. I started hyperventilating and couldn't catch my breath. I felt like he'd run me over with one of the pickup trucks outside, then backed up and run me over again, before throwing me off the roof.

How could he not call his child? There are phones everywhere. I couldn't understand how you couldn't call your child on his or her birthday in this day and age, unless you were an inmate in prison, like me.

Here's the thing. I could have tried to beat the system and break the rules. But I didn't. When some of the women in there ran out of minutes, they would use other inmates' minutes in exchange for commissary items and other favors. They did that all the time. But that's against the rules. Every time you make a call you have to type in your code, and all of the calls are monitored and recorded by the Bureau of Prisons. So if they catch you using someone else's code, it's a big deal, because when they are monitoring and recording the calls they need to know exactly who they are listening to. And again, the way they viewed me in there was like the way they viewed every other inmate. No special treatment. The rules were the rules. And I was determined to follow them.

Besides calling Joe and the girls and my parents and emailing with them and close friends, one of things that helped brighten my stay at Danbury was all the fans who wrote to me while I was in there. Each day when we had mail call, I would get cards and letters from family and friends and hundreds of fans in the United States and all over the world. They wrote to me telling me how much I had inspired them and changed their lives. I found it really amazing that people who didn't even know me took the time to write to me. It really touched my heart. Some of the letters made me cry, because fans told me that they could see how much I loved my daughters and how loyal I was to Joe. I looked forward to mail day each week and just cannot thank my fans enough for supporting me while I was in prison.

While most of my fan mail was from women—moms in particular—I had a lot of men write to me, too. Some of them told me I needed a "real man" like them and to ditch Joe, which always made me laugh. I got a lot of letters and cards from other male inmates across the country, asking me to be their pen pals. I had no interest in talking to these guys, but I would say to the other girls, "Hey, if you want to write to this guy or that guy—here's his info!"

# 7

---

## TV WARS

*N*ow, ever since I'd gotten to Danbury, two of my roommates had fooled around with their girlfriends pretty much every night. I thought it was beyond disrespectful to do that in the same room with me and our other roommates. But there was nothing I could do about it, so I would either stay out of my room as long as I could, or if I was really tired or just wanted to read or write, I would turn my head the other way, climb up to my bunk, and face the wall while I read or wrote in my diary. Thank God for the loud fan we had in our room. It helped drown out the moaning and heavy breathing. The ladies were getting it on so much in there that our room became known as the Boom Boom Room.

Inmates in the dining room or the gym would kid me about it. So would my friends. What was I gonna say? That I had to put up with this every single night? As I said, the one thing you didn't want to be in there was a rat, so I just kept my mouth shut. I was thankful, though, for that fan so I didn't have to hear them.

But I got a lucky break toward the end of my first month when one of the busiest lovebirds got moved out of our room so that another woman could move in. I liked that girl a lot, but I didn't like knowing *so* many personal things about her sex life, if you know what I mean.

The new woman, Katie, was being moved to our room because she had gotten in trouble for using an emergency door and in an area that was considered out-of-bounds—not where she was allowed to go. We got another new roommate, too, Lala, since one other roommate had just gone home. Lala had a lot of friends, so we had people coming in all day long. I really wanted to move to A Dorm because I couldn't take all this traffic in my room all the time. I just wanted more privacy and a little more peace and quiet.

At this point, I was working out three times a day, every day. It was one of the main things that kept me sane in there. I also started doing yoga DVDs every day and taking yoga classes when they held them. I truly feel like yoga changed my life. Besides getting an incredible workout, I was starting to feel really centered. Yoga helped me see things more clearly. I started using yogic breathing during the day, too, when I could feel myself begin to get worried or frustrated. I loved stretching every day, which made me feel so relaxed and like I could deal with anything that came my way. Yoga is my passion. It is going to be a part of my life from now on because I really love it.

The night after I got my new roommates, I did a fantastic Bob Harper workout DVD with Nikki. At least I got some of my frustration out about the chaos in my room. But when I got back, I only found more drama. A bunch of girls on my block came up to tell me that Heaven was leaking information about me to the media—particularly *US Weekly*. They told me that they had also heard that I caught someone smoking outside, which never happened. I felt like I was truly back on *RHONJ*—it was all drama, drama, drama.

Each one of them was trying to prove that she wasn't the one leaking the information. I said, "I don't care. Just be happy. I don't have time for this nonsense." Then Heaven came in and started crying.

"It wasn't me! I swear it wasn't!"

I had no idea who to believe in there, but something told me it wasn't her. Just a gut feeling I had. Maybe it was her tears and how upset she truly seemed.

"Look, people are just trying to stir up trouble. Just ignore it. I do."

"Well, I'm gonna set those bitches straight and tell them that I'm not putting those stories out there!"

"They're just stirring things up because you are leaving soon and they're mad."

I was exhausted from another long day in there and from all the drama, and I just wanted to go to sleep, but I was anxiously preparing myself for my other sexaholic roommate to start doing her thing. But for the first time since I had been there, she got into bed alone and went to sleep.

I wondered if she and her girlfriend had broken up. I found out later that there would be no more boom boom going on in our room anymore, because Katie wouldn't allow it. I heard Katie didn't care about snitching and had told her former bunkies that she wasn't about to put up with that in her new room.

So from that night on, the Boom Boom Room was closed for business—because we had a new bunkie in the house.

> WOKE up THIS MORNING AT 6:30 AM AND the SUN WAS RISING, I could tell that it was going to BE A Beautiful DAY IN DANBURY :) DID YOGA IN the MORNING to stART my DAY, I wisH I WAS Doing YOGA DURING the FIRST SIX SEASONS of HOUSEWIVES of New Jersey, But At least I HAD MY WINE. YOGA is not only good FOR the BODY, it is good FOR the SOUL.

Since I had a mandatory meeting with staff at 3 p.m. the next day, I missed the short line for dinner. When I went to dinner at 4:30, I saw Liz waiting in line. She handed me a plate she had gotten for me, which I thought was so nice. We had a pleasant talk over dinner and then I went to the gym to do some cardio and stretching. Later on I found out that a bunch of the girls were complaining about me, saying that I got dinner before everyone else because I was getting special treatment in there.

*Here we go again,* I thought. I couldn't take a breath without everyone having to say something about it. *Wow,* I thought. *This feels like I'm right back on* Real Housewives *again* . . . I laughed to myself and thought, *Maybe we should do* Real Housewives of FCI Danbury . . .

I called home, which I thought would make me feel better. But

Milania got on the line and kept asking, "Mommy. When are you coming home? When?"

I hated hearing her so upset.

"Soon, honey. Mommy loves you so much. I'm going to see you on Sunday! I'm so excited!"

I still couldn't believe I was away from my girls. This was really the hardest part of being at Danbury. It was killing me that they didn't have their mommy home with them. These were the times when I felt like my anger over being in there—and the extreme sadness I felt—was going to overwhelm me and drag me under. That's when I used what I learned in yoga to breathe deeply to center myself. I was so lucky I had that, because otherwise, I'm not sure what I would have done.

OK, so things didn't go so well that day, but at least I had a big treat to look forward. That night at 11 p.m., Gia was going to be on TV talking about her new song and music video, "Just 13," which is about how she felt about my going to prison.

"Mama said be strong/So against the storm I stand through it all," she sings in part of the song.

Of course, she came on at the very end of the show, but I didn't care. It was so worth it. The music video made me cry. When she started talking on camera, she was so composed and well-spoken, I teared up again. I was so incredibly proud of her. They asked her how she felt with her mom being in prison, and she said she had come to see me and that I was doing really well. She said I had my hair and makeup done and looked amazing.

I called home the next day to check in. Gabriella and Milania had gone skiing, Gia was getting ready for a cheerleading competition, and Audriana was in bed watching TV with Joe. Everybody seemed busy and content, which made me feel better.

I stopped by Diamond's salon, so she could roll my hair in curlers. I sat under the dryer for forty-five minutes. After she wrapped my hair, I put on a kerchief and went to the TV room for movie night.

I was so excited to see the girls the next day. After I had breakfast and went to the gym to do a yoga tape, I started getting ready for my visit from my daughters and my friend Lisa G., who acted as though we went for coffee at Ladurée SoHo in Manhattan when she came to visit, just like old times. We shared stories and laughed like we always did. What I loved about her was that she invited the girls to stay with her in New York City while I was gone, and they shopped, went out to fun restaurants, and did some sightseeing. She even took the girls to playdates, to their soccer games, and to see me while I was at Danbury. I was lucky to have such a good friend I could rely on when I was in there.

I did my makeup and had another one of the girls, Margarita, put braids in my hair on both sides of my face. She was in her mid-twenties, was covered in tattoos, and was in there for selling drugs. She was very gifted when it came to hair, so I loved going to see her. I had brunch at 10:30 a.m.—French toast, scrambled eggs, potatoes, and an apple.

Lisa and the girls arrived at noon. I was so happy to see them! We sat in the chapel/kids' room, and I caught up with each of the girls. I asked how Gabriella was doing in soccer, and she started telling me how well it was going and the latest goals she had scored.

While Milania and I were coloring, I found out that she had hit a tree when she was skiing the day before. No one had said a word to me about it! The ski patrol had to pick her up and carry her down the hill on a stretcher. This was not what I wanted to hear! But thank

God she was OK. I told her to be careful when she was up there on the slopes. *Madonna mia* . . .

Saying goodbye to them was a tiny bit easier than the last time, but still not a walk in the park. When I was bundling Audriana up in her coat, she started crying. Gia, bless her heart, bent down and said softly to Audriana, "Don't cry. Remember we talked about this? If you cry, then Mommy will cry." Gabriella and Milania started comforting Audriana, too.

I was so proud of my girls for being so strong and for helping their little sister get through this surreal, horrible moment—when we had to detach from each other. It seemed so unnatural to me. A mother is supposed to be with her children. I tried to keep so busy in prison because if I didn't, all I thought about was how I was supposed to be home with them. This, to me, was the worst punishment of all. For something I didn't even think I had done.

But whoever said life was fair?

After they left, I went to dinner and then headed to the TV room, because they were showing *Jersey Boys*. Anything to get my mind off Joe and the girls. But the movie had a sad ending, which got me all worked up, so I started crying again when I had a moment alone. I always cried in private. When I called home, though, I felt much better. Joe said he was brushing Milania's hair and that Gia was videotaping him. I loved hearing that. Before I went to prison, I used to do all that kind of stuff, so I thought it was adorable that now Joe was doing it, too. He really picked up and kept marching on after I began serving time. So many husbands would not have been able to soldier on the way he did . . . and for that, I am so grateful.

A little after that, I got the *best* news when I had my team meeting with the camp administrator and my case manager. They told me that I would definitely be leaving the camp on December 23! I was so overwhelmed with joy that I had a firm date when I would be reunited with my family and that we would be spending Christmas together. That news really helped me get through the next months. Spending the holidays with your family is such a blessing. I am one of the lucky ones.

Toward the end of my first month at Danbury, I got my work assignment: wiping down tables in the dining room after breakfast, lunch, and dinner on Wednesdays, Thursdays, and Fridays for twelve cents an hour. I was given a uniform for that, too. I wore a white button-down shirt and black-and-white checkered pants. I expected to be there for at least two hours a day, but there were four of us assigned to table duty. Rina, the woman who worked alongside me, and I finished cleaning our tables in five minutes.

"That's it?" I said to her.

"Yup! We're done!"

The two other girls who were there with us asked if Rina and I wanted to take mornings, since they hated to get up early. They said they would take lunch and dinner.

"Fine with me," I said.

I'm a total morning person, so I didn't mind getting up early for my job. I mean, I was usually already up, so it wasn't a big deal for me. Then I had the rest of the day free.

Since I couldn't do anything there without everybody yapping about it, I soon heard that some of the other inmates were complaining about the job I got.

"Why did she get a cushy job when other women have to clean the toilets?"

Then, of course, the tabloids got wind of it. Here's the bottom line: Anybody who has been to prison knows that there are rules and regulations. We were all treated equally and there was no favoritism. I couldn't get away with anything that anyone else couldn't get away with. I conducted myself in a respectful and dignified manner, and as a result I was treated by the staff and the women respectfully.

In fact, eight months or so into my stay, the officials told me that they appreciated how much I had kept to myself and flown under the radar the whole time I was there. Now, put that in your tabloid and print it.

By now, I had a pack of good girlfriends in there: Tonya, Nikki, Franchie, Katie, and a few others. We hung out all the time. We ate together and watched TV together. I went all the time to Tonya's room in A Dorm, where she would give my hair a colored rinse or paint my nails while we talked. She even did my makeup for me before my family visited me on weekends. We just really clicked and I liked being with her.

We all tried to work out together when we could. I worked out three times a day, and sometimes someone would join me in the morning for the bike and weights or some kind of workout DVD, or at one of the 5:30 p.m. classes, and then come to the gym with me after that. One night, after Tonya painted my nails, Franchie measured our arms, legs, waist, and hips. We were on a mission to lose inches! It looked like we were on our way . . . I could already tell that my body was tightening up and getting leaner and stronger. Ironically, I honestly had never felt so good in my life.

After my nails dried, we all went to Katie's room, where she told me she had heard that the media was looking to pay a hundred thousand dollars to anyone who could get a picture of me in prison. That got me mad. That was *big* motivation for someone to get a picture of me. Where? In the bathroom? In the shower? Now I felt like I couldn't ever let my guard down. I went to the gym and rode the bike as fast as I could to get my frustrations out.

My night got much better after that, though. Gabriella had sent me a long email, detailing every moment of her day, which I absolutely loved. She told me everything. Gia would say a lot in hers, too. Milania? Not so much. She was too impatient to sit there and type out a novel-length email. Honestly, it made me happy to know all my children were out in the world, living their lives.

The next day, Joe and the girls came to visit me and showered me with hugs and kisses and couldn't wait to tell me everything they were up to.

After Milania, Audriana, and I colored, I got up from the table, took my honey aside, kissed him on the cheek, and whispered in his ear how much I missed him—and that I had learned about some new things I wanted to try out with him when I got home . . . He laughed and said, "What exactly *are* they teaching you in here?" I didn't say anything but just gave him a sexy smile . . . The girls in Danbury had also told me about a few things I had *never* heard of before and would just keep to myself . . . *Madonna mia*, I was dreaming of my husband, my Juicy Joe . . .

When it came time to leave, he broke down again. He was sobbing and he hugged me and told me he wished I weren't in there. "I love you, Tre . . ."

I love him so much and it killed me to see him so upset. After a dinner of "triangles"—which look like big wontons that are filled with chicken, peppers, onions, and cheese—I went to Mass at 5 p.m.

Since I had gone to prison, I had been praying every day, reading the Bible, going to the chapel during the week, and attending weekly Mass. I always felt so good when I got out of Mass—like God was really present with me. I needed God's help more than ever these days, and I was glad I had my faith to rely on in there.

It was Milania's birthday. My baby was turning nine! I couldn't call her, but I emailed her, telling her I wished I could be there in person, but I was there with her in her heart. I sent her a prayer, asking God to give her a beautiful year. I cried as I typed the email to her, because I wanted to be there with her so badly . . . It made me feel depressed the whole rest of the day. But I got some emails back from her and she sounded good, so that lifted my spirits.

*B*esides all the parties I was going to at Danbury, another thing I hadn't expected was that you basically had spa services at your disposal there—prison-style. By this time, I had become a regular in Diamond's salon. Tonya painted my nails at least once a week and did my makeup for me before visitation. So I was thrilled to find out that you could also get massages! You could pay someone to do it by buying her items in the commissary—or simply give her one in return.

I'd heard that Camila, a petite, talkative Dominican girl, was the best masseuse in the place, so I asked her for one. I went to Franchie's room and lay down on her bed while she stood at the door as a lookout for the officer on duty because we could have gotten in trouble for doing this. This felt like heaven! Camila's hands were small but strong. She put just the right amount of pressure on my muscles. I had been working out so much and had been stressed out by not being able to talk to Milania, so this felt sooooo good.

Camila was in there for two years for bank robbery. She told us she was so young when she committed that crime that she hadn't known any better. Prison really makes the young ones grow up fast, though. Now she knew better.

"Quick! Someone's coming!" Franchie whispered.

We could all hear the keys on one of the officers' belts jangling down the hall.

I scrambled to pull my shirt down and get up. We just sat on the bunks and talked, like nothing was going on. He walked right by Franchie's room and went to talk to another inmate. When he left, we all looked at each other and laughed. I pulled my shirt back up and sank back into a deep relaxation. This massage was definitely worth a couple bags of chips, Diet Coke, mascara, and shampoo. I would have never, ever have dreamed that I, Teresa Giudice, would literally be *bartering*. But in that moment, I felt what I can only describe as the prison version of content.

I had never read so many books in my life than when I was in prison. I love to read, but it was always hard to find the time to do it because I was always working, taking care of the house and the girls, and running them around all day. After a long, crazy day, I would pass out the minute I got to bed, or when my head hit the pillow after getting busy, if you know what I mean!

At Danbury, I read pretty much every night, after I wrote in my diary. I read Victoria Gotti's memoir, *This Family of Mine: What It Was Like Growing Up Gotti*, *Mafia Prince*, *The Women's Devotional Guide to the Bible*, *The Five People You Meet in Heaven*, Andy Cohen's latest book, *Most Talkative: Stories from the Front Lines of Popular Culture* (I'm in there!), and Jackie Collins's classic *Hollywood Wives*.

(Jackie Collins passed away when I was in prison, which made me very sad. She and I once appeared on *Watch What Happens: Live* together, where she told me she was a big fan. I was floored because I thought she was amazing. She was so much fun and we had a blast on Andy's show together.)

I had also never watched so much TV before in my life. In my former life, I did try to catch the *Housewives* shows on Bravo when I could. Before I went to Danbury, I tried to never miss *Dancing with the Stars*, which is my favorite show. But in prison? I never missed an episode, which was great. I watched pretty much every Bravo show that was on: *Shahs of Sunset*, all the *Real Housewives* shows, *Watch What Happens: Live* (of course), and *American Idol*. I also liked *Suits*, *Mistresses*, and *Law & Order*. In the morning I would always try to catch *Good Morning America* and *Live with Kelly and Michael*. I also tried to watch CNN as much as possible to catch up on the news.

I've never seen more movies in my life than when I was in Danbury, either. My favorites? *The Theory of Everything*, *Safe Haven*, *My Sister's Keeper*, and *The Count of Monte Cristo*, which is now one of my favorite movies of all time. I love how after years in prison, the count goes on to lead a triumphant, fulfilling life. That is what I want, too. I want to be called the Countess of New Jersey! (Just kidding . . .)

As with everything else Chez Danbury, there were lots of unwritten rules when it came to the rooms where we watched TV, but rules you had to know. They had five TVs for two hundred women. There was one for the people who spoke Spanish. Then there were two TVs mainly for sports. I'm not a sports fan at all, but there wasn't anything I could do about it, so two TVs trained on ESPN it was. So really, there were two TVs for everyone else.

I learned very quickly that the inmates gravitated as a group to certain shows and things on TV—and basically took control of that TV. They had a sign-up sheet outside each room so you could write down what shows you wanted to watch, but it wasn't a strict system.

The African-American women would mostly gather in one room and watch shows like *Empire*, *Scandal*, *The Real Housewives of Atlanta*, *Love & Hip Hop: New York*, *Basketball Wives*. I liked a lot of the same shows they would watch, so I was in there a lot with them. They were great. They told me they were happy I was there, which made me feel good. I made some really close friends in that room— and shared a lot of good laughs with them.

Like the African-American inmates, the Hispanic women also watched TV together. (They lost their room months later when they used that area for Skyping.) They took over another TV room and would watch Univision and the *telenovelas* they loved so much. Even though I speak Italian, I don't really understand Spanish, so I wasn't in there much, though I would pop in now and then to say hi to somebody I knew and catch up. The white ladies commandeered another TV room, although women from all backgrounds would come in, depending on what was on. They liked to watch a lot of the Bravo shows, HGTV, *Extra*, the Food Network, *Access Holly-wood*, *Dancing with the Stars*, Lifetime, *Scandal*, *Grey's Anatomy*, talk shows, and the news, so I was in there a lot, too. As for the Asian women, there weren't enough of them to command their own TV, so they were at the mercy of whatever was on in those rooms. I basically just bounced around depending on what was on or which of my friends was in a particular room. Everyone welcomed you.

They were happy you were there—unless there was some kind of disagreement over what people wanted to watch, which happened *all* the time. I would say most of the arguments or fights I witnessed in Danbury were over the TV. The only time everyone came together peacefully was when it was movie time on weekends and holidays. They would only show one movie at a time and the officials selected it and that was it. They would start showing a movie at 1 p.m. and keep showing it until the last viewing time at 6 p.m.

Within the groups of different women, there were cliques, of course. Sometimes one clique wanted to watch a show that another did not. That's when they would start shouting and swearing, and if it was escalating, they would stand up, maybe push each other—and then all hell would break loose.

While the women were territorial over seats in the dining room, when it came to the TV rooms, they created a whole system to keep control over their turf. Every group had a senior member who would dictate what everyone was going to be watching that day. Then there was the Gatekeeper—the one who was always in control of the remote. When that inmate had to go to work or to eat, another one would watch over it—like her life depended on it.

Months into my stay there, someone from the African-American group somehow got control of the coveted white women's remote. They were in that room, kicking back and laughing and watching whatever it was they were watching, when someone from the white group walked in and saw this. Shirl, a bony but muscular woman in her early fifties, who was in there for some con job she'd concocted, went up to the thief who'd dared to take that room's remote.

"Give it back now," she said, standing over the new Gatekeeper, a tall, lanky woman in her mid-thirties, with short, braided hair, who was slouched in her chair.

The woman holding it looked up at her, shrugged, and said, "Sorry. We got it now."

"Give it back . . ."

The new Gatekeeper sat up a bit in her chair and looked around at the others in the room. "Um, hey. We're busy watching a show, so, 'bye, Felicia."

All her conspirators laughed, which made Shirl even more mad. Now this was serious. Besides the Dictator, who chose the shows, and the Gatekeeper, who guarded the remote, every group had an Enforcer, an intimidating inmate, for just these occasions. Shirl went to get the group's enforcer, Butchy, a beefy woman in her late forties, with thick arms and legs and a crew cut, who didn't take crap from anybody.

She strode into the room with her chest puffed up and walked right up to the cocky Remote Thief.

"They told me you have a problem with your hearing," Butchy growled. "Give us back the remote."

When Butchy tried to grab it out of the Remote Thief's hand, the thief jumped up and started yelling at Butchy.

"Fuck you, bitch! It's ours now!"

By now, a bunch of inmates had gathered around them, ready to jump in if fists started flying.

I was watching the whole thing and had had it. I was friendly with both girls and didn't want them to get a shot for a stupid fight over TV.

I stepped in and said, "Look—just give us back the remote. You have your own TV and you know we always watch our shows in here. We don't go in and try grab your remote."

The Remote Thief just gave me a funny look and turned back to Butchy, "Hey. If the remote was so fucking important to you, then you shouldn't have left it laying around. You're shit outta luck!"

I could see the red rising in Butchy's cheeks. I thought she was going to belt her. She lunged at the Remote Thief, who laughed and held the remote high up in the air, so she couldn't get it. By now, members of both groups were shouting at each other. The room was crackling with bad energy and I knew someone was about to get hurt. I moved to the back of the room so I wouldn't be involved in any brawl that was about to break out. Don't forget—I had seen this kind of thing before. But the guards heard all the yelling, ran in there, and broke it up before anyone could take a swing, thank God. Maybe I should bring the guards back to New Jersey, to keep as protection while we're filming. Lord knows we need it sometimes . . .

"What's the problem in here?" one of the guards yelled. "You— over here," he said, pointing to the Remote Thief. She went over and almost started crying as she told the guards how our group ganged up on her and the others and threatened them. She was a regular Meryl Streep.

In all the chaos, she dropped the remote on her chair, and Butchy scooped it up. After the guard in charge assessed the situation, he told the group who tried to take over to get out. The Remote Thief and her girls trudged out of there, cursing under their breath. Shirl waved goodbye to them. Butchy folded her massive arms and gave them a victorious smirk.

"Right is right!" said one of the inmates who lost the battle over the remote. "They left it laying around and we got it. What's the problem?"

"Bitches," we heard them say.

"Fuck them . . ."

Once they were gone, we took our seats in *our* TV room and turned on what we wanted to watch. Nobody paid attention to what was on the screen. We were all still complaining about the nerve they had to try to take our remote. It just wasn't done. They had stepped over the line.

We all forgot about it until the next day, when a bunch of us got called down to the office. Someone in the other group had complained to the guards about us. I felt like I was back in junior high, getting called to the principal's office.

I was thinking, *Why did I get called down? I wasn't fighting. I was trying to stop them from fighting.*

But apparently, someone had told the guard I was getting mouthy. The guard wanted me to explain my role in this and my version of what happened. I started telling him and he said, "Stop. Go over there." He pointed to a far wall. "You talk with your hands, Giudice, and wave them all around. Last time I had you in here, you almost hit me in the face." I said, "Yes, I do. I'm Italian." It was pretty funny.

After everyone took turns telling him what happened, he said, "I've heard enough. Get out of my office."

We skulked back to our rooms, not sure if we were going to get in trouble or not. (We didn't, thank God . . .)

What we did get was control of the remote again. Since the other group told on us, they were now considered snitches, so the whole camp started freezing them out and calling them "rats" everywhere they went. They had tried to take over our remote—and it backfired, big-time.

This wasn't the only fight I tried to stop. I got to know a sweet, quiet girl named Bonita. She and I used to read the Bible together and talk about what various passages meant to us. She was in there because she was accused of helping her boyfriend in a drug deal, when she said she had had no idea she was doing anything wrong.

She said she simply answered the phone at his house and passed it to him when the guy on the other end of the line asked for him. She got six months for conspiracy to sell drugs. I don't know the whole story, but like a lot of what I heard in there, I didn't think that one was fair.

Two days before she was going home, a bully down the hall who had a beef with her from the minute she saw her decided to stir up trouble. The bully was hoping she'd rope Bonita into a fight so that the prison would extend her sentence. The bully got in Bonita's face and started reading her the riot act about Bonita's boyfriend, who the bully hated because he had dissed the bully somehow before she got locked up.

I followed Bonita into her room. I grabbed her arm. "Listen to me. Don't fight her. It isn't worth it."

She went on and on about how that woman had made her life miserable from the day Bonita arrived at Danbury—and how her insults just now were over the line.

"I know," I said. "I get it. You have no idea. But you're leaving in two days. She's mad you're getting out and doesn't want you to leave. Don't take the bait."

I told her to sit down on the bed. I sat down next to her and put my arm around her.

"Just think about your family," I said. "In two days, you will be out of here. She'll still be in here for another six years."

Bonita wiped the tears from her eyes.

"I guess you're right. Thank you."

When I was sure she had calmed down, I hugged her and went back to my room. The tough-ass girl was gone. She continued to harass poor Bonita right up until she left, but Bonita took my advice and ignored her, as hard as it was. We had a going away party for Bonita, and she hugged me and thanked me.

"God bless you, honey," I said, hugging her back. "You're going to be all right."

I didn't say too much to anyone about it, but I was proud of myself for stepping in and protecting her. Yes, I was really learning a lot in here about compassion, and how to approach certain tough situations. Much more than I'd ever thought I would.

When I'd first gotten to my room, I thought I would be living with the same five women who were in there at the time. I didn't know how it worked. But the longer I was there, the more I felt like my room had its own revolving door. With each new roommate, I had to put up with a whole new set of annoyances. Let's just say it is *not* easy living with other people you don't know. I never lived in a college dorm, so I had nothing to compare it to. Now I was living with more than two hundred women, who were usually PMSing at the same time. Wow . . .

I liked Lala, but she was always eating in the room or on her bunk. I got reprimanded when I ate a salad in my room when I first got there, not knowing the rules. But she got there on the same day I did, so she knew the rules. She honestly felt that rules didn't apply to her. She acted entitled, for whatever reason, so our room always smelled like food, had dirty Tupperware containers lying around in it, and candy wrappers on the floor. She was a total slob, which made me crazy.

Then there were the beds. My shoulder was killing me from having to sleep on top of a bar under the mattress. I went and got another massage and it helped a little bit, but the pain came back. I was hoping that yoga would help make it feel better . . . If my shoulder pain kept rearing its ugly head, I was going to have to go to the doctor for it—and believe me, I had no desire to do that, since I probably wouldn't have gotten treated for a long time.

Unless the weather was bad, I saw my daughters pretty much every weekend, as long as one of them didn't have to be somewhere for one of their many activities. They would come with my mom, my friend Lisa G., or with Joe. I always loved their visits but felt drained emotionally after because I hated saying goodbye to them.

A bit after my last visit with my mom, the girls, and Lisa G., I went to a party for one of the inmates, who was leaving after thirty months. Franchie made this great punch and some of the girls made the most delicious popcorn balls! That was probably my favorite thing to eat in there. They would melt caramel and butter in a Tupperware container in the microwave, add in some kind of candy bar, like Snickers, pop some popcorn, and mix it all together. *Delizioso!*

After the party, I went to take a shower, and lo and behold, there was Big Bertha, who had asked me if she could be my bodyguard, getting a peep show from her girlfriend of that week. I said hi to Big Bertha and, despite trying to zoom by her on the way to an open shower stall, got an eyeful of her naked girlfriend. I was like, "Oops . . . sorry!" I may not have loved every second at Danbury, but I have to say, there was rarely a dull moment.

# 8

## TABLOID SPIES

*L*ife got a lot more dramatic for me after the first five or six months at Danbury, if you can believe it. One cold, sunny morning, some of the admins called me into the office to tell me I had to change my schedule. On more than one occasion, someone had noticed a small, low-flying plane circling the prison overhead. Officials had heard a rumor that a media company had hired the plane to take pictures of me leaving the actual building and walking down the outdoor staircase to the gym and track. Apparently, someone inside had leaked details of my daily routine. And because of one reason or another, officials actually ended up putting the entire prison on lockdown, to prevent anyone from going outside. I couldn't believe this. I was still being hunted—even while I was *locked up*. I was sick of it.

What was even crazier was when I found out that one of the inmates, a chunky, thirty-something Latina named Frederica, had sold my schedule and other personal, prison-related information to one of the tabloids for a supposed three thousand dollars! Well, it was actually her husband who sold the information, but she passed it along. I couldn't believe she was spying on me, and selling bits and pieces of my private life to the media, during one of the darkest times in my life. What a bitch. Some of the other inmates told me that she had been trying like hell to get a picture of me to sell to the tabloids, too. She had snuck a phone with a camera inside the prison, which was major contraband. One day, her husband brought a diaper bag to the visitation room, set it down on a table right near me—and I immediately wondered if he had hidden a camera in it. Who knows what people are capable of? I literally had to have eyes in the back of my head, and keep them peeled for potential weasels who could sell details to the media. As if I needed one more thing to be creeped out about.

When I found out that this bitch and her husband were trying to sell a picture of me in prison, I wanted to beat them to the punch. Over the course of my career, I've truly come to understand the often bizarre relationships celebrities have with the media—especially the tabloids. We've got to outsmart them at their own game, and sometimes, that means handing them a story that otherwise would have remained private. And so, Jim made calls to some of the top magazines, and got some huge offers for pictures of me inside prison in my uniform. They would get their story and I would get a paycheck—that would go toward something important, like doing my part to pay off the restitution. Even if they weren't things I would have shared to begin with, at least they were details I shared on my own terms, and were not given to them by some sleazy rat who could profit off totally underhanded and manipulative actions. So there.

Soon after the *US Weekly* cover story hit newsstands—complete with the photos my family and I took during visitation—we were put under lockdown. The guards tore through our rooms, looking for a rumored contraband phone or camera. The guards had gotten wind that one of the inmates was taking illegal photos of me, on the sly, during day-to-day activities. Of course, they found one, and of course, it belonged to Frederica—but they found it in her friend Teetsee's room. I found out later that Frederica had asked her to take pictures of me in yoga class and in the gym—and Teetsee obliged. Teetsee—who was also found with a carton of cigarettes on her—got sent to Brooklyn for having contraband and taking the pictures. At first I thought Frederica got off scot-free, but she got a shot for her part in all this. (I don't know why she wasn't sent to Brooklyn. I'm not sure they knew she had sold a story—or stories—about me or given Teetsee the camera.) I was glad that the guards had found the phone, but I wondered who else was playing paparazzi in there.

After I survived the plane and camera drama, I got some good news in the late spring: I was finally moving! Hooray! One of the counselors called me to her office one pretty April morning and told me I could move downstairs to A Dorm. I was so happy because a bunch of my good friends lived down there, too. I packed up my stuff as fast as I could, hauled it downstairs, and moved into a two-person cubicle with Tonya. My new room had a bunk bed, two rusty lockers, and a rickety chair. If you were lucky, you got a hook so you could hang up your uniform or towel, and I did. The concrete block walls dividing the cubicles were low in A Dorm—maybe five feet tall. If you had a top bunk, you could see over the "walls" into the next cubicle, and believe me, I was thanking my lucky stars I got the bottom bunk. I did *not* need a bird's-eye view of other inmates having sex with each other, because *ew* (while I couldn't see them, I could still hear everything . . . and believe me, I could've used some earplugs half the time).

But it was overall a lot quieter in A Dorm. I didn't have five hundred people whooping it up outside my room anymore at all hours, talking and laughing, or eating a ten-course commissary meal on the bed and leaving wrappers and dirty plastic containers all over the place. Since I knew so many people in A Dorm, we would sit on the steps in the streets and hang out talking. There were days I felt like a teenager again, hanging out with my buddies, passing the time, with nothing much to do except shoot the shit. (Wow, did I learn a lot, too. They told me about G-spots and sexual positions I'd never heard of in my life. My girlfriends back home and I never talked about anything this explicit. This was all new to me, but it made me laugh.)

If A Dorm was like living in an upper-middle-class neighborhood, D Dorm, which was a new discovery on my part and somewhat close to A Dorm, was like living in the slums of Calcutta. D Dorm used to house the dog program, where inmates raised and trained service dogs. Even though the program had ended and the pups had gotten shipped out, the rooms still smelled like dog shit to this day. For real. I felt bad for the sixteen women who lived there. Their metal beds had rusty frames, the mattresses had piss stains all over them, spiderwebs lined the walls and ceiling, and the women had no windows—just a fan.

The nurse's office, which was across from D Dorm, was minuscule, with an old, mold-covered desk in it and some first aid supplies.

The prison ob-gyn occupied the next office over. Supposedly, the ob-gyn spent three or four days a week down the hill, seeing patients in the men's prison. This was the first time I had ever heard of an ob-gyn treating male patients, and I'm sorry, but I laughed so hard when I heard that one that I had tears running down my face. We all did. Literally, what could that doctor have been *doing* down there?

The camp psychologist had his own, tiny office. He had more patience than almost anyone I had ever met and listened to the inmates complain for hours on end. But I heard he routinely offered the same non-helpful, non-advice: deal with the circumstances and make the best of them. So it seemed like kind of a waste of time to go see him. That's why we just bounced things off each other rather than take advice from the "professional"—and anyways, that doctor got to go home every day. I don't think he fully understood what it was really like to be an inmate and live without your loved ones for months—and in some cases, years—on end.

Of course, my birthday rolled around on May 18, and to keep myself sane, I knew I had to treat it like any other normal day. I went about my business, and after reading all the sweet messages from my friends, fans, and family, I went to yoga.

At the end of a yoga session, the instructor will guide you through Shavasana, or Corpse Pose. During this part of the practice, you lie on the floor in total relaxation mode, and though my birthday was no different from any other day, in that position I thanked God for my family and my health and for getting me through these past months. I thanked God every day for all the blessings in my life, including Joe, my daughters, my parents, my family, and my friends. I asked God to keep me on the path He wanted me to be on.

My birthday wish was for health and happiness for all of us and to go home to my family as quickly as possible.

Joe sent me an email that day telling me how much he loves me and how he wants us to grow old together. He told me that God often pairs husbands and wives who are both strong, which is why we are so good together. He would tell me he would never take me for granted again because now that he was taking care of the girls, he saw just how much I did to take care of the house and everything else. He said now he understands just how busy I really was at home, which of course, makes me laugh.

Every day since arriving in prison, I tried to think more positively about things that were happening to me at the moment—and about the future—and on my birthday, this became incredibly important. After reading *The Secret* and learning about the Law of Attraction, I made a vision board, sending the Universe and God messages about all the things I wanted in my life. (My friend Blaire made fun of me for cutting out magazine pictures and taping them to my board. She said it was like I was in kindergarten again. We laughed!) One of the things on the board was a handwritten note asking God to bring me home as soon as possible. Other images and words I put on my vision board: making forty million dollars so I could take care of my girls and help needy children around the world; making yoga DVDs; creating my own shoe, clothing, bathing suit, and children's clothing lines; getting a place in Florida on the beach; opening a restaurant; and a wish for the entire world to be happy and healthy and for everyone to have a place to live, enough food and clean water, and to be with their families.

Here are some other words, phrases, and pictures that I had on my vision board:

Free to Go Home
Lucky
Perfect Future
Fabulous
Family Time!    40 Million

Make History
Believe
Superwoman
           Love + Life
Goddesses of Food
         Queen
Inspire          Family
        Hawaii        Home
Yoga
       Best Body
     Money
Strong Mind, Strong Body

   Abs          Get Fit
Skinny
        Love
Happily Ever After

| | |
|---|---|
| Yoga DVD's | Parents |
| Love | Diamonds |
| Shoe Line | Leopard |
| Black Card | Ferrari |
| Lucky | Rolls Royce |
| | Boats |
| Rising Up | Vacations |
| Private Jet | Money |
| Shoes | Money |
| | Money |
| Milan Cathedral | Beach |
| Helicopter | Abs |
| Islands | Home |
| High Rises | King  Queen |

Peace

Lord

Jesus

Faith          Faith

Faith

I know it's a long list, but I have a friend who tells me all the time: "Dream big and it will happen." It has happened to her. I have seen it. So I was dreaming big! After I got out of prison and had spent time with Joe and the girls and gotten the girls settled when Joe left, I wanted to start new businesses and create an amazing future for me and my family. I knew I could do it. I had to, for them.

*I* had asked my friends not to do anything for my birthday, but Yazmeen, the amazing and loving prison chef I adore, surprised me with a birthday dinner that night! Nikki, Tonya, Franchie, and some others arranged it for me, which was so touching. They were such good friends to me. Tonya has connections with one of the girls who worked in the warehouse—she was able to get fresh spinach for me! I hate canned spinach and refused to eat it the whole time I was there, so for me, this was one of the best birthday treats I could ask for! It was so weird to think about the lavish birthday celebrations I'd had in the past . . . but honestly, this one was as rewarding, in different ways.

Yazmeen made sautéed chicken with spinach over angel hair, which was so delicious. She made me the most amazing salad, too, the kind you would find in a fancy restaurant. She said she wanted to impress me and she did. She even joined us and ate with us, which I loved. She is such a good cook that I hope she opens her own restaurant when she gets out of prison.

My friends gave me cards and gifts from the commissary, like body lotion, powdered pepper mix to spice up my food, and vitamins and supplements like calcium and vitamin D. Nikki and another friend even made me crocheted booties, which was so thoughtful. (Crocheting was so popular in prison, they even had classes and knitting circles. It's never been my thing, but my friends did try to teach me.)

Turning forty-three in prison was all part of my journey—and I know I've said this before, but it really made me appreciate the little things. That celebration was small, elegant, and perfect. For dessert, one of my friends made me oatmeal squares, which I love. Another friend made cookies out of egg whites that looked like tiny lemon meringue pies. We didn't have candles, so we pretended that we did and they sang me "Happy Birthday." It was one of the best days I ever had in there, thanks to the kind women who had become my prison family.

While I loved the commissary, I was grateful that so many of the ladies there offered so many different services to make money on the side. The twelve cents an hour that we made from our prison jobs just wasn't cutting it for most people who didn't have the resources I did outside of prison. I hired a woman named Jenny, who used to be a seamstress, to alter my uniform so it fit me much better. It made me feel good to wear clothes that finally fit me so well. It was well worth the twelve dollars I paid her in commissary items (that was my birthday gift to myself!).

I also paid Jenny three dollars to make me an eye mask, so I wouldn't be woken up every night when the guards shined the flashlight in our eyes. Again, it was some of the best money I ever spent.

Jenny's prices were good, but there was another woman named Hookup, a short, funny, firecracker Haitian woman who sold goods and services for ridiculous prices, like the other commissary queen, Magic, did. One morning after working, grabbing my coffee, and watching the news, which I did every day, I told Nikki I would meet her on the track for a walk. When I got there, one of our other friends was telling Nikki how Hookup wanted to charge her eight hundred dollars to cross-stitch some designs on eight pieces of clothing. That was insane! Everyone else charged ten to fifteen dollars for their services.

Our friend said she had to go, so Nikki and I kept walking. When we walked by the gym, we saw two inmates smoking behind it, like everyone did all the time. We glanced at them, they glanced back, and we just kept talking and walking.

I forgot all about that until later on, when Nikki told me that one of the women, from Brooklyn, stopped her in the computer room. "Hollywood better not snitch on us," she said. "I know you cool, but I dunno about her."

"Teresa isn't like that," Nikki told her. "She minds her business and doesn't care what anyone does."

"She better not or we'll beat her ass."

Whatever. Did they really think I'd tell? What did I have to gain?

Different groups of women in there tended to hang out with each other. The African-Americans, whites, Latinas, Asians, Jewish ladies, and Russians would all hang out with their own kind. But I was friends with people from every group and hung out with everyone. That didn't mean I got along with every single person in every single group.

I made friends with two Russian ladies who were just great. I liked them a lot. But they were friends with two others, Olga and Jerischa, who were nothing but troublemakers. Some of my true prison friends told me that Olga and Jerischa would trash-talk me, saying, "She walks around here like she owns the place. Who the hell does she think she is? Does she think her shit don't stink?" and on and on.

It was so crazy to me how Olga and Jerischa would smile to my face and be so friendly and wonderful when they saw me, but would talk bad about me behind my back. My Russian friends stuck up for me and told them that they were wrong about me. "She is the sweetest girl," they told her.

When I confronted Olga about this, she denied bad-mouthing me, too. "Why would I say something nasty about you?" she said, looking me dead in the eye. "How dare you even accuse me of such a thing!"

I literally was like . . . *Wait . . . am I being filmed for* Housewives *right now?!* It was all so dramatic!

A side note: Jerischa lost more than one hundred pounds while she was in there—in something like nine months. After she slimmed down, she asked her husband for permission to have sex with another woman before she got released because that had always been her fantasy. She chose to fool around with the Stud, who was the prison heartthrob. *Madonna mia*, sometimes prison felt like a *telenovela*!

While a lot of the ladies turned gay for the stay in there because they were lonely, needed a little something something, or wanted to make money, other girls would flirt with the male officers, especially the handsome ones. They would get all dolled up for them and act sexy around the cute ones, which the rest of us thought was hilarious. I even heard rumors that some of the inmates gave the officers blow jobs in exchange for nail polish and other items. I heard talk that some of them even had sex with officers in the woods. If the latter is true, I don't know what they got in exchange for that.

Some women didn't have money for the commissary, which is why they sold inmates laundry, nail, and hair services. I heard that some women even sold their own bodies to other inmates, just to make enough money to buy essentials at the commissary. My heart breaks for women (and men, because I'm sure it happens in men's prisons, too) that have to go down that road just to survive. Sure, some people fool around in prison because they want to and it makes them happy. If so, whatever. But when someone is driven to go to those lengths out of desperation, well, that makes me sad. People who have never experienced the system sometimes think it's like a "free ride." That undeserving people get shelter and food at the expense of taxpayers. After having seen and heard the incredibly moving and difficult stories of some of my fellow inmates, and experiencing just what that food and shelter consists of, I cannot justify that way of thinking. Sure, there are convicted felons who deserve to be where they are. But many of them don't.

I was incredibly lucky to have the necessary funds in my commissary account to allow me to live "comfortably" day to day in prison. I even used some of my commissary money to buy things to send as gifts to my family and friends. We were able to mail anything we bought there. I sent my mom black seed face cream, soap, and body lotion, and my dad jalapeño peppers, because he had a weakness for them. I knew he liked them and wanted to send him something so he knew I was always thinking of him. I also sent my daughters popcorn, caramels, and Cookies 'n' Creme Hershey bars so they could make the delicious popcorn balls other inmates made for me in here. Since Gia is a teenager, I also sent her some Clearasil face wash. I couldn't buy gifts online from in prison from Nordstrom or Neiman Marcus, where I used to love to shop, but I was happy I could send my family and friends little gifts. On tough days, knowing that I could still do things for my family while in Danbury really turned my entire perspective around. I know my girls could go to the drugstore for these things, but somehow, sending them from in there made me feel a little more connected to them.

I also bought little crocheted crosses that my friends made in there, to send to my friends and family to thank them for being there for me while I was in prison. I had someone make a crocheted soccer ball bookmark for Gabriella, a butterfly bookmark for Milania, and flower bookmarks for Gia and Audriana. I also sent some of my Jewish friends, including Andy, crocheted Stars of David. Those were small gifts that I could get nowhere else—Danbury's version of Etsy couture! The women who made these small gifts really changed the energy of prison life. I couldn't have been more grateful for their talents!

Though there were tons of women who brought only positive energy to each day, there were of course plenty of troublemakers. And with trouble comes consequences, doled out by the poor guards. I mean, I had to give those guys and gals credit. They had to break up fights all the time, and had inmates running to them every minute to rat out their enemies over the most ridiculous things, like who stole whose "reserved seating" in the TV room by ripping the piece of paper with their name on it off the chair they had picked out, who gave who the side eye, or who cut in front of who in the phone line. Each prison guard also played the roles of police officer, disciplinarian, psychologist, babysitter, peacekeeper, diplomat, and hand holder, all rolled into one. Once in a while they even had to be firefighters. Literally. In October, one of the women accidentally set a garbage pail on fire by tossing a lit cigarette into it when she thought she heard a guard coming. I think the pail contained rags that were covered with turpentine or something, so the whole thing went up in flames. The guards came running to put out the fire with buckets of water.

I got along great with all the officials and guards. They treated me very fairly. I was respectful to them, followed the rules, and tried to stay under the radar, and they treated me, in return, with respect. Again, I can't even believe I am saying this, but I miss some of them, too. They were good people with a very hard job babysitting a lot of people over there at Danbury Daycare.

# 9

---

## SNITCHES AND SNAKES

*I* made friends with a new inmate who came to Danbury in the summer, who got hit with girl drama the minute she set foot in the camp. Right after she got there, she walked by two women who were smoking cigarettes outside behind the gym. They knew she was new, so they came up to her later on and said, "We are gonna beat the shit out of you if you say one fucking word."

Shannon was a really sweet woman from New Jersey, who was in prison for mortgage fraud. I had a feeling she was a Jersey girl because she came to prison with a spray tan. She had never dealt with anyone like these two thugs in her life. They were part of a new group of tough-ass women who came to prison around the same time. They called themselves the Brooklyn Crew, and caused so much trouble in the dining room by short lining it—going to the meal lines early when they weren't supposed to—that the officials ended early mealtimes. They cut in line for the phones and the computers. They told everyone that they were the new leadership at Danbury. *Lead away,* I thought, *but don't ruin it for the rest of us.*

I felt bad for Shannon because she was so scared. But I wasn't. I realized early on that people respected me in there because I stood up for myself. I didn't run away from anyone and I think they knew I was one tough Italian cookie. No one was going to mess with me, and secretly, I loved that respect. I had transformed myself into someone stronger—mentally and physically.

So I had a talk with the thugs. "Why are you picking on her?" I said. "She's new. She's not going to tell on you. Why would she? She's just trying to get used to the place. Leave her alone."

They gave me some lip, calling me a skinny punk-ass bitch.

I didn't back down. "Are you finished?" I asked after their rant. "Leave her alone."

They cursed me out as I walked away. But they never bothered Shannon again. She thanked me over and over.

"No problem," I said. "Their bark is worse than their bite. They just wanted to test you and see what you would do. They just didn't know you had me in your corner."

We laughed. I was happy to help her because I remembered how I felt when I got to prison. I knew nothing, and it was my fellow inmates—the decent ones—who gave me the lay of the land. Now it was my turn. Just like Nikki had done for me, I gave Shannon a bunch of the things she would need for the first few days. I told her about the official—and unofficial—rules in there and invited her to sit with me in the dining room so she wouldn't have to eat alone. Her smile was infectious and her attitude was full of good vibes. I'm so lucky that she ended up being one of my closest friends in there.

• • •

The longer I lived in Danbury, the more I learned about my fellow inmates and their, um, colorful pasts. One woman defrauded an investor who was mixed up with the mob. Another one had a boyfriend who was a well-known hip-hop producer. One woman who loved to sing was bulldagging everyone she could get her hands on. So we called her Beyoncé and we called her girlfriend at the time Jay Z.

We had a lot of white-collar criminals in there, from doctors to lawyers to politicians. One former politician was in there for supposedly taking a bribe, even though she says she didn't. A lot of women were in there for scamming people—and huge companies—out of millions of dollars or for running credit card games. I also found out that some of the Russian women in there had gotten prosecuted for stealing millions from Holocaust survivor funds. I had no details on any of their crimes because I had no access to the Internet. I couldn't wait to get out and Google them all!

Just as you would expect in prison, there were a lot of power players in there. We called them the "crime bosses." They were the inmates in charge of each of the different departments, including recreation, the kitchen, educational classes and the chapel, the grounds, and the warehouse and commissary. They controlled everything. If they didn't like you, you would never work for them, and if you really pissed them off, you might have a hard time getting the things you wanted.

I liked them all because they were strong women, like me. I never had any problems with them, but I saw how hard it was for troublemakers to get things they needed or wanted when they clashed with the crime bosses.

One of the crime bosses I really liked was Shaniqua, who was considered the godmother of the prison, like the godfather in the mafia. She was the go-to person if you wanted anything. She would tell you how to get it done. Like other leaders in there, she was called in to defuse fights between women. Another crime boss I liked was a girl named Koolaidra. She was a petite Puerto Rican who was in prison for drug-related crimes and for bank robbery. She was one cool chick and, unsurprisingly, was one of the leaders—an unofficial enforcer who was told to watch over me and others if we had some kind of issue with another inmate. Shaniqua would have done it, but she was "hot," meaning she was being watched because she had a temper. While Koolaidra laid low and avoided being on the guards' radar, inmates respected her because she was so tough and never backed down from anything. They said she had "street cred" because she came from a tough background and wasn't scared of anyone or anything. As tough as she was, she was also friends with a lot of people. One of my favorite sayings of hers was, "You bleed just like I bleed." I actually learned a lot about standing up for myself, and for other people, by watching her. People in there told me that if I had stayed there longer, I would have become one of the unofficial "leaders" in there, too, because I was seen as the voice of reason so many times. Yes, me.

GETTING TO KNOW these WOMEN iN HERE HAS TAUGHT ME TO NEVER judge A Book By its COVER. AT THE END OF the DAY EACH of us iS NO Better THAN the next. I LOVE OUR talks iN the MORNING with OUR coffee, it feels Like home, not quite AND the coffee AT DANBURY sucks COMPARED TO MY HOMEMADE CAPPUCINO.

• • •

*O*ne day, I decided I wanted to reach out to my fans and to the people who had supported me on Twitter. I didn't think it would be a big deal. I called Gia and told her to tweet a message for me on my Twitter page, saying, "Thank you everyone for all of the cards, letters, and kind words of support I love, love, love you all xo T!" Some of them even sent me money for my commissary account. It blew my mind that people took the time to do that and were so kind to me. So I wanted to let them know I loved and appreciated them. It was the first time I had tweeted since Christmas, before I went away. I just wanted to let everyone know I was doing OK. I thought it was crazy when I found out that that one tweet made headlines everywhere— and somehow caught the attention of prison officials.

The following Tuesday, I got called down to the office. One officer was sitting behind an old, worn wooden desk and another stood on each side of him.

"We want to know how you were able to tweet something," said the officer at the desk. "Do you have a phone?"

*Mannaggia*, I thought to myself (which means "damn" in Italian . . . Joe loves saying that, too . . .).

"I don't," I said. "I had my daughter tweet that for me. I wanted to thank my fans. Check my locker and my room. I don't have a phone."

But to help clear things up, I asked them if they wanted me to have Jim tell the media that my daughter was the one who tweeted for me.

"Yes, please," they said.

Then they said I could go. I let Jim know about this. I did not want a shot. Another crisis averted.

•  •  •

$\mathcal{S}$ince I got to Danbury, I had been working out three times a day for about five to six hours a day and was getting into such amazing shape. Every muscle in my body was rock hard. I had veins in my arms from all the lifting, planks, and push-ups I did in there. I loved doing Bob Harper's workout DVDs and Travis Eliot and Rodney Yee's yoga DVDs. One Saturday, after visitation, they held a competition between two of the workout classes, with four people on each team. I won the plank contest by staying in place for nine minutes and nineteen seconds!

I was proud of myself. I am very competitive and it felt good to win. But really, in the end, it was just about the workout for me. I love to exercise and always have—and was glad I was getting so much stronger and leaner. I took a running class while I was there, and after six months or so, I became the leader of the advanced group and instructed them on what to do. It felt really good to help other women out and motivate myself at the same time. I love teaching so much that I want to get certified in yoga and start a line of yoga clothes and gear.

Even though I exercised so much while I was there, I only lost eight pounds or so. But I went down maybe two or three sizes from all the running, walking, weights, yoga, and exercise classes I was doing!

I was happy and proud that I was reaching one of the goals I had set for myself when I got in there—to get into the best shape of my life. I have to say, though, that there was one person who wasn't so thrilled with how lean and mean I was getting: Milania. She emailed me and said, "Don't get too skinny or else you will be too bony!!!"

Milania made Joe laugh (and me when he told me later) when she asked him for pasta saying, "What do you want? I'm Italian! We love our pasta!" We would also laugh when she would tell him, "I quit you!" when he would get mad at her.

One night, Tonya and I went to watch TV, put on the movie *Double Daddy* on Lifetime, and were in the middle of watching it when a woman named Abby came in and sat down.

"You know at ten that we are changing the channel," she said, looking right at Tonya.

Tonya didn't like the fact that Abby always tried to take control of this TV room. The movie was going to end at 10 p.m. anyway, but they had butted heads over the TV before. Tonya had been there so long that little things bothered her. That night, she had had enough of Abby.

"Why don't you shut the fuck up and mind your fucking business," Tonya said.

"Mind my fucking what?" said Abby. "I hope I didn't just hear you right. I'm watching whatever I want at ten. And stop being such a bitch all the time."

"What did you just say to me?" Tonya shifted in her seat and was facing Abby, who stood up and got right into Tonya's face.

I was sitting in between the two of them and couldn't believe things got this bad, this fast.

"Calm down!" I said. "This isn't worth it!"

They didn't listen and were both screaming at each other at this point. Abby made a move toward Tonya like she was going to hit her, so one of Abby's friends grabbed her and held her back, while Shaniqua held Tonya back. I knew this wasn't going to get physical because Tonya wouldn't risk hitting Abby and getting shipped out of there and sent to Brooklyn. I'm sure Abby felt the same way.

"Tell your friend here to back the fuck off," Abby yelled at me. "You really need to rein her in!"

I felt like I was being pulled into this fight and was now right in the middle of it, even though I really had nothing to do with it. It was between Tonya and Abby.

"I'm outta here," I said. I wanted nothing to do with their stupid fight over a TV show. All I was concerned with that day was missing Audriana's recital.

While I was walking back to our cubicle, inmate after inmate kept stopping me and asking me about the fight. "What happened? Were they fighting? I heard they punched each other. I heard you punched Abby."

Please. These women thrived on gossip and any drama that went on in there. I wanted no part of it, which was why I was mad at Tonya. This was exactly the kind of thing I tried so hard to avoid. I went back to our cubicle, got ready for bed, lay down, and read some of Joel Osteen's book *You Can, You Will: 8 Undeniable Qualities of a Winner*, which I absolutely loved. He tells you to dream big and pick big goals, to try to do your best with everything and to stay positive—all things I was really trying to do while I was in there. I was glad I was reading such an inspirational book because I felt like I was going to lose my shit at any second. While I was at Danbury, I was trying really hard to keep a lid on my temper and just talk things out. I was upset that we were now the talk of the camp. But I understood why Tonya went off on Abby. She did have it coming to her because she was so possessive over the TV. Even so, I thought the best thing for now was to say as little as possible to Tonya so I didn't say or do anything I would a shot for or regret later on.

Tonya came back into the room about a half hour later and

started to talk to me, but I ignored her. I gave her the silent treatment.

"OK. So you're not talking," she said. "I just want to go to bed." So did I. I just wanted this day to be over.

*J*oe, my mom, and the girls came to visit me the next day, which made me happy and took my mind off my bunkie drama. When I saw Audriana, I hugged her so hard and kissed her over and over.

"I am so proud of you, honey!" I said.

She hugged me again. "I love you so much, Mommy."

"I love you more," I said back.

When my mom, Gia, Milania, and Gabriella got up to go to the bathroom, Joe surprised me by kissing me on the lips, which is not allowed. Kissing in front of other people usually makes me feel embarrassed because I'm so old-fashioned like that, but this time, I didn't care. I missed him so much and this was way overdue! We started making out the way we used to when we were younger. It felt so good to kiss him. We told Audriana to stand in front of us so no one would see us. She thought that was the greatest thing. It was so cute. I think she liked seeing Mommy and Daddy so happy and so in love.

*E*ven though I was still mad about the TV drama, I thought it was behind us. But two days after the big fight, we got called into the head CO's office about the TV incident because Abby had reported Tonya and me to the counselor.

I thought it was ridiculous that I got called to the CO's office, because I didn't have anything to do with this. I thought Tonya would let him know I didn't have anything to do with it, but she didn't say anything. I was shocked because if the tables were turned, I would have said she had nothing to do with the argument.

When he asked each of us what happened, I told him that I was not involved and that this was a ridiculous argument over the TV. He seemed to agree and told us to try and work it all out with the TV and to stop fighting over it. That's what I thought I was doing already . . . but at least I didn't get a shot.

During step class a few days later, my friend Jessica told me that she was sitting near Abby and Tonya in the dining room when Abby asked her if she thought it was wrong drag me into the fight. Jessica said Tonya admitted that she and Abby were the ones who caused the fight—not me—and that she felt bad about it. After step class, I took a shower and was thinking about everything that had happened. I really liked Tonya and didn't want to fight with her. We had gotten along so well all these months and I considered her a good friend.

After head count that night, I decided to read some more of my Joel Osteen book. Tonya came back to the cubicle and didn't say anything to me. We hadn't said a word to each other for five days, but I felt that it was time for us to get beyond this stupid fight and move on.

"Can I talk to you?" I said while she was getting something out of her locker.

She just gave me the side eye and said nothing.

"One of us has to make the first move and say something, so I will," I said.

"You've made me feel really uncomfortable in my own room by not talking to me all week," she said. "You know, you can be a real bitch."

"Sometimes I can," I said. I went on to tell her that I felt like I was dragged into the fight with Abby and that I didn't like how she yelled at me when all I was trying to do was stop them from fighting. She said she could see why I felt that way and apologized. I appreciated that.

"I'm glad we talked," I said, giving her a hug.

"Me, too," she said, hugging me back.

"We good?" I said.

"We're good."

I was happy that we were able to talk things through and make up. But I still felt like I was back in high school with all this girl drama! I also felt like I was back on *RHONJ*, although the drama on the show was nothing compared to what went on in that prison.

I wanted to avoid more trouble in the TV room, so I took charge of writing down what shows we all wanted to watch, since the girl who was doing it before had gone home. I was now the Gatekeeper of the TV schedule, and I took my new role seriously.

I tried to keep the peace, too, when I could. While we were watching TV one night in October, one of the new, young inmates from the Brooklyn Crew got mad because Maria Camila, who had been there forever, had saved seats in the second row by taping her name and her friends' names to the chairs, like she always did. That's how it worked in there. But the new inmate had a problem with that, saying no one's name was engraved on the chairs, so she and her pals were going to sit there. Not so fast, said one of the prison elders, a woman in her late thirties who had been there for ten years. She told the newbie to get up and out of there. At more than three hundred pounds, she meant business!

Now, I don't care where I sit. I grab whatever chair is available. But these two were fighting so hard, for what the young girl considered "turf" and the elder considered "respect," they were close to punching each other out. It was getting tense. Normally I would be the one to walk over and try to break up a fight like this, but since I had so little time to go before I was leaving, I did not want to rock the boat. So I told my friend to go over there and play diplomat. I just yelled from the back row, "Cut the crap!"

While there were some women, like Shaniqua and Koolaidra, who were respected and well liked by so many inmates, there were also ladies in there who just rubbed everyone the wrong way. When one woman who worked in food service left Danbury after being in there for more than ten years, inmates actually stood in the hallways and cheered because they were so happy she was finally leaving. She always told on everyone and caused people a lot of angst. I wasn't a big fan of hers either, but I still felt bad for her when they chanted her name, saying how happy they were that she was finally leaving. On the other hand, she was getting the hell out of there, so I'm sure she didn't really mind either way.

Now that Tonya and I had made up, I thought all the craziness was over. But a week and a half or so after the TV fight, one of the admins called me into his office upstairs to say that the men down the hill wanted him to check on me and make sure I was OK because *they* had heard about the TV incident! Word sure traveled fast around there. I told him to tell them I was fine—and to thank them for looking out for me. I didn't even know these guys, but they were watching my back. Who would've thought . . .

I wished those guys were there a few days later, when fireworks went off inside the prison after *US Weekly* ran an excerpt of the diary I had been keeping there since the day I arrived. In one of my entries, I had written how officers had come up to our floor because an inmate had hit her roommate. I wrote, "She is a crazy lady who fights with everyone."

I didn't say who she was, but when the story came out, a ton of women went up to this woman and told her that I talked shit about her in the magazine. These snitches couldn't have run any faster to tell her about this. This woman was in her seventies and had been in and out of prison her whole life. She was a career criminal. I had heard that she had actually choked her roommate, which is why the officers raced up there.

"You tell Teresa that I am going to get her when she least expects it!" she told the women. "I am gonna beat her ass and slap the shit out of her." People were scared of this woman because she had no problem doing that. She used to run with notorious gangsters and drug lords, so she feared nothing and nobody. She seemed like a nice old lady but was considered hot-tempered—*caliente* in Spanish—and would curse women out in two seconds if they crossed her.

In the middle of this melee, someone told an officer about her threatening me. I got called to the Special Investigation Services, which they called SIS, where they asked me if I felt threatened by her. I said no—how could I really be threatened by a seventy-something woman?

Later on that day, Shaniqua asked me to come to her room. She and I clicked from the beginning. She always looked out for me. I just loved her. She said the old lady wanted to talk to me. When I got there, the old lady was upset and crying. She invited me to sit down on Shaniqua's bed with her. She took my hand in hers, which shocked me, saying she had no problem with me. She said people from SIS had talked to her and she was nervous that they were going to ship her out. I told her she had nothing to worry about with me; that I was cool with her.

"This woman who hates me and wants me out of here is making up lies about me," she said.

"When you see this woman, just look the other way," I said. "Ignore her."

She went on and on about all the women in there who had something against her and why. I listened for a while and finally said, "OK. I am going to go walk on the track now."

"Are we good?" she asked when I stood up.

"Yes, we're good."

I couldn't wait to get out of there. I didn't want any part of this nonsense because I didn't care and because I had so many other things to worry about. Jim was calling me left and right about saving our house, paying the restitution, and other businesses matters I had to deal with. On top of that, I was still doing my best to mother the girls and run the house—from prison. I was still involved in every detail of Joe and the girls' lives from there, just like I was at home. I was on the phone with them every day, making sure they were signed up for their activities, did their homework and long-term projects, ordered costumes for their recitals and competitions, did their chores, and had Joe fill out forms for school. Drama played a role in my prison life, but I tried my best to keep it at as much of a minimum as possible. After all, that wasn't what was important in life.

Even though I was trying to focus on what was important, sometimes other women's relationship drama was just too loud to be ignored. And let's be real . . . it was kind of entertaining! The women in there went through relationships like crazy. It was worse than in high school! The Stud had liked this lady named Delilah for a while. Delilah didn't have the whitest teeth but she had good hair.

She was dating a sweet woman named Rheenie, who had a crew cut and was very butchy.

When Delilah and Rheenie broke up, the Stud started up a short-lived relationship with Delilah, who she had been trying to get with for a while, but Delilah was still talking to Rheenie. One night when I went into the bathroom at about 3 a.m. or so, I saw Delilah running out of one stall (which already had someone in it . . .) and into another.

The next day I told the Stud about seeing Delilah in the bathroom, potentially during a hookup. The Stud started laughing and said, "But I just broke up with her! That didn't take long!"

But this innocent story—one that took less than two minutes to tell—turned into a big drama at the camp. I have a feeling that the Stud ran to Delilah and told her that I had seen her in the bathroom late at night—and that I figured she was with Rheenie. Delilah could be a bitch, so she totally froze me out of everything—including a big luau she threw for the Stud's birthday on the grounds near the volleyball court. (There was sand on the ground so we would feel like we were at a beach or on an island when we were playing volleyball . . .)

Delilah went all out for the party. She spent days making decorations from things she bought at the commissary. When her guests came down the sixty-four stairs that led to the court, she had someone waiting at the bottom, giving out leis she had made for them all out of tissue paper, asking them, "Do you want to get laid?" before handing them over, which made everyone laugh.

Everyone dressed to impress—well really, as best as one could for prison. They donned their best sweats, T-shirts, and new sneakers, wore makeup, and had their hair done.

Rheenie was obviously not invited. She sat on one of the picnic tables on top of the hill with her posse, watching her ex-girlfriend throw this lavish (well, lavish for prison) blowout for the Stud. I felt really bad for her. Rheenie watched the party for more than three hours. After it ended, she went up to the Stud and said, "We had sex today before your party." The Stud started screaming at her, threatening to beat her ass, which got Rheenie all riled up. Someone ran over and told them to stop fighting before the guard saw. The Stud made a beeline to Delilah and broke up with her right on the spot. What a great way to end your birthday party—with a real bang!

The craziness didn't end there. The next day, Rheenie stormed into Delilah's room, grabbed her by the hair, and screamed, "How could you have sex with me and then throw a party for her?" Rheenie didn't know that Delilah was dating—and having sex with—both of them.

I was lying in bed reading a book when I heard all the commotion down the hall. One of my friends walked by my cubicle and said that when Rheenie started pulling Delilah's hair, other girls jumped in and pulled Rheenie off of her. I didn't even get up off the bed, but I said really loud, "I cannot believe all this drama! *Madonna mia!*"

Later on, one of the Stud's girlfriends came up to me and told me that she thought the Stud got her pregnant. I said, "And how did she do that?" She replied, "Cuz girl! She rocked my world!"

This is what I was dealing with (and this one really made me laugh with tears running down my face!).

Soon after that episode, Jim called me to tell me that Joe had arranged to do a three-part special with Bravo about what life was like raising the four girls without me there, called *Teresa Checks In*.

In June, my brother came to see me in prison for the first time, for the special. He came up with my mother and the girls—and a camera crew. They couldn't come inside the prison to film us, but they filmed him driving there and back.

I was so happy to see him. He had called and emailed me during my stay there, but it was amazing to see him in person. We hugged and started to tear up, but I didn't want my mother to get upset, so I told him not to cry. Gia started tearing up, too, when she saw us together.

I missed him so much. We all sat down on the hard, red plastic chairs in the visitation room, and he told me what was going on with Melissa and the kids and what they were doing for the summer. I told him what my girls were doing and a little bit about what it was like in there. I had to be careful because we had lots of ears around us, listening to every word.

A couple of the women recognized Joey and came up to him to say hello and tell him they loved him on the show. One of the older ladies told him, "You are so handsome!," which made us all laugh.

We had such a nice visit and it made me sad when he left because I felt like I'd gotten my brother back.

A bit later, I was watching *Secrets and Wives* on Bravo, when one of the guards came to the TV room, looking for me. "We need to see you, *now*," he said.

He led me to a small room, where a female officer was waiting for me. "Take everything off," she said.

I had no clue why they were doing this—and I was more stunned than angry. I took off my uniform, faced the wall, and did the dreaded squat and cough. When we were done, the guard ordered me to stand in the hall. They were also strip-searching Tonya. When they were done, they put us in a room and told us to sit there and wait.

"Tonya, I don't have any contraband," I said quietly. "You don't either. What's going on?"

"I don't know, but I'm nervous," she said.

While we were waiting, someone walked by and said officers were downstairs, shaking down our room. They were tearing apart the cubicle I shared with Tonya. They flipped the mattresses off the bed, ripped the sheets off, and emptied everything out of our lockers. I had no idea what they were looking for, but I heard later on that someone had told the guards that I had a phone and that they had seen me texting on it. That made me shake my head in disgust because—hello—of course I didn't.

When we were allowed to return to our cubicle, they told us that they hadn't found anything and to straighten the room back up. We put the sheets and blankets back on the beds, put everything back in our lockers, and went to bed. The next morning, I got up at 6:15 a.m. like usual, went to breakfast, and then went to the rec room to watch the news. Just after I sat down, one of the officers came over the loudspeaker asking us to all go outside. We stood there in a line while they patted each of us down to see if we had any contraband—or phones—on us.

"There are so many officers here!" Nikki whispered to me.

"I wonder what they're looking for," I whispered back.

We found out a little later that they were shaking down everyone's room, looking for a cell phone and an iPad. After they finished, they patted us down again when we went back inside. When I got to my cubicle, it had been turned upside down—again. But I thought, *Who cares?* I had nothing to worry about.

After lunch, two inmates I didn't know stopped me in the hall-way. "Yo—what the fuck you think you're doing?" one of the women said to me.

"You the reason for the shakedown with your stupid-ass tweet-ing," said her friend.

She had her hands on her hips then started pointing her finger right in my face. My Italian temper was starting to get going, but I stayed calm, at least on the outside. "I don't have a phone," I said. "My daughter tweeted that for me, and I cleared it up with the offi-cers a while ago."

"Well, they shook your room down again. They must really be looking for something,"

"They can look all they want," I said, "but I don't have anything for them to find."

"Yeah, right. Well, all this shit is your fault."

They were pissed off because they had contraband like nail pol-ish and makeup that was taken away from them. Whatever. Not my problem.

Tonya and I didn't get shots, but two other inmates did—big ones—when one of the officers found cigarettes in the gym while Nikki and I were working out. He acted like the biggest hero. "What would they do without me here?" he said, while we rolled our eyes.

I heard later on that when he started checking lockers, he found a couple of flat irons too, which we weren't supposed to have. This is the stuff they worried about when they had much bigger prob-lems they should have been dealing with—like the drugs, phones, and weapons people snuck inside, and the unsanitary and downright hazardous living conditions we were faced with. The guards were so strict during room checks and would give us heat if our beds weren't made properly. Yet, if they'd looked up, they'd have seen that there were inches of disgusting dust on the pipes over our heads, which were too high up for us to clean. Why didn't they worry about *that* stuff? The cancer-causing, dangerous stuff?

Right after the officer left, two other inmates came down to the gym, then went around back and started smoking, which we could see out the window. I'm not sure where they got the cigarettes since he had just confiscated a bunch of them. Nikki told me she thought one of them had hidden them in her makeup case.

"I'm going to head back to the camp," I told Nikki when I was done on the bike. "Do you want to come?"

"No," she said. "I want to do some more abs."

"OK," I said. "I'll see you later. I want to take a shower and then call home."

As I was leaving the gym, the two smokers came up to me and stopped me. "You aint gonna say nothin', are you?" one of them asked.

"No way," I said. "I don't care what you do. Just don't get caught!"

As I said before, I knew what happened to rats in there. As long as no one was hurting me, I really didn't care what they did. My feeling was that they were doing whatever they could to cope with life in that hellhole. I totally understood where they were coming from, believe me.

After I showered and called home, we had head count at 9 p.m. Tonight we had the Incredible Hulk do our count. We called him that because he was way too muscular—too many steroids, we thought. He would yell at the ladies to keep quiet because he would lose count of how many inmates were in a room if they were all yapping, which they weren't supposed to be doing. We thought that was hilarious.

After head count, I went to brush my teeth and ran into Motor

Mouth. She never fucking shut up! I never knew what to believe with her, either. She was always telling me not to trust anyone, but sometimes she would lie to me. One time she told me she wasn't friends with someone I didn't like in there—someone I thought had ratted me out about the phone I didn't have. Literally, as she was telling me this, Tonya and her friend Gigi were standing behind her, giving me a look like, "She is lying through her teeth."

When Motor Mouth left, Gigi grabbed my arm. "You are way too trusting," she said, telling me something I have been told again and again, even by my daughter Gia. "Open your eyes," said Gigi. "She is a liar. Stay away from her."

Ugh. I didn't care about all this drama involving two-faced women, but at the same time, I did have to watch my back to make sure nothing too crazy was going on . . .

I just couldn't wait to get out of there. I was sick of all of the stupid shit they focused on.

The next day, we had a birthday party for my friend Talia. Some of the ladies surprised her with a dress they had made out of T-shirts! She loved it and ran down the hall to the bathroom to try it on. She came back out and modeled it for us, pretending to walk like a supermodel on a runway—but in the streets at Danbury. We all laughed and cheered for her. I was having such a good time that for a minute, I actually forgot I was in prison. *Those* were the women who fueled my fire during my stay. The women who encouraged me to keep on going, and who made every difficult day just a little bit easier. Just one of my friends in prison could make me forget about the snitching rumors, Motor Mouth, bat-shit crazy old ladies, and wacko guards— and honestly, that's what mattered most to me in the world.

• • •

While I was in there, I started to hear about more and more tabloid stories saying that Joe was cheating on me with different women. What got us both mad was that these "homewreckers" were literally friends of friends. If Joe went out with a guy friend and his girlfriend, the paparazzi would sell the photos in which only Joe and the girl appeared. If he sat across the table or next to a woman at a restaurant who was friends with his friend, they said he was cheating. If he posed for a picture with a woman, they said he was unfaithful. One time, he posed for a fan picture with a woman, and "a source" said he was having sex with her. Her fiancé was literally standing behind her when the picture was taken! I told Joe to say no to having his picture taken with any female, but he was like, "I don't want to say no and be an asshole." That's how Joe is—an easygoing, good guy who doesn't want to be a jerk. But there were so many evil people out there who just wanted to nail him any way they could. I hated that so much.

As I have said before, if I knew for sure that Joe was cheating, if I had 100 percent proof that he had, I would leave him in a heartbeat. I wouldn't be able to stay with him. I trust Joe with my life and am so blessed that he is my husband. I think about him every day and am dreading the day when he goes away to prison. That is going to be much harder than any of these stupid cheating rumors, and so handling that hurdle is what we are trying to focus on getting through.

For Father's Day, I sent him a card with three pages of printouts of positions I told him I wanted to try when I got home. I told him that I had gotten very flexible in there from doing so much yoga. I thought he would like seeing those printouts—and he did! He emailed me when he got the card, saying he laughed out loud because I had *never* shown him anything like that before in my life—and that he couldn't wait until I got home . . .

In late July, I was in yoga class at about 9:15 a.m. when we were all told to go into the dining hall. Someone said there were eight cop cars outside on one side of the building and a bunch more on the other side. They patted us all down before we were able to go into the dining hall. While we waited in there, they brought in a couple of German shepherds.

"What are they doing?" I asked Shaniqua.

"They are sniffing for drugs," she said. "This is what they do when they think someone has shit they shouldn't have in here."

They kept us in the dining room for more than two hours. It felt like it was a hundred degrees in there because there was no air-conditioning inside that room. We were dying. We had to wear pants, which made it even hotter for us.

After a bit, they brought the dogs outside and were looking everywhere. I had heard that that was where inmates hid drugs and other things. Finally they let us out. It was too hot to work out, although I walked around the track from 7:45 p.m. to 8:45 p.m. just to get some air because I felt like I couldn't breathe inside the building. I couldn't fall asleep that night because it was so hot. I kept getting up to wet towels to put on my head and neck. It was brutal.

I prayed that night for God to bring me home to my family and get me out of this hellhole. I hated it in there. For all the people out there who wanted to see me punished and suffer, well, they got their wish. But I wasn't going to let that get me down.

I found this saying in one of the Joel Osteen books that said something like, "Father, thank you for taking me further, faster. Thank you for turning my water into wine." If I ever needed God to turn my water into wine, it was now. I really didn't know how much longer I could hang on. But I knew I had to.

When Fourth of July rolled around, I told my family not to come, because of the traffic. Joe and the girls, my parents, and his cousin Teresa and her boyfriend went to the shore house. I tried to keep busy, but it was hard not to think about how I was missing such a fun holiday. Anyone who knows me knows that summer is my season. I love everything about it: the warm weather, trips to the beach, spending time outside, getting to wear bikinis(!), and just relaxing. The year before, Joe and the girls and I had gone down to the shore house for the Fourth. We cooked out on the grill, went to the beach, and had friends over. I love watching the fireworks from our deck.

I tried to keep busy so I wouldn't think about my family. I worked out, had lunch, and then walked on the track. I had to take a moment in my cubicle, though, to cry, thinking about how much I wanted to be with them. I kept asking God why I was there and away from Joe and the girls. I said, "Please answer me, God." I was told that if you ask God for something, He will eventually answer you. All I wanted was for God to bring me back home. I couldn't stop crying all day, whenever I could find some time alone, thinking about my family and how much I missed them.

I made it through the Fourth of July not knowing there were more fireworks coming my way because of a woman I referred to as the Stalker and another one I called Trouble. They started something up that led to a huge fight between me and Tonya. I liked the Stalker at first, and thought she was fun to hang out with, until she started to follow me everywhere, even into the bathroom, trying to get as much information about me as she could. It was really weird. She and Trouble would make nice with my family in the visiting room while trying to pump them for info on me. I was like, "Are you kidding me?"

In the late spring, a new inmate came to Danbury who knew one of my close friends back home. She kept telling people that she couldn't wait to meet me and tell me that we had a mutual friend.

The Stalker and Trouble got wind of this before I did and, of course, started asking New Girl all kinds of questions about me. When Tonya found out about this, she told me to be careful around New Girl. "She's talking shit about you," she said.

"And?" I responded, "I don't even know this person. Who cares?"

I told Tonya I would tell my friend back home about all of this when I got out of prison, but I ended up adding that friend to my email list because I needed to talk to her about something else, totally unrelated. When I emailed her, she asked me if I had met her friend, New Girl. I told her that New Girl was talking smack about me, and of course, my friend got mad.

My friend back home said something to New Girl, who was friends with Shaniqua. New Girl got really upset about this. She said she didn't want to start trouble with me at all. Shaniqua was mad, so she confronted the Stalker and Trouble about it, and wow did they get into it. They were all screaming at each other.

Tonya was furious that I had told my friend about it, because now the Stalker and Trouble knew that she had told me. The rumor had come full circle, and she was pissed. "You are leaving in December, but I have to still live with these people!" she said. I told her that I didn't mean any harm—that my friend asked me a question, and I answered it like a grown woman, not thinking it would be a big deal.

"You lied to me!" she said, screaming in my face. "You said you were gonna talk to your friend after you got out! Now you've made trouble for me in here!" I told her that I hadn't lied.

After dinner, I was walking the track when Shaniqua came up to me, asking me what happened with Tonya's friend. She said trouble was brewing. I was like, "What now?"

Tonya was standing near the track with Trouble, watching all of this. She looked pissed off. "Get over here, Teresa," she said in front of about twenty other inmates.

I did not like the tone of her voice, and you know by now how much that gets me mad. When I walked over to her, she started questioning me about everything that had happened. I didn't like that she was doing this in front of Trouble, who had a big mouth. One of the biggest in there.

"I'm not doing this right now," I said to her as I turned and walked away.

"Who the fuck do you think you are?" she said. "Don't you walk away from me! Come back over here, you fucking bitch!"

I turned around but kept walking.

"You heard me, bitch. Get back here!"

I turned around again and she yelled something out, but I couldn't hear her. No one would tell me what she said, either.

Finally, I said, "all the drama!"

"No, Teresa, *you* are the drama!"

I laughed and kept walking until I got back down to the track.

While she was screaming at me, every woman out there had stopped dead in her tracks, not wanting to miss a second of the latest episode of *Danbury Daycare*. I hated being in the spotlight like this. My blood was boiling. But I just kept going. I was proud of myself for not getting into it with her. The old Teresa would have wanted to grab her and drag her down the sidewalk. But I didn't want to take the bait. It just wasn't worth it to me. I didn't want to get a shot for fighting with her, and I wanted to change how I reacted to people who were firing at me.

I walked over to Nikki, who'd been inside the gym when all this was going on. Everyone was already talking about it, so she had heard the story.

"Are you OK?" she said.

"I'm fine. I'm just shocked at what Tonya said. I had no idea she was like that. I really thought we were friends. But she went too far."

I went back inside and watched *The Real Housewives of Orange County* to try to take my mind off Tonya. After head count, I took a shower and went back to the cubicle. I climbed into bed and shut out the light.

Tonya came in fifteen minutes later. She climbed up into her bunk. She leaned her head over her bunk and told me she was sorry. I stayed calm even though I was almost as mad as when I flipped that table way back when. "I cannot believe you said that to me in front of all those people," I said. "I don't want to be involved in any drama in here at all. I don't want people talking about me, and now, because of this, they're going to talk about this fight for the next week. You know how they are."

"I was just really mad that you caused me so much trouble," she said.

"Well, next time you need to handle it a lot better than you did today," I said. "I'm going to sleep now."

I shut my eyes and rolled over to get comfortable, but with my adrenaline pumping, I was wide awake. I was so furious that she had done that to me. While I felt sad about trusting yet another person who let me down, I was proud of myself for walking away. That was huge for me. A turning point. All the inspirational books I was reading in there, all the praying and Bible study groups I was going to, and the yoga and meditation I was doing, had totally changed the way I reacted to things. I almost couldn't believe it. I finally fell asleep, thanking God for looking out for me and helping me get through all of this.

Soon after, though, Tonya and I talked things through and I realized that she had a great point. Long after I left, she would still have to deal with these women, who could be vicious. I was sorry that things had gotten so tense with us, but I was also grateful for such an amazing lesson in restraint, understanding, and forgiveness. I was glad things were all right with Tonya and me again, because she meant a lot to me in there.

Throughout the summer, Joe and the girls kept telling me about that Bravo special, *Teresa Checks In*. They were so excited about it. I was, too, but at the same time, I was upset about it. I didn't want to watch them on TV. I wanted to *be* there with them—and for a while, I sat there feeling sorry for myself, until a friend of mine in prison wisely said, "Hey girl. Everyone in here is dying to know what is going on at home without us there and how our kids are doing—and you are gonna *see* them! No one gets to do that, so you are damn lucky!" She was right. While I knew I would be crying when I saw it, I also wanted to see my home, my girls, and my husband all living their lives. I couldn't wait to see the inside of my home—which I hadn't truly seen in months. I pulled myself up by my bootstraps and forged on—because that's what prison had taught me to do—looking forward to the first airdate.

About two weeks before the first episode was set to air, I got in trouble with the prison for calling home and having the production company record my voice while I was talking to my family. They gave me a shot because they said I'd had "unauthorized contact with the public."

I had no idea I was doing anything wrong. I just called home and the production company filmed Joe, the girls, and my parents talking on the phone with me. Joe did the show because we needed the money. He was doing everything he could to save our house from foreclosure.

Now I was nervous. I didn't know what they were going to do to punish me. I found out a few days later that they were taking away my phone privileges for thirty days. I cried when they told me that because Joe, the girls, and my parents were my lifeline in there.

The good thing, though, was that they had just allowed us to Skype for the first time ever. I could talk to my family for twenty-five minutes straight. So even though I couldn't call them regularly, I could still communicate with them here and there—and see them while I was talking to them. Thank you, God.

On the morning of the special, I raced to the TV room to put the show on the list so we could watch it. But other women had beat me to it and put it on the list to make sure that we got to watch it, which was really nice. I loved that they did that for me and that they wanted to see it!

I was nervous all day long. I was praying that I would get through it. One of my friends got to one of the TV rooms early to save a bunch of us seats. It was crazy, though, because they were still showing the movie *Taken 3,* which ran past 8 p.m., when the special started. We all ran to another room to see the beginning of the special, then raced back upstairs to the rec room to see the rest.

The minute I saw Joe and the girls, I lost it. Oh my God—I missed them so much. Nikki held my hand and one of the other girls came over and hugged me. They were cheering when they heard me call the family from Danbury and were crying when they saw the girls, Joe, and my parents break down in tears. All the ladies watching kept saying that Gia and Milania looked just like me and that Gabriella looked like Joe. Others were saying Gia looked just like Joe. And they kept saying that Audriana was still a baby, which, if you know me by now, made me cry.

What I loved about watching the show with the girls was that everyone in the room—not just my friends—was crying, laughing, hooting and hollering, which was so fun for me (and so different from watching the show in my family room at home with Joe and the girls!). During commercial breaks they would ask me questions about who was who on the show—and of course I filled them in.

I ran into a lot of looney tunes in Danbury, but the wonderful people I got to know so well—and the little family we created—meant everything to me. We held each other up and helped each other to the finish line, where our freedom was the ultimate reward. I will never forget how much those girls were there for me. We were there with each other every single day and spent more time with each other than with our own family members.

I saw how much they cared that night, when they watched the show with me and hugged and kissed me and told me they were there for me because they knew how hard this was for me. I can't put into words the love I felt that evening.

When I saw my dad on TV, I started crying again. He had never visited me in prison because it was too painful for him to see me in there. It literally broke my heart that I'd had to go away. His health wasn't the greatest, so we worried about him visiting and seeing me in there. While I talked to him all the time on the phone, it was good to finally see him and know that he was OK and that he looked healthy (and so cute in his jeans . . .). I started crying, though, when he had to step away from the kitchen when Gia broke down while she was talking to me. That tore my heart to pieces because I don't ever like to see any of them upset over me, especially my dad.

One of the reasons my dad still cannot believe I went to prison is because he always wanted Joey and me to walk the straight edge of the knife. My dad still doesn't understand why I had to go to prison. Neither do I. But one of the things I learned in prison was not to dwell in the past. I now understand the importance of living in the moment and looking ahead to the future. As my journey took me closer and closer to home and away from that hellhole, I couldn't look back, only ahead.

One of the things that I was so grateful for when the special aired was that they showed the memorial Joe made for his father on the side of the house, near where his dad died. They filmed Joe planting a tree there in his father's honor and toasting him, saying, "To the greatest father, grandfather, and greatest everything. I love him. Cheers, Dad!" It made me feel like I was there, with my family, holding that grief with them. I wanted to help celebrate his life, too, and with the special, I felt like I could in some way.

I gasped out loud when I saw Gia come down the stairs on the show for her eighth-grade prom. She looked absolutely breathtaking. I got emotional when I saw Joe holding back tears then, too, seeing Gia with her hair and makeup done so beautifully, looking so grown-up. I'll admit that I did laugh when I saw him show her date, Dante, who is a good friend of hers, how to dance with her by holding hands at arm's length. It reminded me of my father! I laughed even harder when Milania yelled out to them when they were leaving to keep their hands to themselves. Oh, my Milania. She is so funny and always has me laughing. I love her to pieces.

She would also email me when Joe punished her for doing something naughty and ask me, "Why did you have to marry Daddy? He is so mean!" I always replied, "If I didn't marry Daddy, you wouldn't be here." "Oh no," she would say. "I would still be here." I laugh every time I get that email from her.

I was proud of the girls while watching the special. They showed the world that they were doing just fine and were adjusting very well to their mommy being away. They are strong, like me and Joe, but I wish they never had to go through any of this. Out of all of us, me going to prison was hardest on the girls, not me and Joe. The girls are the ones who got punished the most, not us.

Joe tried to keep everything as normal as possible for them, which is why they were able to do so well with it all. I wanted to do the same, which is why I told Joe that prison was like being in a low-budget spa. After the special aired, people were pissed because they thought I was living this cushy, locked-up life. Let me tell you, prison was nothing like a low-budget spa. It was hell. But again, I didn't want him to worry about me while he was home taking care of our four daughters. I didn't want to tell him anything negative about that place because I wanted to put his mind at ease. I also didn't want him to inadvertently let the girls know how horrible it really was in there. I was fine. I could handle it. I wanted to take the brunt of it all so they wouldn't have to, because I love them so much.

I tried to savor every second of the show. I couldn't get enough of seeing Audriana, who is so precious and adorable, or Gabriella, who is the sweetest. She is so poised. Such a little lady. They all are. I was also so proud of Gia, who is so put together. It blows my mind how well-spoken, grounded, and mature she is. Thank you, God, for such beautiful, wonderful, loving daughters. I know this sounds crazy, but I loved seeing my three youngest girls' sweet little bare feet and their cute little toes when they were sitting on the couch. It's a mommy thing . . .

I was also glad that viewers got to see a little more of the Joe I know and love. My Joe is so sensitive, has such a big heart, and is such a good father and husband. That's why I love him so much. What they didn't show enough of was how much he laughs! He would call me and say something like, "I'm at the friggin' Apple store getting Gia's phone fixed—again," and then laugh at how he was now the chauffeur, assistant, chef, hairstylist, homework helper, and everything else. As he laughed, he'd say what he always says when life is sweeping you along for a hell of a ride: "Whaddya gonna do?"

I loved seeing them when they all gathered around the kitchen table to talk to me on the phone. They all looked so adorable. I wanted to give them one giant hug from Danbury. My beautiful family . . . God bless them all . . . I planned to watch the special over and over again when I got home, because I think I missed a lot because I was so emotional.

My brother and I were getting along better when I was in prison, thank God. I always enjoyed talking to him on the phone and hearing from him on email. I knew it was hard to come see me, his big sister, in prison. When he sat with me in that visitation room, we really were the Joey and Tre from years ago. Any hurt or pain from the past had just disappeared. I cried when I saw him break down when he got back in the car after coming to see me for the first time. That's when

I knew, deep in my heart, that things were going to be better between us. He wasn't acting for the cameras. This was Joey, with his heart on his sleeve, reeling over seeing me locked up in there and having to leave—without me. I had no idea that it would take me being in prison for us to finally break down those walls between us. But as I have seen in prison over and over again, God works in mysterious ways . . .

Melissa and I were also in a good place when I went to prison. I appreciated her being there for my girls when I was gone, like the time she took them for mani-pedis while they filmed the special. My hope was that we would continue to get along when I got out. I wanted to feel close to her again and I was hoping she did, too. But these things take time. And that's OK.

After the special aired, a lot of people at Danbury asked me who had emailed me or called me while I was in there. I emailed with Joe and the girls, of course; with Joe's family including his sister, Maria, his sister-in-law, Sheila, and his cousin, Teresa, who helped Joe so much while I was gone; and with my close friends, including Kim R., Lisa G., Rosanna H., Lisa F., Linda B., Rose C., Leah B., Tracey C., Nicole P., Dana T. and Dana L., Priscilla, David, Josephine A., Anna D., Giovanna D., Julie B., Tina S., Jackie R., Robyn K. and Christina, Diane P., Andy Cohen, and my brother, Joey. I love them all for keeping in touch with me.

I kept in touch with Dina, who took Audriana to the American Girl doll store in New York City for her sixth birthday, which made me so happy. My brother and my mother came to see me, along with Lisa G. and some of my other friends. Rino Aprea called Joe all the time to check on me while I was in prison, which was so nice. His wife, Teresa, and her sister, Nicole, asked about me, too. Melissa sent me notes and pictures of our kids. My niece, Antonia, and my nephews, Gino and Joey, sent me cards.

After the three parts of the special aired, things calmed down for me in there and it was back to business as usual. I wasn't the center of attention anymore, and wanted to have a little fun. I had an adorable Latina girl named Cinnamon put cornrows in my hair (which I called corn rolls at first!). I had seen other girls with them and thought they looked cool. Everyone was laughing along with me and started calling me the OG: Original Gangster. Who would have thought: Teresa Giudice, an OG!

I laughed when I looked in the mirror, thinking about how I would never have gotten cornrows in my real life—my life back home. I wondered how that would have flown on *RHONJ*. I never could have pulled this off in Jersey. I felt like, *Yeah, I'm in prison and doing what everybody else here is doing because I am a part of all this, too.* These were my girls. My prison sisters, whether they were black, white, Asian, Latina, or Russian. I will never forget them and all that we went through together.

The whole thing with the cornrows made me laugh, which made me feel so free. Sometimes, you don't realize how bogged down you are until you laugh till your stomach hurts. It's in those moments that I knew I would come out of this whole ordeal stronger. A better person. Ready to take on the world.

My family came to Danbury that day for an event they throw in the fall called Oktoberfest. It was amazing. They held it in back of the camp, and I couldn't wait for my family to see the track, where

I had spent so much of my time at Danbury, walking, running, and just thinking everything through. I can't believe I am even saying this, but I knew I was going to miss that track. It was another thing there that had kept me sane and was a lifeline for me.

At the Oktoberfest, my daughters and I held hands and walked up one of the hills and then ran back down to Joe. They loved doing that and were laughing the whole way down. My family is just so beautiful. And stronger than I ever knew possible.

October 23 was quite a day for me. Not only was it my sixteenth wedding anniversary, but it was the day that Jim was able to save our house from foreclosure. He had worked nonstop with the bank to make sure we could keep it. I was so happy and relieved when he told me we could stay in the house. Later that night, Joe called. He and the girls had dinner with Dina at our house. He was also relieved that the girls and I could continue to live in our house, the house they had always known. I knew we would be okay. We always had been, and always would be. In recent months, I had found myself thinking, amid all the stress, difficulties, and bullshit, *God, am I thankful for this life.*

I wasn't thankful, though, for the lack of sleep I got on Halloween. I don't know what was going on, but it was *crazy* in there that night! The girls were bouncing off the walls, running through the streets, hooting and hollering and having so much sex! My cubicle was near the bathroom, and I had never seen so much action go on in there in all my months at Danbury. Honestly, I think there was an orgy going on. I had never seen so many feet in those stalls before. We always said, "What happens in Danbury, stays in Danbury," but really? I tried so hard to go to sleep, but I couldn't. As I watched pair after pair of ladies run to the bathroom to do God knows what, I kept thinking, *I can't deal . . . I just can't.* I found out later that two lovebirds actually broke the sink off the wall after having sex on it! Thank God I was getting out of there soon . . .

# 10

---

# TURNING THE TABLES

It was early December. A gorgeous morning. I got up at 6:15 a.m. like usual, went to breakfast and had my oatmeal with raisins, and did my yoga (I can't start my day without it now), before going to sit outside to drink my coffee, which had become my morning ritual. When I first got here, I didn't even know you were allowed to sit outside, let alone drink your coffee out there. I liked to call it my "coffee time." I wondered how much longer I would be able to sit outside without freezing to death.

As I sat there, thinking about how beautiful it was out, my buddies Tonya, Shannon, Shaniqua, Blaire, Josie, and Nikki joined me outside. Most of them got up later than I did and always made fun of me for being such an early bird. But I loved being around them because we always laughed the whole time. I love being around positive people.

We sat around talking about the big newsflash of the week: how we heard that a bunch of inmates were being sent to the Federal Metropolitan Detention Center in Brooklyn after throwing a big bash with a hundred dollar cake and lit candles. I heard that four lieutenants raced up to the room where they threw this party and demanded to know where they got the candles and how they lit them. For four lieutenants to charge into a party like this, I knew it had to be serious. I was just glad that I was not there because I heard that everyone who was there was getting shipped to Brooklyn. (In the end, they didn't. They got moved and they got shots.)

The conversation then turned to how I was leaving in a matter of weeks. My friends told me how happy they were that I was finally getting out, but said they would miss me so much. "It's not going to be the same without you, T," said Shaniqua. I told her I was going to miss them all and that I loved each and every one of them for being there for me and helping me get through this nightmare. "What I will miss most is how much you make me laugh!" I told them.

"You want to laugh some more?" said Blaire, who started doing a skit with Josie about me and Tonya, acting out how much of an "old married couple" we were, which made us roar. They called us the Bickersons, because we always bickered—but in a loving way. Tonya had truly become one of my closest friends there and I was happy we were so comfortable with each other. Our stomachs hurt so much from laughing so hard. I had tears in my eyes. It was just so silly. Just what we needed in there to break the monotony.

We also talked about how, for the first time ever, I got to help cook dinner for all the inmates! I was so happy to be back in the kitchen. I helped the ladies there make tofu with stir-fry vegetables (with the biggest pan I have ever seen!), as well as meatloaf, rice and peas. It took me a little bit to get used to using the equipment in that huge kitchen, but I had so much fun! I cooked along with two other

Italian ladies, so we spoke Italian the whole time, which I loved. I even got to help serve the meal. It was a great way to wrap up my stay there.

It was nice to sit there and chat with the girls. We had gotten to know each other so well over these many months. We had had our ups and downs, like we would have had anywhere, but somehow we'd made it work. I lived at home throughout college, but I imagined dorm life was a lot like life in prison: you rode the highs together; you laughed together; you argued with each other; you pissed each other off; you got stressed-out about things and vented to your fellow students to get you through the day. We did a lot of complaining in there—about the living conditions, the food, and other inmates, but through it all, we truly needed one another. But at least we had each other to lean on. Of course, I say this all with a grain of salt: I never forgot that some of the women in there were hard-core criminals who would sell their mother for a dollar if they could. But not my friends. They were good people.

The other girls were getting really cold, so they decided to go inside. "Hey, T," Shaniqua said. "You comin' in?"

"No," I said. "I'm gonna stay out here for a bit."

They headed inside. I curled my legs underneath me and held on to my coffee cup with both hands to keep warm. I looked at the acres of rolling hills that had became barren now that the leaves had fallen off the trees. I had loved looking at the open land surrounding the camp starting in the winter, when I got there, when the hills were completely white and it looked so peaceful out my window; then in the spring, when it turned bright green; in the summer when it got hot and brown and then in the fall, when there was an explosion of red, yellow, and orange. It was almost winter again. I had made it almost a year in Danbury, and had come full circle. I had actually survived prison. I learned so much while I was confined within those four walls—not only about myself, but about other people. I never knew I would be able to turn such a horrible situation into a positive one—one that would teach me how to be a stronger person.

I thought back to how scared I was before I turned myself in, and during my first weeks at Danbury, wondering how Joe and the girls were going to handle life while I went away for so long. I remember being nervous about how the other inmates were going to treat me—and whether I would be totally skeeved out by the place. I remember being surprised at how fast I got used to living there. I made friends right away with a great group of girls, who showed me the ropes and helped me find my way. I got into a routine and was able to accomplish the goals I set for myself. I read. I watched TV. I learned to be adaptable and strong. I vowed to live every day like it was my last when I got home.

I wanted to stay in touch with some of the girls I'd met when I left. I wondered what it would be like when I got out and they were still in there—and then what it would be like when we were all out. I was hoping my relationship with some of the girls I was the closest to—like Nikki, Tonya, Blaire, Shannon, Josie, Franchie, Koolaidra, Katie, Shaniqua, and some others—would stay the same, or as close as possible to what we had when we were in there. But we all knew that as intense as things were at the time, we all would be released, move on, and go back to our lives. The relationships we shared there would never be the same again. But that was OK. I was just glad that they were there for me to help me through one of the toughest times of my life—and I hoped that they felt the same about me.

The one thing I never got used to in prison (besides the food!) was missing Joe, the girls, my parents, my family, and my friends. The hardest part of prison was trying to live with that aching feeling in my gut that never went away. Some of my Danbury friends told me it would get easier, but it never did. I felt guilty for being away from Joe and the girls. I knew how much they all needed me. Even though we had tried so hard to keep me out of prison, in the end that's where I was sent and there was nothing I could do about it. All I could do was stay strong for myself and my family. I learned that no matter how tough things become, you can get through anything with strength and resilience.

As I sat there, thinking back over the past year, one thing that became a lot clearer to me was that I had sometimes let negativity cloud my vision during some of the traumatic things that had happened to me in the past six years. But that's not who I am. In my heart of hearts, I am a positive person. I always have been. So while I was in prison, I realized that I needed to reach way down and find that sunny spirit that always looks at the glass as half-full and view the world through those eyes. It's just better that way.

I was touched when some of my fellow inmates came up to me and told me that they liked being around me because I was so upbeat and gave off such good energy. They told me that they were inspired when they saw that I tried to see the best in every situation. Wow. Once I got past the shock and horror of being in prison (and let me tell you, it took a *long* time to accept my fate in there), I was happy to help give other women the strength I have and to share my positive outlook with them, telling them that like me, they would get through all this, too.

I also thought about how I had survived my time at Danbury. I've always liked nice things, even when I was young, and always worked hard for them. But once I started becoming famous, I started wanting even more: better clothes, shoes, purses, and the like. Spending almost a year in a federal prison definitely brought me back down to earth. I learned that I can live anywhere—in any conditions, no matter how depressing, dreary, and horrible I think they are—and make the best of it.

I guess one of the biggest things I was reminded of in prison was something I had always known, but had forgotten: that sometimes you have to put things in God's hands, trust in Him, let go, and move on. Just like that. Doing that makes the burden easier.

Maybe God wanted me to have some time to step back, do some thinking, heal, and evaluate everything around me, because it had all become so out of control and chaotic. I mean, look where I ended up. Maybe He wanted me to clean house and start fresh.

One of the most profound things that happened to me while I was in prison was that I saw firsthand how God was with me every step of the way. He never let me down, always protected my children, my parents, and my husband. I know that everything happens for a reason, and with God's love and strength, I knew that this experience, too, would pass. My family would reunite and we would be stronger than we ever were.

As I neared the end of my sentence, I worried about what life in prison would be like for Joe, even though he was always very stoic about leaving. He said that he planned to just go in, do his time, and get out. But still, as his wife, I worried. I was also concerned about how the girls would deal with their dad being gone for forty-one months. They adore their daddy and need him in their lives. So do I.

I wanted to show my girls, through my example, how to be strong in the face of tough times and to always carry their heads high and with dignity. When I got out, I knew they would be watching me as I worked hard for a better future for them. I had so many plans! I realized that I needed to make better decisions for myself when it came to my personal relationships, and also my businesses. Our future depends on it.

*O*ne of the things that kept me going in Danbury was daydreaming about what I planned to do as soon as I got home. It was going to be one of the happiest days of my life. Jim had planned on picking me up because I would be leaving in the middle of the night, just like I did when I arrived, to avoid the media. I couldn't wait to hug and kiss my daughters, and cuddle in bed together like a family, just like we did the night I left. I wanted to hug them all so tight for so long. I knew we would be crying, but this time they would be tears of joy and relief that we had made it through this hellish year and were back in each other's arms again.

Showering in my own (clean!) bathroom and scrubbing the scent of prison off of me would be an absolute luxury. I wanted to use my favorite bath products and just stand there under the hot water for as long as I wanted to. I wanted to dry off with my fluffy towels, put on a thong (no more granny panties!), a *real* bra, and my favorite leopard-skin pajamas. I was also looking forward to a sink that worked like normal. I had always taken the running water in my house for granted. Not anymore.

On that first morning back home, I wanted to go downstairs to my own kitchen, where I knew Joe would make us a healthy breakfast of eggs, oatmeal, and fresh fruit. The girls would probably set the table for us, making it look beautiful, because they know how much I love that and enjoy eating together as a family.

I thanked God for keeping me safe during my stay at Danbury and for protecting Joe, the girls, my parents, and our family and friends. I prayed for Him to protect us all in the weeks before I was released. I also thought about all the people who hated us, wished the worst for us, and actually did things to try make our lives miserable and trip us up, before Joe and I got sentenced and while I was in prison. I prayed for them, too—that they would find peace in their hearts and learn to just let things go and not be so bitter and hateful.

Our family had gotten so much closer since I left for prison, and though I feared what was to come when Joe was gone, I knew we'd be safe. I knew we'd be all right. I thanked God for that, too.

As I sat there thinking about what it would be like when I got home, I stared up at the big, beautiful blue sky above me. The funny thing about the sky, and the sun, and the stars is that they all look the same no matter where you are, whether you are in prison or at home. Even though I had been away from the people I love the most, I knew that wherever they were at that moment, they could see the same vast sky I did. We are always together in our hearts. After all, it's where we belong.

# 11

## EXCLUSIVE BONUS CHAPTER: HOME, WHERE I BELONG

The last three weeks leading up to my December 23, 2015, release were the longest of my life. The hours and minutes dragged by. Time wasn't ticking by fast enough. I just wanted to go home. Even my front-row seat to the never-ending girl drama didn't help to pass the time much. Oh, some of the inmates still had their moments. They were still fighting over everything from contraband flat irons to their latest girlfriends, but I had little interest in their antics. Now that the end of my stay was in sight, I was antsy to get the heck out of there and go home.

During that last stretch, inmates started getting busted left and right for all kinds of things, especially contraband diet pills and, surprisingly, even makeup, so the tension was high. The girls who had thrown that big party, complete with lit candles, had put the guards on red alert. They became so strict that inmates were starting to get strip-searched after every visitation (including me—*Madonna mia!*).

By this time, I was over all the bickering, snitching, and embarrassing prison procedures. I made a point of laying low and staying out of the nonstop nonsense swirling around me. With my sentence almost over, I didn't want to do anything to get a shot. Some inmates got mad when other girls were leaving, out of jealousy, I guess, and tried to make trouble for them. I didn't know if they could extend your sentence or ship you out to another facility if you got in really big trouble, so I kept to myself and ignored anyone who wanted to start something up. I had too much on the line.

I was thrilled that the countdown to the number of days leading to my release was growing smaller and smaller, but the one thing I knew I'd miss were the amazing—and hilarious—friends I made on the inside. During my last few weeks, one of my friends broke the guard-induced tension by offering up some of her best advice: using a grape to help us do our Kegel exercises. She said it would help strengthen our chuckalina muscles. *What? A grape? What if it got lost up there? How would you explain that to the doctor?* We roared. Another one of my friends even suggested I get a sexy fishnet, crotchless cat-suit to wear to bed for Joe right when I got out. (I never did . . .) It was moments like these that chipped away at the monotony but also made me feel sad about leaving my friends behind.

By this time the whole prison had gotten into the holiday spirit. Christmas was definitely in the air. Inmates decorated their rooms and cubicles with whatever makeshift ornaments they could create out of commissary items, while the officials put up three Christmas trees throughout the facility. My girls filled me in on the holiday preparations they were busy doing in my absence. Every time I hung up with them, I couldn't believe I'd be home so soon. It was all so surreal.

\*   \*   \*

The last week in there was definitely the hardest, because the end of my stay was just around the corner, but at the same time, it felt like it was taking forever to arrive. Though leaving was all I could think about, I didn't talk about it much, if at all. I didn't want to make a big deal out of getting out when I knew other girls would still be in there—especially during the holidays. Other inmates would come up to me every day and ask if I was excited to leave. Of course I was, but I just said, "I'll get excited when I am actually out of here."

While I was thrilled and relieved to be leaving, it was also bittersweet: I knew once I got out that the countdown would begin for Joe's own surrender date. I couldn't sleep much that last week, thinking about him going away and what life would be like without him, especially for the girls, who need their daddy. I am a worrier. I always have been. I tried to put it out of my mind, and was able to during the day. But at night, when the prison was quiet and I was alone with my thoughts, my mind was racing.

Since parties were now banned, my friends couldn't throw me a going-away bash like we had done with some of our other friends who had left. But they still did what they could to make things nice for me. They made me a card that said "You are a Survivor," and gave me a drawing of all of us hanging out in my cubicle, which we did all the time. They asked one of the ladies in there to draw it. It's something I will treasure forever. When I got out, one of my friends had it framed for me. I want to hang it somewhere special.

Finally, the day I had waited for since the moment I set foot in the prison arrived. I woke up at 6 a.m., ate breakfast, had my coffee and worked out, as usual. I couldn't believe this day was finally here. It seemed strange, almost, because I had gotten used to being in the camp for so long now. This had become my life, but not a life I ever thought I would be leading—or leaving behind.

After I had finished packing the things I was taking home (including the inspirational books I found comfort in, that I knew I'd send to Joe when he went to prison), I had my last dinner with my friends: a healthy salad with tuna. Soon after, we all went to bed. I couldn't sleep at all, so Shannon stayed up all night with me, straightening my hair and doing my makeup. Jim was coming to pick me up at 5 a.m., but told me to be ready around three to give me time for final processing. (Joe stayed home to take care of the girls.) I was leaving in the dead of night, just like I had come in, to avoid the media and the paparazzi that I knew were chomping at the bit now that this day had finally come.

Tonya, Nikki, Blair, and Josie set their alarms for 3 a.m. so they could get up and see me off. I had been dreading saying goodbye to them for a while. I thought back to the emotional night I said goodbye to my girls and to Joe before I surrendered in January. The minute I walked through the camp doors for the first time, all I could think about was how I couldn't wait to go home. Now, here I was, steeling myself for yet another difficult goodbye—this one to the girls who had become my family, a family I never expected to gain when I first arrived.

Finally, one of the guards came to get me. It was time to go. My friends grabbed the boxes I was taking home and walked with me as I made my way through the sterile hallways, up the stairs and through the double doors that led to the visitation room, from where I would be exiting the prison. I looked around that cold, stark room, thinking of all the things I had done in there, from seeing my family when they visited for the first time to breaking up fights over the TV—and how I would never see it again. Thank God.

When we got to the doors that would lead to my freedom, my friends stood in a circle around me. I said goodbye to them, one by one. They hugged me and told me they were going to miss me. Shannon was sobbing, saying she would miss me so much. "But these are also tears of joy," she said. "I'm so happy you're going home to your family." Her words, and those of all my friends, meant so much to me. "God bless you, honey," I told her, trying to hold back my own tears. "I will miss you so much, too."

Then came one of the toughest goodbyes for me. My roommate and I had become really close. I really love her and knew it was going to hurt like hell to leave her behind. Tonya and I held each other and tried not to break down. We're tough girls, you know?

"We'll see each other soon, OK?" said Tonya.

"We will, sweetheart," I told her.

"Love you," she said.

"Love you more."

When I got to the exit, I turned around and hugged them all once more. "I love each one of you. One day, when we're all out, we'll all see each other again."

The guard said we had to go. I blew my beautiful friends a big kiss. "I love, love, love, love you so much! Goodbye!"

"Goodbye, Teresa!" they said in unison. I know this sounds like a Lifetime movie—and honestly, in that moment, it felt like one. I was stepping out of prison life and into the one I was meant to live: on the outside.

With that, the guard led me to a white van that would take me down the hill to Receiving and Discharge for final processing and one more round of fingerprinting.

I thought back to how terrified I was when I set foot in that stark, dungeon-like place last January. I could never have gotten through this experience without my faith in God, that's for sure—and the friends I made.

Jim said he would be there at five on the dot, but when I finished the discharge paperwork, he still wasn't there. I didn't know he was driving around trying to find a Starbucks because I was dying for "real coffee," as I had told him. I was done with the instant coffee I had started my morning with every day at the camp.

When he finally pulled up, two female guards escorted me through a series of doors to a gate outside. As soon as I saw him I said, "You're late."

"You're busting my balls already?" he joked. "It's only 5:01!"

That made me laugh for the first time since walking out of the camp, which felt freeing as a now-former inmate.

I zipped back into the prison building (just for a moment!) to change out of my greens and into the clothes that Gia and my friend Lisa G. had packed for me, and walked back out, feeling liberated, knowing I would never have to go back in there as an inmate. After we took my picture by the prison fence, I quickly slid into the back-seat of Jim's car, anxious to begin the drive home. The windows were covered with garment bags so the paparazzi couldn't get a shot of me, and we had a security detail follow us to make sure the photographers didn't get out of hand. That made me feel better, but still, it felt strange to have this much security just to drive me home.

As Jim led our motorcade of five cars, including ours, down the prison driveway, he handed me a gas station version of the "real coffee" I told him I wanted.

"This is all I could find," he said, handing me the steaming cup. "It's a cappuccino. Starbucks is closed right now."

I took a sip. "This is the worst thing I have ever tasted!" I said, laughing.

"This is as close to cappuccino as you're gonna get at this hour," he said, smiling at me in the rearview mirror.

"They have better coffee in prison!" I joked. "But thank you for trying. I appreciate it—and everything you've done for me. It means the world to me."

After settling into the backseat, I asked him for my cell phone. Wow, did it feel weird (and thrilling!) to hold it after waiting for it for almost a year. I found myself staring at texts I had gotten on January 5, the day I went to prison, but had never seen because I had to give Jim my phone, since they weren't allowed. It was eerie seeing a year's worth of messages. It was like I had fallen off the face of the earth, which I kind of did, and then here I was, back again.

I called home and talked to Joe, who had been up since two, telling him I couldn't believe I was talking on my cell phone to him and that I was on my way home. When Gia woke up, I talked to her, and then eventually to Gabriella, Milania, and Audriana. I could hear the excitement in their voices—*this was for real*. Mommy wasn't just calling home. I was actually *coming* home.

I couldn't help but get teary-eyed while I was talking to them. I started to cry but stopped because I didn't want to upset them. It was emotional enough. We had all waited for this moment for so long.

After I hung up, I began to lie down on the backseat when the car swerved, knocking me into the door.

"What was that?" I asked Jim.

"Friggin' paparazzi are everywhere and they're being *very* aggressive," he said. It was raining, pitch-black out, and really foggy, so it was hard to see the road ahead. We were going at least seventy on slick roads. I did not endure almost a year of prison only to crash on the way home. What a story that would be!

One of the cars chasing us tried to sandwich itself between us and one of the security cars that was now ahead of us to snap my picture through the windshield. They were shooting with blinding flashbulbs, which made it extra hard for Jim to keep the car in our lane, but he did. I almost screamed when the driver cut Jim off, almost taking off part of our bumper in the process, but he swerved and missed the car just in time. Our car was jerking so much that I thought we were going to crash. I got scared, crouched down, and started praying.

"We've got to be safe," I kept saying.

"We will," said Jim. "We're all right. We're in good hands."

I didn't know it at the time, but the four cars in our security team had formed a barrier around the speeding car, surrounding it to prevent it from coming too close to us. Jim told me our security team was prepared to run the car off the road to keep me safe, if it came to that. At this point, all I wanted was make it home in one piece!

This went on with other paparazzi throughout the almost two-hour drive from Connecticut through New York and on into New Jersey. It became a game of cat and mouse. One car would fall back and another would jump in.

But Jim knew we would be fine. He told me later that before he picked me up, the lead security guy told him that high-speed car chases like this could get very dangerous. At one point, someone on the team brought up Princess Diana's fatal, paparazzi-induced car crash, but he told the group, "We're not going to let that happen." And they didn't.

By the skin of their teeth. At one point, one of the security cars and a pap almost crashed when the other car kept swerving in and out of our lane and an SUV on our security team wouldn't budge. Thank God Jim didn't tell me that until afterward.

When there was a lull in the action, I asked Jim to put on the radio.

I popped my head up from the backseat while we listened to Christmas music. "Silent Night" came on the radio and I started tearing up. I kept telling him how strange it felt to be driving down the highway when I had been in prison just an hour before. Soon, I'd be home.

I ducked back down when he said yet another pap was approaching our car. These guys were tireless. I kept asking Jim where we were. When he told me we were passing New York City, I got excited. I had had so many great times there and would be back again, thank God.

When he told me we were in Franklin Lakes, I knew we were getting close. Jim had an advance team on my street telling him what was going on, saying there were reporters and photographers waiting, so I stayed down in the backseat. Even though I was in the best shape of my life, scrunching down in a ball in the back of the car was not fun—or comfortable.

When we finally pulled onto my street, I was beyond elated. I couldn't wait to get home! All I wanted to do was hug Joe and my girls, turn the shower on all the way to hot (with great water pressure!), and crawl into my luxurious bed.

I was still crouched down in the backseat to avoid the paparazzi when we pulled into the driveway so I didn't see the welcome home signs that the girls had taped to the front door—or the black Lexus waiting for me with a big red bow on top. People said later that Joe "surprised" me with a new car, but I knew all about it. It doesn't take a genius to figure out that I need a car while Joe's away, so we talked about leasing this one while I was still in prison (plus, he doesn't have a license). And if you're wondering about that bow, you'll have to ask Lexus—they put it on the car.

When Jim pulled into the garage, I couldn't have jumped out of that car fast enough. I raced into the kitchen, where Joe and the girls (and *RHONJ* cameras!) were waiting for me. I was home!

This was one of the most amazing moments of my life—it's hard to even put it into words, because no words are big enough to describe how much emotion I was feeling. I was overwhelmed to be home. This is what I had waited for all year.

"Hi honey," said Joe, with tears in his eyes. "Welcome home." I burst into tears, covering my face with my hands. As soon as I stepped into the kitchen and saw the girls I just lost it, and so did they. The girls came at me all at once and we were all crying and hugging each other. It was an incredibly emotional moment, one I will remember for the rest of my life.

The kids started yanking me in a million different directions, showing me around like it was the first time I had been in my house. They wanted me to see how neat they had kept their rooms while I was gone. They were so proud! The house looked exactly the way I left it, which made me happy. My family kept telling me the whole time I was at Danbury that they kept the house spotless and organized—exactly the way I like it—especially when visitors came over. This, of course, warmed my old-school Italian heart.

Keep in mind that our tearful, heartfelt reunion took place while the cameras were rolling. Some people asked me later if it was hard to literally walk through my own doors after being in prison for almost a year and immediately be on camera. Honestly, having the producers and crew there felt natural—they are part of my family. It was fantastic to see them because I missed them, too. I have known some of them for years. A lot of them were even there when Audriana was born. At this point, I honestly don't even notice the cameras anymore. And plus, I knew I had to get right to work after being away for so long.

After my "house tour," we all had breakfast together. I told the girls I loved the signs they hung in the entryway and the kitchen that read MERRY CHRISTMAS, MOM! in beautiful green lettering with hints of red. Joe helped the girls put up and decorate the tree. The house felt like a Christmas wonderland, and I knew Joe and the girls had put so much effort into having it ready for the holidays before I got home.

Joe made me an omelet with fresh spinach! It felt so good to sit down with my family. The girls had set the table beautifully, just the way they know I like it. I ate very little, though. I was so overwhelmed by being back with my family that I just couldn't eat that much. But I loved that Joe did that for me—and remembered the spinach.

After that, I spent a little one-on-one time with each of the girls. Audriana and I sat down at the kitchen table to play the game Trouble, which we used to do when she visited me in prison. I cuddled with Milania and Gabriella in their rooms, and talked with Gia on her bed to catch up on what was new with school and cheerleading.

During my home confinement I had to wear an ankle bracelet. With its thick black rubber band and plastic square monitor, it looked like a giant watch—one you couldn't take off. I also had to follow certain rules while under house arrest: I couldn't leave without permission and had a 10 p.m. curfew. Most importantly, my home confinement would end on February 5, 2016—a little over a month away. It felt weird to have something strapped to my ankle, and someone dictating when I needed to return to my own house, but the parameters of my home confinement were the least of my concerns. I already felt so free being out of prison: I could wake up when I wanted, eat when I wanted, and see my family all the time. I felt liberated in a way I hadn't felt in almost a year—I'd gladly take a bulky ankle bracelet and follow the rules that were set for me. It was a blessing compared to where I had been.

I kept the ankle bracelet covered with pants and didn't wear dresses until I had it taken off. It's not like I was hiding it, I just didn't want to show it off. I wanted to respect the law by being discreet about it.

As part of my home confinement I had to ask the probation officials permission whenever I wanted to go somewhere. I had to provide my schedule a week in advance and stick to it. If I left the house and didn't tell them, the officials would know about it. That was fine. I had already gotten the OK to go to Joey and Melissa's house for Christmas Eve, and to Joe's sister's house for Christmas. Abiding by the schedule was fine. The hardest thing about it was when the girls would call me on the spur of the moment and say, "Mom, come pick me up." If something wasn't on the schedule, I couldn't go. I would be filming a lot, since that was my job and I was allowed to work. I had already gotten permission to do what was necessary to fulfill my responsibilities to *RHONJ*, such as going to other cast members' houses and to outings we were filming.

I was absolutely exhausted because I didn't sleep the night before and had tossed and turned most of the week thinking about Joe leaving. By now it was early afternoon. Since the film crew had taken a break, Joe and I were going to take a nap. Audriana wanted to take one with us.

But first, I wanted to take a shower. I have to say, my shower is the best ever. The water pressure is very strong, unlike the trickle I used to get in prison. I let the water run down my back for a little while. It felt like heaven, especially since I was used to taking freezing-cold showers in prison. (I loved that I didn't have to ask anyone to flush the toilet to get hot water.)

I slipped into my favorite leopard print pajamas and slid between the plush blanket and leopard print sheets with Joe and Audriana. I had just nodded off when Joe woke me and told me he had to show me "a surprise" in the other room, if you know what I mean. He couldn't wait and neither could I . . . Before we knew it, the crew was back and we had to start filming again for the rest of the day. I got dressed—this time into comfy sweats. After the film crew left, two of the other most important people in my life came to see me: my parents. My mother had tears in her eyes when she walked through the door. She hugged me and said in Italian, "I'm so happy you are home where you belong." My father put those strong hands of his on my shoulders and looked deep into my eyes, telling me he loved me in Italian, before giving me one of the biggest hugs he ever has in his life. "I love you more than anything in this world," I told them in Italian. "I'm so happy you are doing so well. I need you in my life."

I always tell them I need them, because I do. I tell them to take care of themselves because I can't live without them. I was so grateful to have them both right in front of me, healthy and happy. We sat in the kitchen, drank cappuccinos I made, and caught up for a bit about my being back home, what the girls were up to, and our Christmas plans before they had to leave. My parents raised me to stand by family always—and I am so lucky that that's what they did for me throughout my whole ordeal.

I didn't have to worry about making dinner that night because Rino Aprea graciously sent dinner over from Ponte Vecchio, his restaurant in Brooklyn. He sent over enough food to feed everyone on my street. We sat around the table and feasted on lobster fra diavolo and other delicious Italian dishes. He and his wife, Teresa (who were both on *RHONJ* with us the season before), kept in touch with Joe while I was at Danbury, checking in to see how my family and I were doing. We appreciated that so much. I was grateful to everyone who kept in touch with me while I was there, with calls, letters, care packages, emails, and visits. It meant so much to me, and I'm not sure I would've been able to keep the faith if we didn't have loved ones by our side, supporting us every step of the way.

After the longest (but best) day ever, all six of us piled into my king-sized bed, which we filmed for the show. After the crew left and the girls fell asleep, Joe and I snuck downstairs and lit a fire in our great room. He put a blanket down and we sat in front of a roaring fire, talking and catching up, just the two of us, for some much-needed alone time. Our marriage has never been stronger. We are still so in love. Being away for almost a year made us appreciate each other even more. Spending time together after being away for so long was something new, which always adds spark to a marriage. I just wish I didn't have to go to prison for us to ignite a new flame in our relationship—but what's done is done, and we aren't looking back.

One thing led to another, and before I knew it . . . It was so romantic. I had dreamed of *this* moment, too, for a very long time. I was in the arms of my husband, just us. It was truly blissful. After we put out the fire and crawled back into bed with the girls, I laid my head down on my pillow and thanked God for the blessings He has given me. I was *finally* home.

The next day was beyond busy because I had to get ready for Christmas! I had so much to do, including wrapping gifts for *everyone*. I got up early and we had breakfast as a family. As I stood there, sautéing eggs in olive oil, I realized it felt like I had never left. I was right back where I left off: cooking breakfast for the girls, running around gathering things they needed for the day ahead, and scolding two of our dogs, Bella, and the newest addition to our family, Frankie, an adorable German shepherd who was born while I was away, for jumping on the couch.

One thing's for sure, I couldn't have been more excited, because I was having a glam day after a year away! We were taking our annual holiday photo at the house that day and I wanted to look good after almost a year in prison. My aesthetician came over to give me a facial, followed by my hairdresser, David, and then my makeup artist, Priscilla, one of my best friends. We started shrieking when we saw each other. Feeling that Chanel, Stila, and MAC glide over my freshly cleansed skin? Ahhhhh . . .

Joey came to pick us up because I didn't want any of the photographers still staked outside my house to get my picture while I would be driving us over there. I was so happy to see everyone! We spent a while hugging and kissing hello. It was so great to see Melissa and my niece and nephews, and, of course, my parents. Melissa made the night so beautiful for us. We had dinner, opened gifts, and listened to carolers who came to the house to sing to us. It felt so good to spend time with my family. I loved seeing my parents so happy.

Things with Joey and Melissa, I'm thrilled to say, were great. While I was in prison, I had said I wanted things to go back to the way they were between us before the show started, and that's what happened. After such a difficult year, the negativity between us just seemed to vanish, thank God. Just as my parents did, Joey and Melissa told me they would be there for the girls and me when Joe left for prison, which meant so much to me.

The only downside to Christmas Eve with my family? I had to

hide from the paparazzi lurking outside. Since Melissa and Joey's house has so many windows, photographers kept trying to get my picture, so I kept my back to the windows. *Mannaggia!*

When we got home, I tucked the little ones into bed. When they were asleep, Gia and I tiptoed into the game room to wrap the gifts I had asked her and Joe to buy for them. As we sat there wrapping for more than an hour, she made me laugh when she said, "Ma, I can't believe how much work it is to buy all these gifts and then have to wrap them all! I can't believe you do this every year!" Yes, my love, a mother's work is never done . . . but I love, love, love, love it all!

I felt so blessed on Christmas morning. I was so grateful to be home with Joe and the girls, who raced down the stairs to the foyer the second they woke up to see what Santa—and Joe and I—had gotten them. Audriana, Milania, and Gabriella screamed with joy when they unwrapped the hoverboards Joe and I gave them. They tore the boxes open, jumped on top of them, and started zooming all over the house. I tried one out too. (I was pretty good at it and wanted one of my own!) Later on, Milania made me laugh when she started zipping around the house, picking up the discarded wrapping paper and putting it in a big garbage bag. I got worried, though, when I thought the girls were going to crash into the furniture and the walls. Joe made me laugh even more when he said it was good to hear my voice throughout the house, because I kept yelling, "Be careful!!!" *Oh, Madonna mia!*

We had a beautiful breakfast together as a family, went to church, and then to Joe's sister Maria's house. I was so happy to see everyone again and for us to sit down to a wonderful dinner with Joe's family.

I hosted New Year's Eve, which was a lot of fun. I love staying home so this was a perfect night for me. We ordered food from

Rino's restaurant because I wanted to keep it simple and easy. Just before midnight we went outside and released a bunch of black and gold balloons into the peaceful night sky. As we watched them float upward, we heard a big bang out of nowhere. We all looked at each other like, "What was that?" Maria got emotional, saying that was their father, who died in 2014, letting us know he was there with us. Joe and Pete started tearing up, too, and hugged each other, Maria, and their mother. We still miss him so much.

Just like last year, before I turned myself in, at the stroke of midnight Joe and I held each other close, with tears in our eyes, happy to be together but still worried about the future. Last New Year's Eve, we got emotional thinking about the hard year we had ahead of us. This year, while we were grateful to have put 2015 behind us, we knew we had another tough year ahead with Joe leaving in March. I tried to put it out of my mind, but I couldn't.

January was a whirlwind of taking care of Joe, the girls, and the house—and filming nonstop for *RHONJ* Season 7! Even though I am more low-key now than ever before, I am *still* somehow surrounded by drama. *Madonna mia!*

In prison, I had a set routine so I was able to exercise three times a day, like clockwork. But now that I was filming all the time—day and night—while taking care of Joe and the girls, my schedule was all over the place. I tried to fit in a yoga class when I could, but I wasn't going regularly. I needed it! I have been working on getting certified in yoga so I can teach. I can't wait . . .

On February 5, my home confinement ended and I had my bracelet taken off! I had finally finished out my sentence! I was so relieved to have *that* trying chapter behind me. One of the first things I did was take a Jacuzzi bath! I filled the tub with rose petals and soaked in it for as long as I could—without the bracelet!

I was also busy doing interviews for this book, which came out February 9! One of my first interviews was a one-on-one with Andy on *Watch What Happens: Live* the night the book was released. Before that first interview, I had dinner in Manhattan (no asking for permission this time!) with a bunch of friends before heading to the *WWHL* studios. It was great to see Andy, who gave me a huge hug when he saw me and had his staff order us mini cupcakes with the cover of the book on them!

I hosted a bunch of book signings and was thrilled beyond belief to see my fans! When I got to my first book signing at Bookends in Ridgewood, New Jersey, I couldn't believe how long the line was. My fans told me how they had rooted for me while I was in prison and how happy they were that I had finally gotten out. They gave me beautiful bouquets, including a dozen roses, as well as rosaries, prayer cards, and other touching gifts. One fan almost made me cry when she gave me a guardian angel pin, saying, "God bless you. Here is an angel to watch over you." My fans are really unbelievable. The best in the world.

The book party Gallery Books threw for me at 49 Grove in Manhattan was such a great night. Joe and I took a limo to the party with Melissa and Joey. The place was absolutely packed with everyone I love, from friends to family to fellow housewives.

We had invited some of the cast of *Mob Wives*, but they didn't come because our dear friend Angela "Big Ang" Raiola, who had been battling cancer, wasn't doing well. I was devastated. I had gotten to know her over the years and just loved her. How could you not? She had a huge heart and was always a ray of sunshine wherever she went. She was also one of our biggest supporters during our legal crisis, so while I was excited about the book release, I was really sad that her condition was deteriorating rapidly. We got word that she passed the next day. I just couldn't believe it—such a warm and loving spirit, gone. May her soul rest in peace.

I was so nervous when I had to make a speech that night. I was shaking like a leaf when I had to get up in front of everyone! After a beautiful intro from my publisher, Jen Bergstrom, I thanked everyone there, saying, "To see so much support and love . . . oh my God! I'm gonna cry again! I've been crying all day. Thank you so much for coming out. It means so much to me." I had to keep interrupting myself to fan my eyes (no way did I want to let my makeup run for the cameras, despite my happy tears!).

I told everyone that when I first got to "camp," I wasn't sure if I wanted to write a book. At first, all I was doing was keeping a diary because one day I wanted to show my four daughters what I went through while I was away. But people in there, I explained, were trying to steal my diary, so I called Jim and told him I was going to give it to him for safekeeping. At the time, I told him, "Don't read it." So guess what? He read it! He thought it would make a great book— and the rest is history!

For the rest of February and March, Joe spent as much time as he could with the girls and me. We went on a couple of date nights, including on Valentine's Day—our last one for a long time. We enjoyed a quiet, candlelit dinner, laughing over something the girls had done and catching up on what we were each doing that week. As we held hands over the table I couldn't help but think I would be losing him in a few short weeks. I started to tear up, but didn't want him to see me upset, so I just stared down at my salad until I could compose myself.

I knew that going away was weighing on him heavily, too. Joe always gets up a little later than I do, but one morning in March when I woke up, I found him in the great room watching TV. Since I know him so well, I knew he was down there because he couldn't sleep. I knew he had a lot on his mind.

I tried to stay upbeat for everyone else, especially Joe, but deep down I just felt so sad. It would hit me most when I was home alone, cleaning, doing laundry, or washing the kitchen floor. I felt an overwhelming wave of grief wash over me, because I'd realize that going forward I'd be alone for a very long time. That feeling of despair was just so hard to shake. I would call my mother or a girlfriend to talk, but even then, that deep ache wouldn't go away. In my heart of hearts, I knew that Joe's leaving was going to be one of the hardest things I would ever face in my life. It's a lot to deal with and you can't prepare for it, no matter how hard you try.

My family and friends tried to cheer me up by saying he would be close by, in Fort Dix, which is about two hours from our house, and that I would still be able to talk to him every day, God willing. But that's not the same as snuggling with him at night before we went to sleep, sharing a laugh or a hug, or just having him by my side while we made breakfast in the morning. Joe has been my rock for most of my life. He is my best friend. I love him with all my heart. I barely made it without him during my sentence. Now we would be separated again. I am crying as I write this now, and wonder when this terrible aching will go away. I hope it lessens once he goes in, but I don't think I will feel myself again until I have him home with me again, for good.

Before I went to Danbury we didn't talk about my leaving with the younger girls that much. This time around, we approached the looming surrender date differently. We talked with the girls a lot, telling them Daddy would be leaving soon, and asking them how they felt about it. I told the girls we would call him every day, Skype with him if we could, and visit him every opportunity we had. There wasn't much else I could promise them because there wasn't a lot we could give them in a time like this. We just had to accept it for what it was and keep going.

Joe spent a lot of one-on-one time with each of the girls, telling them how much he loved them and would miss them when he was gone, but that he would be OK. Gia is very close to her father, so she was devastated that he wouldn't be around every day, but was holding up as best as she could. Though she is one of the strongest young women I have ever met, it breaks my heart that she has to deal with all this at such a tender age.

Gabriella broke down, sobbing, when she and Joe were talking in her room one day. She kept crying and holding on to him, saying she would miss him so much. As a mom, this was hard to see. If I was hurting as much as I was, I couldn't imagine their pain. When Joe came out of her room he was in tears and said he had to go do something in the garage. I hugged him and let him go have some alone time before I sat with Gabriella on her bed and just held her, telling her we would do the best we could while Daddy was away.

Milania had a really tough time with it, too. She likes to mask her emotions by being "spirited," let's say. But she also broke down when she and Joe spent alone time together, saying she wished he didn't have to go.

Even little Audriana came to me one day while I was waxing the dining room table, saying that her heart felt so sad because Daddy was leaving soon. I took her in my arms, kissed her, and told her it would be all right. But would it? I didn't have the answer to that. But I didn't let her know that's how I felt. As a mama bear, I have to protect them the best way I know how. In reality, though, we were forging ahead blind—there's no rulebook for dealing with something like this.

When I did start to find myself sliding into a funk, I tried to look at the little positive there is in a situation like this. Being apart from Joe would further strengthen our marriage, as it had when I was away.

After I got out, I heard more stories about Joe's supposed cheating. It makes me sick to my stomach to keep hearing these rumors when they are not true. In early March, we went to Mount Airy Casino Resort in the Poconos for a book signing. We invited a bunch of our closest friends to join us for dinner and to hang out—friends who are like family.

So I was shocked (but was I, *really*?) when stories ran afterward saying that Joe was drinking up a storm and cozying up to a mystery woman. We all laughed when that came out, because every woman who was there is like a sister to Joe. I may have laughed, but I was also ticked off that there were yet more stories out there about Joe fooling around—and saying that we are getting divorced. Again.

There's only so many times I can say the same line over and over: if we didn't want to be with each other, we wouldn't be. End of story. (People also told me about stories they read saying I got pregnant before Joe left for prison, asking me if I was! *Oh, Madonna mia!*)

The other silver lining to this whole situation, if you can call it that, is that Joe would not be able to drink while in prison. He has always enjoyed his cocktails and his homemade wine, but after I left for Danbury he told me he started drinking more and more each night to ease the pain of what we were going through as a family. If I'm being honest, I worry about him. I think that being in prison will help him with his drinking and improve his health. He has even said so himself—and all I can hope for is that he is able to find the strength to get through the difficult days ahead.

\* \* \*

Even as we were bracing for Joe's leaving, regular life kept us busy, and then some. Gabriella gave me quite a scare one Saturday when she had a friend over and they decided to fry some Oreos in oil.

I had just started talking on the phone in the next room when I smelled something burning. I told my friend to hold on while I raced into the kitchen. Smoke was billowing out from a pan on the stove, which Gabriella had covered with a lid. When I took the cover off, it burst into flames. I instinctively threw water on the fire, not realizing that would make it worse because of the burning oil. The flames shot up the hood of the stove and across my ceiling! I ducked down to avoid the flames and yelled to Gabriella to call 911. I thought the house was going to burn down! After all we had been through!

With the fire alarm blaring in the background, I told Gabriella, her friend, and Milania to get out of the house immediately. Thank God the dogs followed them out. If they didn't, I would have run back in to get them. They are my babies too. I told my friend on the phone, breathlessly, that we were all OK and that I would call her back! She had no idea what was going on and told me later that she was worried sick.

The flames had gone out by the time the fire department got to the house. The firefighters helped us get rid of all the smoke that had filled the house by placing huge fans all over. They also tested the ceiling to see if there was any remaining heat or embers in the walls. That fire left my ceiling charred and black . . .

Despite Gabriella frying up sweets in our kitchen, I wasn't indulging in *anything*, but I found the pounds starting to creep on a little bit in the two months I had been home. Not a lot, but I definitely noticed it. I was going out a lot more and eating more than I did in prison, and slacking on the exercising (after all, it's next to impossible to work out three times a day at home!). Joe, of course, always likes the way I look, but after I started to put some pounds back on, he realized he missed my pre-prison ass!

The last couple of weeks before Joe left was a whirlwind of get-togethers with friends and family, including a guy's night out that his uncle arranged, and big family functions. Joe's first cousin, who is his goddaughter, got married in mid-March. Gia was a bridesmaid and Joe brought the bread and wine to the altar during the Mass. The wedding was a blast! Joe and I danced for hours! We laughed together and with our family, and for a moment in time I forgot that Joe would be leaving us soon.

That feeling went out the window when Joe began dancing with the bride. He didn't realize it, but all eyes were on him, including Gia's, who started to cry. When I saw her standing there, weeping, I started up too. Pretty soon, everyone who was watching Gia started crying, knowing she was upset over her dad leaving.

In those last two weeks, Joe and I tried to spend as much alone time as we could. We would head off to . . . *cuddle* when the girls left for school. I took him for a massage, which he loved. We went out to lunch a lot, too. I knew we needed to keep up some feeling of normalcy, otherwise the reality of what we were facing would be too hard.

We were enjoying quality time together, until photographers started camping outside the house about a week or so before Joe left for prison, hoping to catch him leaving early. He was planning to get there at the exact moment he had to surrender, not a minute sooner, so they were wasting their time. They followed me everywhere, which I found *so* annoying! They even followed us around Virginia the weekend before Joe left, when we took Gabriella to the 2016 Jefferson Cup, one of the top youth soccer tournaments in the country. The paparazzi are relentless! But we all had the most amazing weekend. I wanted to give Joe and the girls the very best memories they could hang on to while he was gone.

Two days before Joe left, one of his closest friends, John, hosted a get-together at his restaurant, Blu Alehouse, in Riverdale, New Jersey, for more than one hundred people—including almost fifty kids! My girls had a blast riding the restaurant's mechanical bull the whole night. (Joe and I jumped on it together. I loved hanging on to his hard, muscular body! It reminded me of holding on to him on a jet ski years ago.)

John made it such a special night, especially for our girls. He told us he wanted to make the evening all about the kids, because he knows how important family is to us.

Early in the evening, Joe made a toast, saying, "Stop making me cry . . ." One of the many, many things I love about Joe is that while he is tough and strong, he isn't afraid to show his emotions. He has so much love in his heart, which I could see when he spent time talking to his cousins, aunts, uncles, and friends who all adore him, like I do. Though the night started out happy and festive, it ended in tears as everyone said their goodbyes to Joe. When Gia, Gabriella, and Milania saw people getting upset, they started to cry, too. Audriana said, "I don't want Daddy to go. I know everybody is crying because he is leaving." I comforted the girls the best I could, but felt like nothing I did could ease their pain—the same pain I was feeling.

When we got home that night Audriana was so wound up that she wouldn't go to sleep. I lay down with her in her bed and tried hard not to fall asleep because I wanted to spend time with Joe. We only had two more nights together, which I still couldn't believe. It was like a bad dream. After she fell asleep, I tiptoed out of her room into the hallway, where I could hear Joe crying.

When I got to our bedroom I said, "Hon, was that you crying in the hallway?" He nodded his head and said yes. He said he had been checking on the girls before he went to bed, like he has done every night since they were born—and especially when I was away. "I won't be able to do this anymore for a long time," he said. "I am going to miss them so much." That broke my heart. I held him and thought, *This is pure hell*.

The day before he turned himself in was a whirlwind. The girls and I wanted to spend as much time with Joe as we could before he left. Milania stayed home from school because she couldn't bear to leave her father. Normally, I send my girls to school no matter what, unless they have a fever and are really sick. But this was different. My little one wanted to be with her daddy as long as she could and I was totally fine with that. She took his leaving very hard, so I thought it would be good for her to spend one-on-one time with Joe. (Gia can't really miss school because she is in high school. Gabriella doesn't like to miss school because she is such an earnest student. I thought it would be good for Audriana to go.)

That night, Joe's family came for dinner. We laughed over fun times we had shared with Joe, and when they said goodbye to him, we cried, knowing what was to come. He told me later that having his family there made him feel good. When they left, Joe and I put the girls to bed. He spent time with each of them, sitting with them, holding them in his strong arms, and telling them how much he loves them. The girls couldn't stop crying, which was hard on Joe—and me. He was shaking when he left Gia's room. "I can't take this," he said. He was a mess. I have never seen him so heartbroken. He was crying as much as he did when he lost his father.

After the girls fell asleep, we went downstairs to sit on the couch in the great room, talking about the kids and how they would do without him here—and how much we loved each other. He took me in his arms and told me he couldn't imagine anyone else by his side; that he appreciated everything I do for him and how strong and loving I had been throughout our whole ordeal. I broke down, burying my face in his chest and telling him he is the love of my life and that I felt the exact same way about him. I lifted my face from his chest, looked into his eyes, and said, "Despite everything, we are so lucky, Joe." After all, we had found each other.

We headed to the bedroom for our last night together, and despite it being a bittersweet evening, I have to say it was one of the best nights we ever shared. We didn't have the chance to be alone the night I left for prison because I had to leave at midnight, so I was grateful for this moment, just the two of us.

The next morning was beyond difficult because I knew I only had mere hours left with Joe. We all got up early and had breakfast together. Joe held each of the girls before they left for school. Seeing them sobbing in the very spot where they had greeted me when I came home from prison stirred up horrible memories of the night I had to leave my family. I broke down in tears as the six of us stood there together with our arms around each other, just trying to get through the pain.

After the girls left, Joe and I had some time to ourselves and spent time talking because we knew it was going to get crazy soon. It did. More than thirty of our family and friends came over to say goodbye. The house was packed. Joey and Melissa came over, too, which meant a lot to me.

At about 9:45 a.m. or so, everyone left except for Joe's brother Pete, two of his uncles, two of his cousins, and Maria, who were going to drive him to prison. Weeks before, I told Joe I wanted to take him, but he said no; he thought it would be too hard for him to say goodbye to me there. But in the end, I ended up going—I needed to see where Joe would be living during this next chapter of our lives.

We were planning on leaving around 10 a.m., since he had to surrender at noon. Joe grabbed his coat, stood in the kitchen, and looked around one last time. I will never forget the look on his face. It was indescribable. I knew the loss and pain he was feeling all too well, and my heart broke all over again. I put my sunglasses on so no one would see my red, swollen eyes, and with a deep breath, Joe and I left the house. With Bravo cameras and paparazzi lenses on us, we walked to Pete's truck, where we hugged and kissed each other once more, before we slid in the backseat. I snuggled up against Joe during the entire ride. We tried to keep it positive for him, so we were laughing and telling stories the whole way there. He kept rubbing my leg and holding my hand really tight and kissing me on the cheek, which made the thought of saying goodbye to him even harder.

My heart was pounding as we pulled onto the grounds of Fort Dix. I wasn't sure if I could muster up the strength to say goodbye to the man who is my everything. All those memories of leaving him in January 2015 and every time he visited me in prison came flooding back. I barely made it through those goodbyes and now I had to face the same agony all over again.

We all got out of the truck. *This is it,* I thought. I waited for everyone to say goodbye before I had my turn. I tried to be strong for Joe as I hugged him one last time. I didn't want to let him go. I told him I loved him so much and would miss him, but that we would talk soon. "I love you, too, honey," he said. "I'll call you as soon as I can." And with that, he did what he had to do and headed toward the imposing building to surrender.

I stood there as he approached the prison doors, with tears streaming down my cheeks. He looked back one more time. I knew how painful this was for him. It was hard for all of us and would be until he was finally back home with us, where he belongs.

The car ride home was quiet: it was a blur. I felt painfully numb. When I got home, I lay down in my bed. I was completely drained. I said a prayer asking God to watch over Joe in prison, and over the girls and me while he was gone. I stayed strong for the girls when they got home from school, which was hard because they were all crying. I thought it would be easier when Joe went away, since I had already done it. But this time it was much harder for me and the girls, because as Gia explained, we had been through this before when I was gone and knew how hard it was going to be.

Right after Joe left, the girls began pitching in around the house. Audriana and Milania rolled the garbage cans to the curb for me that night, just like Joe used to do. All the girls helped me clean the house. Milania made Joe and me laugh when she told us she was going to be in the best shape of her life after feeding the dogs and doing some of the yard work Joe used to do. (Her responsibilities increased tenfold when one of our other dogs, Stella, another German shepherd, had puppies a few days after Joe left. *Oh, Madonna mia!*) But she also touched my heart and made me cry when she found one of Joe's shirts I was going to bring to the dry cleaners, and asked if she could keep it because it smelled like Daddy. Those moments break my heart.

I was thinking back to good times I had spent with Joe when his cousin Teresa texted me.

I have to say, as an outsider, I hope I can find the love you two have for each other. Very inspirational, like the movie *The Notebook*. Very rare nowadays to stand by each other through it all. It is a true love story. God bless.

That gave me chills. What Joe and I do have is special. More than special. We have known each other our whole lives and have been through so much together. We are raising four beautiful daughters together and, despite everything, we are so blessed.

*A*s time wore on, I thought about Joe every day and night, until finally, on the Friday after he surrendered, he was able to make his first call! I was so relieved to hear his voice; it helped ease some of the pain. Thank God I had my cell phone with me! I was so relieved that he was OK! After we talked a little bit and he told me he loved me, he spoke to the girls, telling them he loved them, too, and that he missed them all so much. He was extra lovey-dovey, which made the girls happy—and gave me peace of mind.

Joe told me he had made friends right off the bat. He is so likable and go with the flow—just a great guy—so I knew he would be all right when it came to getting to know people. One of the first inmates to greet Joe was Apollo Nida, who was on *The Real Housewives of Atlanta* and is also serving time at Fort Dix. I was relieved that Joe wasn't facing prison alone.

When I hung up, the girls told me how happy they were to hear that Daddy was fine. They couldn't wait to see him. Neither could I.

The kids ran up to their rooms to play and do homework, and after I made sure they were settled, I stood alone on the balcony in my foyer. I stared out of the massive window, thinking that once again I had to dig deep down and find the inner strength that had gotten me through so many difficult times before. I knew I needed to find the courage within myself again to get us through this next difficult part of our lives and keep us moving forward. Just as I had done when I sat in that barren cell in the men's prison at Danbury, waiting to be taken to the camp, I knew I had to be strong. Just like that harrowing time in my life, I knew I had no choice.

After all, I am a survivor.

# ACKNOWLEDGMENTS

---

FROM TERESA GIUDICE:

First and foremost, I would like to thank God for blessing me and protecting me and my loved ones.

I want to thank my mother and father for instilling in me their old-world values and traditions that have made me the person I am today. *Mamma e Papà, vi amo con tutto il mio cuore.*

I want to thank my husband, Joe, for being the love of my life and my rock, and for being the amazing Mr. Mom I always knew you were. I love you.

To my four beautiful angels, Gia, Gabriella, Milania, and Audriana: I love you more than I can put into words. You make my heart smile and I am proud to be your mother every single day. I love each of you to infinity and beyond.

To my brother, Joey: This story is just as much yours as it is mine. Our family will always come first. Nothing else matters. I love you.

To my mother-in-law, Filomena: Thank you for all your help

with the girls and for being a wonderful Nonna. I want to give a special dedication to my father-in-law, Franco Giudice. You will always be in our hearts. We love you and will miss you always.

To Cousin Teresa: Thank you for doing so much to help Joe and our daughters. You are amazing. You are what family is all about.

To my sisters-in-law, Sheila, Maria, and Melissa: Thank you for looking out for the girls and having all of those playdates with the cousins. Family is everything.

To my brothers-in-law, Pete and Duma: Thank you for your strength and for being there for us.

To my wonderful nieces and nephews, Antonia, Gino, Joey, Miranda, Simona, Lilliana, Sianna, Julianna, Alessandra, and Olivia: Your Zia Teresa loves you all to the moon and back.

To John and Kim, Rosanna and John, Lisa and Dana: Thank you for showing Joe and me the true meaning of friendship over the years.

To Dina Manzo: Thank you for your amazing friendship and for always being loyal to me and for being a wonderful godmother to Audriana.

To Lisa G.: You have been an amazing friend, not just to me, but to my four daughters as well. You're like the sister I never had. Love you, girl. And I would like to thank your wonderful family for the kindness they have shown to my family.

To my make-up artist, Priscilla DiStasio, and my hair stylists, David Antunes and Edyta Gross, who did my hair for the photograph on the book cover: Thank you for always being there and remaining loyal throughout the years. You are such true friends.

To my bankruptcy attorney, Carlos Cuevas: Thank you for everything. I am so happy to be working with you.

To my lawyer and friend, Jim Leonard: Thank you for coming

into my life and helping me when I needed someone like you the most. I wish I met you sooner. Thank you for always looking out for me.

To my very special friend, Victoria Gotti: Thank you for always being there for me and for helping me to stay strong.

To Andy Cohen: Thank you for always having my back and for all of your support. I'm really sorry I pushed you at the Season Two reunion.

To Lucilla D'Agostino, Caroline Self, Jacob Huddleston, and everyone at Sirens Media, as well as Frances Berwick, Shari Levine, Todd Radnitz, and everyone at Bravo, thank you for continuing to believe in me and my family.

To my fellow Housewives who reached out and were there for me: Lisa Vanderpump, Nene Leakes, Dorinda Medley, Jill Zarin, Teresa and Rino Aprea, and Nicole Napolitano: I want to thank all of you for your support. It means so much to me.

To Louise Burke, Jennifer Bergstrom, Nina Cordes, Jennifer Robinson, Jennifer Weidman, Elisa Rivlin, Liz Psaltis, John Vairo, Alysha Bullock, Susan Rella, Jaime Putorti, and everyone at Simon & Schuster/Gallery Books, and to Frank Weimann and everyone at Folio Literary Management: Thank you for believing in this book and for helping me to share my story with the world.

To Portrait Artistry by Linda Marie, Neal Clipper from Abbey Photographers, Michael Todd, Steve Gardner, Andrew Coppa, and Dave Kotinsky: Thank you for the photos. You do amazing work . . .

To Dana Levine, her amazingly inspirational son, Matthew, and the entire Levine family: I love you all and thank you for allowing me to be a part of your lives.

To Anna D., Rose and Leah, Nicole P., Linda B., cousin

Josephine, Diane P., and everyone who took the time to come and visit me at Danbury: You don't know how much that means to me. Thank you.

To Aunt Anna, my godmother Domenica, Cousin Christina G., Dana T., Julie B., Tina S., Giovanna D., Jackie R., Cynthia I., Robynand Christina, Maritza and Jose Z., Gina A., Steve D., Stacey G., Karianne F., Cindy K., Alisa Maria D., Julie R., Rosanna N., Kim D., Julie J. Robyn K., Mrs. Monaghan, and Tracey C., every one of your cards, emails, or pictures you sent me of the girls helped me get through this. Thank you.

To Roxanne at allabouttrh.com, thank you for always taking the time to check the facts and caring enough to get it right.

To the ladies at FCI Danbury: Keep your heads held high and your minds strong. I will never forget the time we spent together.

To all of my amazingly loyal and supportive fans from all over the world, who never turned their backs on me and have been with me on this crazy journey, including all of the Trehuggers out there and my superfans Michele Scapeccia and Jason Kelly: I love, love, love, love each and every one of you.

And last, but certainly not least, to K.C. Baker for allowing me to open up to you and spread my wings with you as an author. We laughed, we cried, and somehow, we got it done. You have a huge heart and I am so thankful you are in my life. I cannot thank you enough.

I Love, Love, Love, Love You All . . .
XO
Teresa Giudice
2016

FROM K.C. BAKER:

When I agreed to help Teresa write her memoir, I had no idea that I was about to embark on one of the most exciting, fun—and intense—journeys of my entire life. What a ride it's been!

Like Teresa, I would like to first thank God for all the blessings in my life and for always looking out for me and my children.

I am so grateful to my dad, Jim; my mom, Grace; and my sister, Jennifer (who is fondly known as Jackie) for always rooting for me, giving me the most amazing advice and for just being there for me. I couldn't do the things I do and be the person I am without your unending love, support, and encouragement. I love you so much.

I also want to thank Aunt Gerry, Jeffrey, cousins Peter, Vic, and Lynne, and the rest of my big, beautiful family for all your support and love.

I want to give a huge thank you to the stellar team at Gallery Books and Simon & Schuster, including Louise Burke, Jennifer Bergstrom, Jennifer Robinson, Liz Psaltis, John Vairo (who designed our gorgeous book jacket!), Marla Daniels, Loan Le, the amazing production team—Alysha Bullock, Susan Rella, and Jaime Putorti—and most of all, my editor, the incomparable Nina Cordes. I couldn't have asked for a more talented editor, who always stayed calm no matter what came our way. You made this project an absolute pleasure . . .

I want to give a big thank you to my agent, Jacqueline Flynn of Joelle Delbourgo Associates for your sage guidance and for the many calls you took from me during this project. I also want to thank Teresa's agent, Frank Weimann of Folio Literary Management, who was an integral part of this book. Thank you both for being there for me.

I am incredibly grateful to the amazing staff at *People* magazine,

292          ACKNOWLEDGMENTS

including Norm Pearlstine, Jess Cagle, Dan Wakeford, J.D. Hey-
man, Kate Coyne, Cynthia Sanz, Alicia Dennis, Elaine Aradillas,
Mary Green, Gail Kaufman, Sharon Cotliar, Liza Hamm, Liz
McNeil, Alex Brez, Linda Marx, Samantha Miller, Nicole Weisenee
Egan, Charlotte Triggs, Mary Margaret, Kim Hubbard, Wendy
Hanson, Jeff Nelson, Jackie Fields and the beauty and style teams,
Hugh McCarten, Emily Strohm, Janine Rubenstein, Celine Wojtala,
Sara Nathan, Aaron Parsley, and the rest of the entire People crew
for your words of encouragement for this project and for the huge
outpouring of support I got from you after a massive fire I had at
my house while writing this book. (The timing couldn't have been
worse . . .) I am so blessed to be able to work with such talented,
smart professionals—who also have huge hearts. You are the best in
the business in every way.

I want to also thank my friends, my BFF Sherry Fragomeni,
the amazing Debbie and Jim McAleavey and their children, Patrick
and Caroline (who took me and the kids in after the fire), Madeleine
Fromageot, Terri (who is like a sister) and Bill Bachlechner, Frank
Gallagher, Nicky and Tom Migacz, my longtime PIC Amy Kellogg,
Teresa Superfan Lora Heck, Michelle Centeno, Lara Walden,
Dawn Davies Rice, Henry and Kathy Smalls, the Ivanoviches, Ruth
Denomme, Greg Marconi, Chris Kapteina, Doug Alderman of
Carpentry Unlimited, my cousins Tracey and Gene Cleri, Allison
Snyder, Courtney Kudey, Alex Rauso and the volunteer fire depart-
ment in my town, my insurance agent, John Delveccio, my insurance
adjuster, Darren Toth, Sarah and Wayne Baker, and countless oth-
ers, for being there for me while writing this book and after the fire.

I also want to thank the wonderful people I met and got to know
while writing this book, including Joe, Gia, Gabriella, Milania; and
Audriana Giudice; Teresa's parents, Antonia and Giacinto Gorga;

Joe's sister, Maria Fazliu; Priscilla Distasio; and Lisa G. I can't thank you enough for all the help you gave me with this book, gathering the pictures and fact-checking. *Molte grazie!*

I am so grateful to all of you and so many others, but I would like to give a special thank you to the following people:

My son and daughter, Cameron and Lindsay, who were there for every second of this journey with me and then some: Thank you for being so patient and putting up with me as I worked 'round the clock on this book. I love you both so much and am so proud and blessed to be your mom.

Jim Leonard: Where do I even begin? There is no way we could have done this book without you. I am so glad to have met you and to have worked so closely with you. Thank you for being there every step of the way and for always putting out so many fires. You are amazing . . .

And most of all, of course, I want to give a big hug to Teresa. Thank you so very much for bringing me on this adventure with you. I had the time of my life. I was so happy to get to know the real you—a great girl with a big heart and immense inner strength, who opened up to me so much and always made me laugh. You showed me your true colors with your concern and offers to help me and the kids after my fire. You also gave me the opportunity of a lifetime. I am so glad to call you my friend.